**Breaking Up Is Hard To Do**

This publication is based on research that forms part of
the Paragon Initiative.

This five-year project will provide a fundamental reassessment
of what government should – and should not – do. It will put
every area of government activity under the microscope and
analyse the failure of current policies.

The project will put forward clear and considered solutions to
the UK's problems. It will also identify the areas of government
activity that can be put back into the hands of individuals,
families, civil society, local government, charities and markets.

The Paragon Initiative will create a blueprint for a better,
freer Britain – and provide a clear vision of a new relationship
between the state and society.

# BREAKING UP IS HARD TO DO

## Britain and Europe's Dysfunctional Relationship

EDITED BY PATRICK MINFORD AND J. R. SHACKLETON

with contributions from

PHILIP BOOTH • MARTIN HOWE • PHILIPPE LEGRAIN
DAVID MAYES • PATRICK MINFORD • KRISTIAN NIEMIETZ
GWYTHIAN PRINS • SEAN RICKARD • MARTIN RICKETTS
J. R. SHACKLETON • MATTHEW SINCLAIR
CHRISTOPHER SNOWDON • RACHEL TINGLE
ROLAND VAUBEL • RICHARD WELLINGS • GEOFFREY WOOD

Institute of
**Economic** Affairs

First published in Great Britain in 2016 by
The Institute of Economic Affairs
2 Lord North Street
Westminster
London SW1P 3LB
in association with London Publishing Partnership Ltd
www.londonpublishingpartnership.co.uk

The mission of the Institute of Economic Affairs is to improve understanding of the fundamental institutions of a free society by analysing and expounding the role of markets in solving economic and social problems.

A CIP catalogue record for this book is available from the British Library.

ISBN 978-0-255-36722-6

Many IEA publications are translated into languages other than English or are reprinted. Permission to translate or to reprint should be sought from the Director General at the address above.

Typeset in Kepler by T&T Productions Ltd
www.tandtproductions.com

Printed and bound in Great Britain by Page Bros

# CONTENTS

# THE AUTHORS

## Philip Booth

Philip Booth is Editorial and Programme Director at the Institute of Economic Affairs and Professor of Finance, Public Policy and Ethics at St. Mary's University, Twickenham. He was formerly Professor of Insurance and Risk Management at the Cass Business School, where he also served as Associate Dean. He has an undergraduate degree in economics from the University of Durham and a PhD in Finance. He is a Fellow of the Institute of Actuaries and of the Royal Statistical Society. Previously, Philip Booth worked for the Bank of England as an adviser on financial stability issues. He has written widely, including a number of books, on investment, finance, social insurance and pensions, as well as on the relationship between Catholic social teaching and economics.

## Martin Howe

Martin Howe QC specialises in European Union law, particularly in the field of intellectual property and the free movement of goods and services between Member States. His practice regularly involves appearances at the European Court at Luxembourg. He has published extensively on EU legal and constitutional issues, including (jointly authored with Brian Hindley) the IEA publication *Better Off Out? The Benefits or Costs of EU Membership* (1996, revised 2001).

## Philippe Legrain

Philippe Legrain is a writer and thinker. A visiting senior fellow at the London School of Economics' European Institute, columnist for Project Syndicate, Foreign Policy and CapX, and independent consultant, he was economic adviser to the President of the European Commission and head of the team providing President Barroso with strategic policy advice from 2011 to 2014. He has also been special adviser to World Trade Organisation Director-General Mike Moore and trade and economics correspondent for *The Economist*. Philippe is the author of four critically acclaimed books. They include *Immigrants: Your Country Needs Them*, which was shortlisted for the *Financial Times* Business Book of the Year 2007, and *European Spring: Why Our Economies and Politics are in a Mess – And How to Put Them Right*, which was one of the *Financial Times*'s Best Books of 2014.

## David Mayes

David G. Mayes is Professor of Banking and Financial Institutions and Director of the New Zealand Governance Centre at the University of Auckland Business School. He is also Visiting Professor at the University of Buckingham. His main areas of research are the regulation and governance of the financial sector and financial firms, on which he has published widely. He has focused particularly on cross-border issues and on the process of closer integration, especially in Europe. He has worked extensively in and with central banks and financial regulatory authorities in many countries. He is an Editor of *The Economic Journal*, a Fellow of the Law and Economics Association of New Zealand and a member of the Australia and New Zealand Shadow Financial Regulatory Committee.

## Patrick Minford

Patrick Minford is Professor of Economics at Cardiff University, where he directs the Julian Hodge Institute of Applied Macroeconomics. His main research interest is in macroeconomic modelling and forecasting. Between 1967 and 1976 he held a variety of economic positions, including spells in East Africa, industry, HM Treasury and its delegation in Washington DC. From 1976 to 1997, he was the Edward Gonner Professor of Applied Economics at Liverpool University, where he founded and directed the Liverpool Research Group in Macroeconomics; this built the 'Liverpool Model' of the UK, which was influential in forecasting and policy analysis during the 1980s. During the 1990s he also undertook part-time roles in the UK administration: he was a Member of the Monopolies and Mergers Commission from 1990 to 1996, and one of HM Treasury's Panel of Forecasters ('Wise Men/Persons') from 1993 to 1996. He was made a CBE in 1996. His published work includes books, journal articles and op-ed pieces in the area of macroeconomics and related policy issues.

## Kristian Niemietz

Kristian Niemietz is Head of Health and Welfare at the Institute of Economic Affairs. He studied Economics at the Humboldt-Universität zu Berlin and the Universidad de Salamanca, graduating in 2007 as Diplom-Volkswirt (MSc in Economics). He also studied Political Economy at King's College London, graduating in 2013 with a PhD. During his postgraduate studies, Kristian taught Economics at King's College London.

## Gwythian Prins

Gwythian Prins is Emeritus Research Professor at the London School of Economics, Visiting Research Professor and Visiting

Professor of War Studies at the Humanities Research Institute, University of Buckingham, and was previously Fellow in History at Emmanuel College and University Lecturer in Politics, University of Cambridge. He is currently a member of the Strategy Advisory Panel of the Chief of the Defence Staff and a member of the Royal Marines Advisory Group.

## Séan Rickard

After studying economics at the London School of Economics and Birkbeck College, Séan embarked on a career as a professional economist and in 1987 was appointed Chief Economist for the National Farmers Union. In 1995 he joined the Cranfield School of Management as a senior economics lecturer and was appointed MBA Director and Director of Graduate Admissions. Between 1995 and 2012 he was a government academic economic advisor on food and farming policy. Since retiring from Cranfield to concentrate on his consultancy, Séan Rickard Ltd., he has taken up a number of visiting lectureships and is a visiting research fellow at the Royal Institution. He continues to write and speak on food and farming matters.

## Martin Ricketts

Professor Martin Ricketts is Professor of Economic Organisation and was formerly Dean of the School of Humanities at the University of Buckingham. He is also Chairman of the IEA's Academic Advisory Council. He has a DPhil from the University of York (1980) and was Research Economist at the Industrial Policy Group from 1970 to 1972 under the direction of John Jewkes. He was Research Fellow at the Institute of Social and Economic Research, University of York (1974–77). He has published in professional journals on the new institutional economics, the theory of the firm, entrepreneurship, public choice, aspects of public finance and housing policy, and has authored several books. He was Economic Director of the National Economic Development Office (1991–2).

## J. R. Shackleton

J. R. Shackleton is Professor of Economics at the University of Buckingham and Research and Editorial Fellow at the Institute of Economic Affairs. He studied economics at King's College, Cambridge and the School of Oriental and African Studies. He taught at Queen Mary University of London, has worked as an economist in the civil service and has been Dean of two business schools. A specialist in labour economics, he has published many books and academic articles and appeared frequently on radio and television.

## Matthew Sinclair

After studying Economics and Economic History at the London School of Economics for his undergraduate and master's degrees, Matthew Sinclair joined the TaxPayers' Alliance. He became their Chief Executive and led major research projects including the 2020 Tax Commission – a joint project with the Institute of Directors investigating the potential for strategic tax reforms – and organised award-winning campaigns, such as the MashBeerTax campaign, on issues from energy prices to business rates. His work on climate policy has included reports on the EU Emissions Trading System, renewable energy subsidies and green taxes. During his time at the TaxPayers' Alliance, he cemented his role as a key critic of the efficacy of UK climate policy by writing the book *Let Them Eat Carbon*, published by Biteback Publishing in 2011. He joined the economics consultancy Europe Economics in 2014.

## Christopher Snowdon

Director of Lifestyle Economics at the IEA, Christopher Snowdon is the author of *Selfishness, Greed and Capitalism, The Art of Suppression, The Spirit Level Delusion* and *Velvet Glove; Iron Fist*. He has authored a number of IEA publications, including *Sock Puppets, The Proof of the Pudding, The Crack Cocaine of Gambling, Alcohol and the Public Purse* and *Drinking, Fast and Slow*.

## Rachel Tingle

Rachel Tingle is a visiting lecturer at the University of Buckingham, where, amongst other things, she teaches a course in the Economics of Europe. She has had a varied career as an economist and journalist, which has included working in the City; in economic consultancy; for a number of senior Conservative politicians; and in television, print and web journalism. For many years she specialised in writing about the interface between economics, politics and Christianity and has written hundreds of articles and two books in this area.

## Roland Vaubel

Professor of Economics at the University of Mannheim, Germany, Roland Vaubel has a BA from the University of Oxford, an MA from Columbia University, New York, and a doctorate from the University of Kiel, Germany. He has been Professor of Economics at Erasmus University Rotterdam and Visiting Professor of International Economics at the University of Chicago (Graduate School of Business). He is a member of the Advisory Council to the German Federal Ministry of Economics and Technology. He is associate editor of the Review of International Organizations and a member of the editorial boards of the *European Journal of Political Economy, Constitutional Political Economy* and *Cato*

*Journal.* He is also a member of the Academic Advisory Council of the Institute of Economic Affairs.

## Richard Wellings

Richard Wellings is Deputy Director, Academic and Research, at the Institute of Economic Affairs and Director of IEA Transport. He was educated at Oxford and the London School of Economics, completing a PhD on transport policy in 2004. He is the author, co-author or editor of several papers, books and reports, including *Towards Better Transport* (Policy Exchange 2008), *Which Road Ahead – Government or Market?* (IEA 2012), *The High-Speed Gravy Train: Special Interests, Transport Policy and Government Spending* (IEA 2013) and *Seeing Red: Traffic Controls and the Economy* (IEA 2016).

## Geoffrey Wood

Geoffrey Wood is Emeritus Professor of Economics at Cass Business School in London and Emeritus Professor of Monetary Economics at the University of Buckingham. A graduate of Aberdeen and Essex Universities, he has worked in the Federal Reserve System and the Bank of England. Overseas he has advised several central banks and national treasuries. He is currently a director of an investment trust and an adviser to several financial institutions, two pension funds and the Treasury Select Committee of the House of Commons; he was also adviser to the Parliamentary Banking Commission until the Commission ceased to exist on the publication of its report. He has authored, co-authored or edited over forty books and has published over 100 academic papers. His fields of interest are monetary economics, monetary history and financial regulation.

# FOREWORD

Many of those who believe in free markets support Britain leaving the EU (Brexit). But such people do not do so because they desire isolationism. On the contrary, they believe in freer trade and less regulation of business. Furthermore, their support for Brexit also does not mean that they are against international institutions. Such institutions can serve a number of purposes. They can, for example, restrain national governments from imposing trade barriers or barriers to the employment of non-nationals. International institutions can also help to solve problems where there are spillover effects or externalities, such as in the case of environmental matters.

There are also many free-market supporters of the status quo who believe, on balance, that the EU promotes free trade and free markets and, in some areas, does so unequivocally.

The authors of this book were asked to examine a particular policy field and determine, from an economic or political economy point of view, what the appropriate role of international institutions should be. They were then asked to relate this to the reality that exists under the status quo or that might exist if Brexit occurred. In doing this, the volume can help achieve three objectives. First, it provides an analysis of the role that international institutions should play in the economic life of a free society. This is important, and rarely discussed in policy debates. In general, policy discussion tends to revolve around how to tweak the status quo – should we have more EU involvement in climate change policy or military intervention by the UN in this or that case, for example.

Second, the authors implicitly lay out what a renegotiation agenda ought to look like if a country (whether Britain or not) wishes to reform the EU in a liberal direction, now or at some future time. At the time of writing this foreword, it is clear that David Cameron's agenda is not nearly radical enough, though it remains to be seen whether even that will be achieved. Indeed, it is not clear that the proposals of the UK government will even take the EU in the right direction. Any serious agenda to create a new settlement should start from first principles and take into consideration for what purposes the institution should exist. This would provide a benchmark against which success can be measured.

Third, the authors provide a framework within which the practical options of remaining with a reformed EU and Brexit can be analysed. There are some authors who do not believe that international institutions are at all important in the area they discuss. Others believe that international cooperation can take place through bespoke, informal or ad hoc mechanisms, and that the EU itself need have no role. Presumably, in these cases, Brexit would be the logical way to get the best policy outcome. Another group of authors believes that a reformed or slimmed-down role for the EU would be satisfactory, or that the restraints that the EU currently puts on member states are really important in guaranteeing economic liberalism. As far as these areas are concerned, a renegotiated (or, in some cases, unreformed) EU would be the best option.

One interesting issue is raised that perhaps transcends the discussions of particular policy areas. Rather than trying to renegotiate a better deal when it comes to labour market regulation or agriculture, it might be better to try to reshape the institutions of the EU. There might be wider support for that, and, in the long term, better institutions could lead to better policy.

Overall, this is an important and unique contribution to the discussion about Britain's relationship with the EU. In the white noise of the referendum debate, serious long-term analysis of the precise role that international institutions should play in a free society, grounded in the context of the reality of the EU's current role, is refreshing. Its relevance will long outlive the referendum on Brexit that is likely to take place in the next 18 months.

The views expressed in this monograph are, as in all IEA publications, those of the authors and not those of the Institute (which has no corporate view), its managing trustees, Academic Advisory Council members or senior staff. With some exceptions, such as with the publication of lectures, all IEA monographs are blind peer-reviewed by at least two academics or researchers who are experts in the field.

PHILIP BOOTH
*Academic and Research Director*
*Institute of Economic Affairs*
*Professor of Finance, Public Policy and Ethics*
*St. Mary's University, Twickenham*
January 2016

# SUMMARY

- UK voters face an historic choice between remaining within the EU or leaving and seeking a different type of involvement in the world economy. Such an alternative is clearly possible: the UK has many advantages in an international context as a result of its historical alliances and involvement in international institutions. This book looks in detail at the arguments about the future of our relationship with Europe. As such, it informs the debate about whether the UK should remain in the EU or should leave. Furthermore, it examines the form a reshaped EU should take if a renegotiated Union was shaped by sound principles of economics and politically economy.

- In many areas, such as defence, environmental policy and some aspects of transport, some degree of international cooperation is desirable because of public good spillovers. However, such cooperation often involves cooperation beyond the EU, and this need not be directed by Brussels. Still less do such spillovers lead to the conclusion that we need 'ever-closer union' in Europe.

- Reform of institutions such as the European Parliament, the European Commission and the European Court of Justice is arguably more important than specific areas of policy – and is likely to find greater support from our European neighbours.

- Renegotiation is an extremely difficult process, which could conceivably be more effective from outside the EU: if the UK signalled its intention to leave, negotiations could focus on the positive aspects of cooperation rather than the negative aspects of integration.

- Free trade is the ideal, but the European Union prevents the UK from opening up trade with other parts of the world. This probably costs us around 4 per cent of GDP as a result of trade diversion and distortions to the UK economy. The EU needs to be much more open to trade and reduce its tariff and non-tariff barriers, which remain far too high.

- Despite recent concerns, the free movement of labour within Europe is a positive feature of the EU, and we should be careful in renegotiation not to damage the principle that Europeans should be able to live and work in other countries. Similar principles apply in areas such as agriculture, employment regulation and lifestyle prohibitions. Many UK politicians are at least as opposed to liberal principles as EU regulators, and we need to ensure that any repatriation of government powers leads to a genuine shift to market liberalism.

- In banking and financial regulation, the EU has shown very damaging centralising tendencies, exacerbated by the financial crisis. Banking structures should be simpler, banks should be allowed to fail, but there should be overnight resolvability and an enhanced 'lender of last resort' function. The EU emphasis on enhanced capital and supervisory regulation is wrong. In the field of other financial services, such as insurance, the EU needs to move back towards mutual recognition rather than impose common rules.

- The Common Agricultural Policy is expensive, holds back innovation, raises prices to consumers and serves special interests; the Common Fisheries Policy has had an adverse impact on the UK and has a very poor record with regard to the conservation of fish stocks. Significant reform in both these areas is unlikely, but some degree of repatriation of policy could prove beneficial.

- The role of supranational institutions (which need not be the EU) in transport policy should be confined to some aspects of emissions, air traffic control and cross-border travel. Some EU interventions, such as the open-access rules on railways, go beyond what is necessary to allow the integration of services across borders. The EU should not be imposing an inappropriate structure on the railway industry; rather, it should let the market determine its shape.
- In climate policy, the EU has been attempting the impossible: setting its own targets on the assumption that an effective global policy will emerge. Its emissions targets are unrealistic, the Emissions Trading System has been ineffective and subject to fraud, and its emphasis on renewable energy has been expensive and ineffective. Perhaps a better focus for its efforts might be supporting fundamental research into new technologies, though this might equally be conducted at the national level.

# TABLES AND FIGURES

# 1 INTRODUCTION

## Patrick Minford and J. R. Shackleton

The relationship between the UK and the EU has never been completely untroubled. However, this book is published against a background in which both the UK and the EU as a whole are facing existential crises, which would not have been thought likely, or even possible, a few years ago. Across the EU, the seemingly inexorable movement towards 'ever-closer union' has run into major problems that have set European neighbours against each other in a way that has never occurred before in the decades since the Treaty of Rome.

The euro zone crisis has shown what happens when ill-matched economies enter into monetary union without proper preparation and commitment. The cavalier way in which Greece and some other Southern European countries joined the euro zone has had dire consequences. These were predicted at the time, not least by British economists, but political imperatives overrode such concerns. The financial crisis has now forced euro zone governments to face up to the massive fiscal problems of the weaker members, and the political fallout of the required responses has been dramatic.

Less predictable, perhaps, was the migration crisis set off by the consequences of the Arab Spring, the collapse of governments in Iraq, Syria and Libya, and the rise of the Islamic State of Iraq and the Levant (ISIL). Millions of people have been displaced by war in the Middle East and are seeking, by one means or another, refuge in Europe. The struggles of EU countries to handle the influx of refugees, plus that of economic migrants from many other parts of the world, has placed severe strains on the principle of free movement within Europe – a basic feature of the European ideal since the beginning.

Here in the (still just about) United Kingdom, we face a referendum on EU membership, the outcome of which appears more uncertain than ever. The attempt by David Cameron to renegotiate the UK's terms of membership, always likely to be a difficult task, will not have been helped by other members' perceptions that the UK has stood back from helping resolve Europe's other problems. At home, the strongly pro-EU Scottish National Party has threatened a new referendum on independence should the EU vote go in favour of Brexit. The UK Independence Party polled four million votes in the May 2015 general election. Some of these votes were at the expense of the Labour Party. Following its poor election performance, Labour has swung dramatically leftwards under the leadership of Jeremy Corbyn. This has opened up doubts about Labour's previously strong support of EU membership. At the same time, although the Conservative Party is perhaps more eurosceptic than it has ever been, there are still considerable divisions about the appropriate relationship with Europe. Only the Liberal Democrats remain overwhelmingly pro-EU, although they are a greatly shrunken force after their disastrous general election results.

This volume attempts to step back from the immediate political battlefield and to consider longer-term issues about the appropriate relationship between Britain and the EU. It is not a eurosceptic treatise, but it is certainly not blindly pro-EU either. Instead, it is intended to clarify the choices available. Working from first principles, the authors were asked to provide their take on appropriate regulatory frameworks, legal arrangements and international commitments for promoting a liberal market economy in the various areas where the EU currently has substantial powers.

These powers, or competences, are set out in detail in 32 review reports commissioned by the coalition government. The reports, which also summarised over 2,000 submissions from interested parties, are a valuable source of information. However, given the politics of the coalition, no real conclusion was reached. In summarising the work at the time of the publication of the final seven reports, Foreign Secretary Philip Hammond contented himself with generalities about the importance of subsidiarity and proportionality, and the need for the EU to focus on areas where, in the banal cliché of government statements, it 'adds genuine value'.[1]

In the IEA tradition, our authors, unlike the coalition's competences reviewers, were asked to go back to first principles. They were asked to go beyond reviewing the field and to make judgements: not judgements about what is currently politically possible, but about where we need to be after renegotiation is concluded. Some authors believed that, in respect of the area of policy they analysed, we would be better off if we were not in the EU; others believed that there is a legitimate EU role in policy, but that it should be radically reformed; and some authors were content, more or less, with the status quo. We hope that their analysis will provide readers who have a vote in the forthcoming referendum with a conceptual framework to help them judge the revised membership terms that Mr Cameron intends to put to the electorate.

The next section of the book sets out first principles – four chapters that look at fundamental issues concerning the relationship between the EU and its members, in particular the UK. This is then followed by a series of essays on particular policy areas.

---

1  See https://www.gov.uk/government/news/final-reports-in-review-of-eu-balance -of-competences-published (accessed 10 October 2015).

## Principles

In his chapter, Martin Ricketts applies economic reasoning to the process of assigning powers and responsibilities to different levels of government in the EU. He starts from the proposition that one of the state's basic roles is the provision of public goods. For some such goods, the existence of international spillovers suggests that the appropriate locus of decision-making is above the nation state, although Ricketts concedes that detailed examination of cases may call this into question. In some cases, decisions should possibly be taken at a higher level than the EU: for example, some defence issues are better determined by NATO than by the relatively feeble European capability. In many cases, however, appropriate jurisdiction is clearly at the national level, and there is little economic justification for 'ever-closer union'.

Using Coasean reasoning, Ricketts draws an analogy between decisions to assign competences between states and the EU on the one hand and firms' decisions to merge (often as a result of high transactions costs) rather than continue to rely on contractual relations between individual firms on the other hand. The important issue for the EU is 'the complex one of determining the relative bargaining costs, agency costs and effectiveness of different collective decision-making processes'.

Ricketts places great emphasis on the benefits from competition between jurisdictions over such matters as taxation and regulation. The argument in Tiebout (1956) that factor migration and 'exit' will reveal preferences better than a voting system may have been based on restrictive assumptions, but Ricketts feels it was essentially correct. He rejects claims that competition leads to a 'race to the bottom'. He argues that such claims – which lie behind the promotion of many of the EU's 'shared competences' – reflect producer interests. Many health, safety and environmental costs, for example, are truly local, and EU harmonisation may act as a barrier to trade and encourage rent seeking.

Roland Vaubel's contribution examines the institutions of the EU from the angle of the UK's renegotiation stance. He argues that negotiations should focus on these institutions because there is much wider support among governments for limiting centralising powers than for reversing specific policies. Vaubel emphasises the need to reform the European Court of Justice (ECJ). He argues that the Court is the 'lynchpin of the system': the judges misinterpret the European treaties because they have a vested interest in centralisation at the EU level, for instance in relation to financial regulation. The Commission's role as initiator of legislation and enforcer/prosecutor breaches the principle of the separation of powers. The European Parliament should, in his view, be reduced in size, and a second part-time chamber added, with a veto over centralising legislation and consisting of members selected by lot from national parliaments.

Four types of institutions, Vaubel proposes, are needed for international cooperation: international courts or arbitration tribunals; international public prosecutors to monitor and enforce compliance; international fora to negotiate these commitments; and an independent international competition authority. Importantly, he argues that such cooperation should not necessarily be confined to the EU. Like Ricketts, he argues that wider cooperation through the North Atlantic Treaty Organization (NATO) or the Organisation for Economic Co-operation and Development (OECD) may sometimes be more appropriate.

Vaubel points out that EU institutions differ from the ideal because the 'founding fathers' of the European movement intended to use the common market as a stepping-stone to political integration, setting up institutions that went far beyond what was necessary to abolish national barriers to trade and capital movements. This theme is taken up by Gwythian Prins, whose contribution traces the origins of 'The Project' of European union to the generation of Monnet, Salter and Hallstein, who reacted against the horrors of World War I.

Prins emphasises that Monnet and his colleagues, seeing that a direct move to a united Europe was unlikely ever to be agreed by independent nations, promoted a 'creeping federalism', epitomised by the *acquis communautaire*, the ratchet principle by which all integration is essentially a one-way process. Prins sees the lack of a true European identity as the fundamental flaw in Europeanism and the autocratic rule of the EU elite as a cause of the hollowing-out of democracy in Europe. Increasing integration and centralisation has 'deepened the gulf between rulers and subjects'. The current crisis in Greece is only one aspect of a wider disillusionment with the EU, also manifested in Spain with the rise of Podemos and even, perhaps, in the election of Jeremy Corbyn as Labour Party leader.

For Prins, the issue is not simply, or even mainly, the economics of EU membership. He argues that the UK's worldwide political and strategic interests are increasingly likely to be more important than belonging to a federal state founded on the ghosts of the past.

In an important chapter, Martin Howe spells out the legal framework for exiting the EU (relatively straightforward) or renegotiating the terms of membership from within (much more difficult).

Withdrawal from the EU is possible under Article 50 of the Treaty of European Union. The state concerned notifies the European Council of its intention to withdraw. Negotiations then take place on the arrangements for withdrawal and the state's future relationship with the EU. At the end of two years, the state ceases to be part of the EU, whether or not those negotiations have been completed. Howe shows that the negotiation of transitional and any continuing arrangements would be demanding but that there would be a strong mutual interest in maintaining a free trading relationship.

UK domestic law, much of which now builds on European Directives, would need to be amended, as otherwise whole areas of regulation would potentially be wound up without replacement. It would not be sensible, for example, to have no laws on the licensing of medicines if and when we were no longer signed up to the European Medicines Agency. Howe argues that we can use mechanisms ('Henry VIII powers') rapidly to unravel and replace EU legislation – the same mechanisms that have been used to incorporate EU rules into law without Parliamentary debate.

He also discusses the areas in which we have international agreements with the wider world mediated through the EU and shows how these obligations could be handled. In discussing post-exit relations with the EU, he opts for developing a Swiss-style series of bilateral agreements on particular areas of interest, rather than adopting a relationship on the model of Norway, which is obliged to implement burdensome regulatory requirements without the Norwegian government having a vote in framing them.

If Howe is optimistic about the prospects of the UK following a possible Brexit, he is pessimistic about negotiating exemptions from various forms of regulation while remaining an EU member. He points out that many such changes (for example, in relation to employment law) would require an amendment to EU treaties, and that there is unlikely to be wide support for this, with many member states regarding 'Social Europe' as a key element of the union. Even if sufficient support were forthcoming, the process of ratification would take years and could subsequently be derailed by the changing political complexion of member countries' governments.

Thus Howe advocates a 'zero plus' approach to renegotiation: the UK should indicate its intention to exercise its right to give notice of withdrawal and then see what shape of future relationship mutual interests would dictate. The result could be that the UK ends up retaining its formal membership but with much wider exemptions and opt-out protocols than could be achieved by negotiating wholly from within.

## Policies

The free movement of labour is one of the central features of the EU, dating back to the Treaty of Rome. At the time of writing, however, the EU appears to be tearing itself apart over the issue of mass migration from the Middle East and Africa, with the Schengen Agreement having been temporarily suspended, Germany and a number of East European countries at loggerheads and Britain pursuing a policy of its own.

In this turmoil, it is important not to lose perspective. In a challenging contribution, Philippe Legrain sets out a powerful classical liberal case for free mobility of labour between nation states. He points out that few would now quibble over the benefits of free movement within countries – a principle that was not, however, universally held until recently[2] – yet many baulk at unconstrained cross-border movement. But Britons themselves move abroad in substantial numbers: the number of British expats working abroad is much greater than the number of American expats, for example, despite the US's much larger population. And certainly, Legrain notes, they value the freedom to relocate that the EU offers: British people list the freedom to travel, study and work elsewhere in Europe as one of the top benefits of EU membership.

Legrain stresses that most migrants wish to work, and their energies are likely to promote entrepreneurship, innovation and economic growth in host countries. In the UK, immigrants make a substantial net contribution to government revenue, take on jobs that native workers cannot or will not do and, by

---

2   Even in England, the Tudor Acts of Settlement (which tied poor relief to place of residence) inhibited internal migration: these were not repealed until the nineteenth century, and even then not entirely. A similar provision still exists today in China, where entitlement to welfare benefits is linked to place of birth and has been used by the authorities to deter migration from the countryside to cities (*The Economist* 2015).

expanding the numbers working, relieve the burden of the ageing population.[3] But this is not a purely instrumental argument: the freedom to move is a fundamental liberty that should not be abridged unnecessarily. Legrain argues that it would be better if this freedom were extended to the world as a whole, but he points out that our acceptance of the EU's principle of free movement within Europe does not preclude the UK from pursuing a 'first-best' solution by opening immigration up more widely and pursuing agreements to allow our people to work in other non-EU countries. Although free movement of labour within Europe is often considered analogous to the single market in goods and services, Legrain points out an important difference: our membership of the EU's customs union prevents us from negotiating trade agreements with other non-EU countries, while nothing prevents us from extending free movement of labour beyond the EU.

Thus, Legrain argues that, from a liberal perspective on migration, EU membership is 'pretty much ideal', while talk of leaving the EU to gain control over our borders is 'illiberal and economically harmful'.

If free movement of labour is one defining feature of the EU, two others are the Common Agricultural Policy (CAP) and the customs union (which involves a common external tariff and no tariffs between member states) protecting European manufacturing. In his contribution, Patrick Minford evaluates the costs of these policies to the UK.

Minford points out that tariffs are only one barrier to trade employed by the EU and its members: others include 'anti-dumping' duties, quotas and tacit 'self-restraint' by non-EU states

---

3 Legrain downplays the argument that immigration causes pressure on public services and housing (the same reasoning would limit internal migration) and argues that the 'cultural' objections to migration are weak: Britishness is increasingly, and rightly in his view, based on civic values rather than ethnicity.

intimidated by the threat of EU action. He calculates that effective rates of protection are markedly higher than nominal tariff rates.

Using a computable general equilibrium model, Minford estimates that the total cost to the UK of the protection of agriculture and manufactures is over 4 per cent of Gross Domestic Product. The UK could thus gain significantly from leaving the EU. Resources would switch away from manufacturing, which might be reduced to a small rump of design- and high tech-intensive products. This would not, in Minford's view, be a bad thing: service employment would rise to compensate and overall living standards would increase. He sees no case for artificially maintaining our manufacturing sector in the absence of clear evidence of divergence between the social and market values of manufacturing output.

It follows that, if the UK should leave the EU, Minford does not believe that we should tie ourselves into a free trade agreement with the EU, which would effectively keep us within the customs union. Such an agreement would maintain the distortions (and costs) created by our membership, but give us no voice. We would be better off if, like other smallish countries such as New Zealand and Singapore, we pursued a policy of free trade.

The issue of employment regulation is one that has exercised many British critics of the EU. Particular attention has focused on issues such as the Working Time Directive and the Temporary Agency Workers Directive, which have forced costly changes to employment practices on UK employers.

In his contribution, J. R. Shackleton critically analyses the arguments put forward for regulation in this area and describes the political pressures in most parts of the continent for 'Social Europe'. In fact, the EU's jurisdiction in this area was rather limited until the Maastricht Treaty of 1992, and the UK had an opt-out until Tony Blair's government accepted the 'Social Chapter' in 1997. Even today there are many areas of employment regulation where the UK has freedom of manoeuvre, and this has meant it has chosen to be rather less restrictive over matters such as employment protection legislation than most other EU members. This is why the UK's job creation record has been so good and its unemployment record much better than the EU average.

However, in recent years domestically inspired regulation has sharply increased over such matters as the National Living Wage, auto-enrolment in pension schemes, an apprenticeship levy and so on, while some European Directives, such as that covering parental leave, have been 'gold-plated' (in other words, UK legislation has gone significantly beyond what the EU requires). This leads Shackleton to conclude that leaving the EU would probably do rather little to liberalise the UK labour market. It is difficult to see that much originally EU-driven legislation would be repealed unless a fundamental shift occurs in the attitudes of politicians and the general public. The ideal is definitely less regulation coming from the EU, but the fact that this ideal has not been attained is not the main factor preventing the UK from having more liberal labour markets.

In his detailed examination of the evolution of the CAP, Séan Rickard reminds us that the CAP remains the EU's most expensive policy, accounting for 40 per cent of the EU budget, while (as Minford shows) it raises consumer prices by protecting inefficient farmers across the continent.

Over time, the form of EU subvention to farmers has changed, and the decoupling of support payments from production has led to some modest 'renationalisation' of the CAP, as the introduction of co-funded 'Pillar II' payments has allowed national or regional input into policy. However, prospects for radical reform of the CAP are remote. Strong political support for the hazy vision of 'family farms', plus well-organised farmers' lobbies, makes it difficult to see how any reform could succeed that does not involve similar sums of support money being allocated.

Rickard believes that leaving the EU would bring some possible improvements, such as a more positive attitude to genetically modified (GM) and other new technologies and a greater focus on productivity and competitiveness. The ideal if we were to remain in it would be a much reduced role for the EU in agricultural regulation and price fixing. The example of New Zealand shows how a liberalised agriculture with little government financial support can be successful in the world economy. However, as with employment regulation, domestic pressures in the UK are likely to mean continued government intervention, and 'transitional' financial support for farmers would probably drag on for years.

The management of sea fisheries was originally something of an 'add-on' to the CAP: agriculture was defined in the Treaty of Rome to include the products of fisheries. However, apart from a price support system for fish similar to that of the CAP, little was done to develop a common policy for fishing until the planned enlargement of the European Economic Community (EEC) (which would bring in several important fishing nations) at the beginning of the 1970s. At that point the Community effectively declared the fish stocks in the 200-nautical-mile zone around its coasts to be a shared resource, to be managed by a Common Fisheries Policy. Rachel Tingle's chapter sets out its depressing history.

Tingle argues that the need for some sort of managed approach to fishing arises from the marine version of the Tragedy of the Commons: where resources (in this case fish stocks) are rival in use and non-excludable, they will be overused. But the EU's policies over many years have been contradictory and ineffective, and over-fishing has been rife. By 2008 the European Commission estimated that 80 per cent of fish stocks in EU waters were being fished above their Maximum Sustainable Yield, compared with a global average of 25 per cent.

The system of control, inspection and sanctions has been inadequate for much of the last 40 years: with catch data being incomplete and unreliable, the inspection system being poor and few sanctions being imposed on those breaching quotas. In particular, quotas have been set too high, as the problem of the Commons has been played out within EU fisheries committees, rather than on the seas.

The UK fishing industry has suffered particularly badly because of the manner in which fishing rights have been carved up and the way in which the large EU structural funds, meant to bring about a staged reduction in EU fishing over-capacity, have been used to modernise many of the fishing fleets, particularly that of Spain.

Tingle argues that the UK fishing industry would probably fare much better if we left the EU, as our government could then take full control over UK fishing waters and administer them in the national interest as Norway, Greenland and Iceland have done. If we remain in the EU, fisheries is one area where we do not need, for economic or environmental reasons, to have a joint EU policy. It is an area of policy that should be repatriated to national level. Nation states could then manage fisheries at the most appropriate ecological unit for the fish stock concerned and experiment with making quotas more fully tradable.

The EU plays an increasing role in transport policy: its effects have been mixed. In some areas (uneconomic politically inspired infrastructure projects, excessive emission standards, unrealistic plans for switching freight from roads to rail and water) it has clearly imposed heavy costs on businesses and consumers. There are some benefits including savings from harmonisation of regulation and increased cross-Europe competition: one particular success has been aviation policy, in which state subsidies have been reduced and low-cost airlines are free to compete across the EU.

Kristian Niemietz and Richard Wellings see a need for international cooperation over some issues, such as transport emissions, air traffic control and cross-border rail travel. However, it is not necessarily the case that this cooperation needs the EU to be involved: bilateral agreements between states might be feasible. Moreover, some such cooperation could also involve non-EU countries.

European regulation and investment decisions involve bureaucratic and political processes and an insufficient role for markets, in their view. An example is railway regulation, in which the superficially attractive 'open-access' policy has undermined property rights and prevented vertical integration – which emerged as the most efficient structure in the nineteenth century.[4]

Niemietz and Wellings would like to see a radical programme of deregulation, and believe, where state intervention remains necessary, that there should be a bias towards political decentralisation. This would lead to better use of local knowledge, reflect local preferences and facilitate competition between different countries and regions.

They see a role for transregional and transnational cooperation, but this should cluster around specific areas and be assessed on a case-by-case basis. Integration should not be an end in itself in transport policy. Such cooperation and integration also does not have to take place through formal political institutions, so there would not have to be an EU role in transport as such. If Britain remains a member, EU competence in this area should be dramatically reduced.

The EU has responded to the financial crisis with enhanced capital and supervisory regulation, with the creation of a Single Supervisory Mechanism under the European Central Bank, a Bank Recovery and Regulation Directive and other proposals. However, David Mayes and Geoffrey Wood argue that this approach has been mistaken.

As the UK is contemplating a new start in its relationship with the EU, they draw on the lessons of banking history to make

---

4   Though it could be argued that this policy may protect the industry against the complete renationalisation of the railways currently proposed by the Labour Party.

a case for going back to first principles. In nineteenth-century Britain, cash (on security) from the privately owned central bank ensured that one bank running out of cash did not lead to panics and the failure of other banks. This support was on some rare occasions supplemented with private consortia acting to cover losses. The system did not need substantial detailed regulation from the state.

In modern conditions, there needs to be ready overnight resolvability so that the financial system can be kept operating without a break. In this context, banks must hold adequate 'loss-absorbing capacity', bank structures should be simpler and there should be an enhanced 'lender of last resort' function.

Mayes and Wood point out that no system can remove all risk of bank failures and crises. But a simpler system on the lines they discuss is preferable to further detailed regulation: a lesson that needs to be learnt whether we are in or out of the EU.

In the related area of financial services, such as insurance and securities transactions, there has been a movement away from the principle of mutual recognition of diverse regulatory regimes across Europe and towards increased centralisation of regula-tion at the EU level. Ostensibly justified by the desire to promote free trade in services within a single market, the danger is that this may lead to more regulation and higher costs for consumers. The single market promoted by the EU is not a 'free market' by any means.

As Philip Booth reasons in his chapter, there is in practice lit-tle check on centralisation and excessive regulation: a unanimity requirement for new regulation is probably necessary to provide this. Within the EU, the UK should press for a return to greater use of mutual recognition and the resolution of disputed regu-latory issues through the ECJ, which should adjudicate only with a view to removing restraints on free trade.

More fundamentally, if countries wish to obtain the advan-tages of unifying regulatory systems, they can in principle do so through intergovernmental agreements. This could be done amongst EU countries or involve countries outside the EU, but it would be a process that would not need to involve the EU as an institution. The EU-specific role in relation to these aspects of financial services should simply be to remove barriers to trade. If we left the EU, we might face higher trade barriers, and it cannot be assumed that domestic businesses would be less heavily regulated than they are currently.

Climate policy is a major area of EU responsibility that was never envisaged at the time of the Treaty of Rome. It currently consists of targets for emissions reduction, the Emissions Trading System, renewable energy subsidies and green taxes. There is also a range of requirements for greater energy efficiency (for example, in regulations setting requirements for average fuel efficiency in motor vehicles).

Matthew Sinclair argues in his contribution that the EU has been too ambitious in terms of setting targets and ineffective in devising detailed policies. Too often, he claims, the UK has gone along uncritically with the rest of the EU: indeed, it has sometimes been responsible for putting forward or promoting some of the policies he decries.

The Emissions Trading System has been subject to massive fraud, and the carbon price has been subject to excessive fluctuations, caused partly by over-allocation of emissions allowances. Renewable energy subsidies have been poorly directed, with the most expensive energy sources receiving the most subsidy, and are proving so costly that governments are having to cut back on them. Green taxes have in practice led to confusion: are they there to raise revenue or to alter behaviour?

Sinclair argues that in some ways EU climate policy is attempting the impossible: it is assuming that an effective *global* policy can be instituted and trying to organise Europe's 'share' of such a policy. In reality, no effective global policy is ever going to be implemented. The EU should recognise this and instead focus on directly supporting research into new technologies that could reduce greenhouse gas emissions intensity (an intervention that could be initiated unilaterally but, if successful, affect emissions globally) and promoting adaptability and resilience in the face of global warming. This could be an area where the UK might form better policy on its own.

There may be some economic arguments for EU intervention in health matters to help protect against communicable diseases and pollution, issues that transcend borders. There may also be EU single-market and consumer protection concerns over problems such as non-prescription and counterfeit medicines. The European Health Insurance Card could be justified in relation to free mobility of labour. But, as Christopher Snowdon argues in his chapter, in European law there is no basis for (and little interest in) integrating healthcare provision or preventing non-communicable disease.

Snowdon focuses instead on the growing field of 'lifestyle regulation' – in particular, attempts by government prohibitions, taxes and subsidies to get people to cut tobacco and alcohol consumption and change their diets to reduce the prospect of obesity.

He points out that this overtly anti-market agenda threatens to limit personal freedoms. In the context of the EU, however, the interesting issue is that measures such as tax rises, advertising bans and minimum pricing can conflict with free trade and the single internal market. In fact, the European Court has usually held that the single market trumps lifestyle regulation where such regulation threatens competition across the EU. An example of this is the recent European Court opinion against the Scottish attempt to introduce a minimum per-unit alcohol price.[5]

---

5   The Scottish Parliament voted in 2012 to set a minimum price per unit, but in September 2015 Advocate-General Yves Bot concluded that minimum pricing was 'difficult to justify' as a means of curbing excessive alcohol consumption: it was a breach of trade rules. This opinion was accepted by the ECJ in December.

Direct legislation by the EU has been limited: examples include the Food Labelling and Nutrition Labelling Directives, and the recent Tobacco Products Directive. Fear of adverse legal judgement has meant that the European Commission has avoided some types of intervention (such as a cross-EU ban on tobacco retail displays) but has gone ahead with other, arguably less significant, prohibitions such as that on menthol cigarettes.[6]

Snowdon points out that the Tobacco Products Directive has been rationalised as an attempt to harmonise regulations and promote the single market, but its real aim has been to create a larger area of competence for the EU and allow more initiatives to cut smoking.

A particular concern highlighted by Snowdon is the way in which the European Commission funds a large number of activist organisations that promote lifestyle interventions. This funding enables activists to have a high profile promoting policies that the EU cannot currently endorse; by attempting to influence political debate in this way, the Commission is arguably behaving unethically.

In reviewing lifestyle regulation, Snowdon finds that the British (and Scottish) governments are frequently more draconian than the EU has so far proved to be. UK consumers have thus to some extent been protected against their own governments' legislative appetites. And, although taxes on tobacco and alcohol are arguably far too high in the UK, they would probably be higher still without the possibility of consumers legally importing significant amounts of these goods for personal use, and smugglers importing larger amounts illegally.

He concludes provocatively by pointing out that Brexit would only benefit those consumers who want to smoke, drink alcohol

---

6    There are no national differences between consumers of menthol cigarettes, and no particular country's retailers lose out disproportionately. There are thus no obvious grounds for objectors to take legal action against prohibition.

and freely choose what food they eat if British legislators become more liberal: an unlikely prospect. If we were outside the EU, British governments – whether Conservative, Labour or Coalition – would likely be more interventionist, restrictive and bureaucratic lifestyle regulators than the EU. Currently, the EU role in this field is, on balance, beneficial. It restrains governments from imposing burdens on their peoples. In an ideal world, and in the renegotiation, there is no need for great changes in this area of policy.

## Change has to come

One common thread running through these contributions is that the goal of 'ever-closer union' – understandable in the generation that pioneered European integration – is no longer a useful guide to the future development of the EU.

Our authors suggest that, although there are some areas where cooperation with our European neighbours can bring positive benefits, there are many other areas where there is no clear reason for such heavy EU involvement. Greater freedom for nation states might allow them to pursue constructive relationships with others outside the EU (and, for that matter, arrangement with EU members outside EU structures) as well as allow their domestic policies to promote economic liberalism and respond more effectively, where necessary, to local and regional concerns.

Furthermore, even where there is a case for an EU competence – in some transport matters and in climate change policy, for example – the policies chosen have often been confused and ineffective. This is in part the result of decision-making processes and institutions that are badly designed and give too much influence to special interests. So, in these areas, even though a case for an EU competence can be made, the objectives might be better achieved through other forms of cooperation.

Bringing about change from within the EU is very difficult because of the culture of the *acquis communautaire*. It may be, as Howe suggests, that the only way to get effective reform is to vote to leave the EU, and then negotiate for a new partnership that would allow the UK and EU to build on the positives rather than endlessly squabble over the negatives.

Such a process might also bring greater clarity to the UK electorate, who often blame the EU for policies that our politicians may often approve of or even be largely responsible for. Several of our authors have pointed out the way in which UK politicians are as much or even more committed to potentially damaging policies than their European equivalents.

Most authors concur that the problem of our relationship with the EU is often not only the particular economic and social policies pursued by the EU (which are often supported, rightly or wrongly, by our own politicians), but also the manner in which decisions are made, and the constant emphasis on Brussels' centralising mission.

In personal affairs, marriages that become too inward-looking, and where a dominant partner is used to getting his or her own way, begin to sour. Where the other partner was once happy to defer in matters such as whose parents to spend Christmas with, or where and when to take holidays, he or she may increasingly come to resent more and more decisions being made on their behalf. Unless the dominant partner can loosen up, be less controlling, allow the spouse to make decisions for themself and have the occasional night out with friends rather than doing everything as a couple, the divorce court may beckon.

The contributions of this book are diverse and not easy to summarise. But this last analogy may help us to frame the referendum discussion. It is clear that the UK and the rest of the EU have many common interests that can benefit from cooperation; this book's contributions are in effect an analysis of the form that such cooperation should take. The problem that arises in the

UK–EU relationship concerns the desire for dominance from the EU partner. The EU demands a commitment to 'ever-closer union' and the *acquis communautaire* is a ratchet where power always accumulates nearer to the centre. Yet the EU's institutions do not appear to be well adapted for the decision-making apparatus of a modern state; there is poor accountability to electorates as well as an inability of opponents of state measures to challenge them in open and effective debate. Instead, the EU is heavily preyed on by lobbying from vested interests.

Furthermore, the political philosophy of the elite that dominates EU decision-making is 'social democratic', by which is meant a well-meaning but excessively managerial and bureaucratic socialism, albeit pursued through regulation rather than state ownership or by tax and redistribution. A liberal belief in markets, though occasionally mouthed, does not run deep.

The EU elite is impatient with dissent; the ECJ is its agent for suppressing it. For a UK with a long history of resistance to dictatorial powers, starting with Magna Carta through the Cromwellian wars to modern Parliamentary democracy, subjection in the twenty-first century to an EU superstate looks increasingly unacceptable.

Thus, in the renegotiation process, the emphasis should be on reform of the institutions. But what competences, ideally, should such reformed institutions have when it comes to economic life? If we are to have a more economically liberal Britain, then restraints on the use of powers by national governments to restrict freedom of movement or to introduce regulations that inhibit trade are generally desirable. In some areas, the EU has such powers and uses them in a way the authors of this book believe is desirable. In other areas where the EU has competences, it should be stripped of them – this would include fishing and labour market regulation. In a large group of further areas, such as financial markets regulation and climate change policy, the EU role should be minimised. These should be the priorities for renegotiation.

In the absence of a substantial package arising from the negotiation process, voters will have to continue to put up with the incursions into their domestic affairs of what many of them regard as a superstate – or they will have to vote to leave. Voting to leave could bring many economic benefits, but only if economically liberal policies are adopted domestically. It could also bring costs if domestic governments decide to regulate those activities (such as migration) in which the EU currently has a restraining role on states.

The referendum will give the UK's verdict. This book sets out a range of parameters by which the British people can frame their decision.

## References

*Economist* (2015) Managing migration; no riff-raff, 26 September.

Tiebout, C. M. (1956) A pure theory of local expenditure. *Journal of Political Economy* 64: 416–24.

# 2 ASSIGNING RESPONSIBILITIES IN A FEDERAL SYSTEM

Martin Ricketts

## Introduction

In 1777, the thirteen newly independent states of America drew up the Articles of Confederation. Article III set out the purposes of this 'firm league of friendship' – 'for their common defence, the security of their liberties, and their mutual and general welfare'. Ten years later, the same language appeared in the Constitution of the United States, which aimed to 'establish Justice, insure domestic Tranquility, provide for the common defence, promote the general Welfare, and secure the Blessings of Liberty …' Section 8 of the first Article lists the delegated powers that were considered necessary for these purposes, including the power to collect taxes (in proportion to the population of each state) in order to regulate commerce between the states and with foreign nations; to borrow and coin money; to establish post offices and post roads; to introduce patent protection and copyright 'to promote the progress of science and the useful arts'; and to conduct foreign affairs, including the support of military forces.

Two hundred and twenty years later, the Treaty of Lisbon sets out a more detailed list of 'competences' for an EU. As in the case of the US Constitution (which replaced the Articles of Confederation in 1789), the powers are 'governed by the principle of conferral'[1] and (echoing the tenth amendment of 1791) 'competences not

---

1   Title, 1, Article 5(1) 'Consolidated Treaties'.

conferred upon the Union in the Treaties remain with the Member States'.[2] In other words, the individual states are regarded as conferring upon the Union certain specific delegated powers, while retaining for themselves an open and unspecified list of remaining competences. Exclusive competence[3] is granted to the Union in the areas of the customs union, the rules governing the internal market, the common commercial policy, monetary policy for members of the euro area and the common fisheries policy. With the exception of the latter, these correlate with the commerce and monetary clauses of the US Constitution. In addition to these exclusive competences, there is a class of 'shared competence'[4] in which both individual states and the Union as a whole can act. This class includes areas such as (inter alia) some aspects of social policy, agriculture, the environment, consumer protection, transport, energy, safety and public health matters. The Union may also act in research, technological development and humanitarian aid and may 'support, coordinate or supplement' the actions of member states in human health, industry, culture, tourism, education, sport, training and civil protection.[5]

This extensive list of exclusive and shared competences naturally gives rise to the question of what principles, if any, lie behind it. When would we expect to see individual states finding it advantageous to enter a federation with powers to impose rules binding for all its members, and when would we expect a state to remain aloof? Does economics provide any tools for identifying the circumstances in which leaving states to make unilateral decisions will produce generally superior outcomes (defined by various possible normative criteria) to joint decisions? If joint decisions are potentially beneficial, what decision rules should be adopted?

---

2   Title, 1, Articles 4(1) and 5(2) 'Consolidated Treaties'.
3   Part 1, Title 1, Article 3, Treaty on the Functioning of the European Union.
4   Part 1, Title 1, Article 4, Treaty on the Functioning of the European Union.
5   Part 1, Title 1, Article 6, Treaty on the Functioning of the European Union.

It is immediately evident that such questions are the province of 'political economy' broadly conceived rather than of standard microeconomics. States are themselves made up of many people with differing interests, so identifying some form of coherent collective interest for each one presents problems of its own. Furthermore, when collective decisions are made, questions of legitimacy arise that are not entirely a matter of rational analysis (which is not to say that the legitimacy of a collective process is unrelated to its ability to serve the rational interests of its participants). Institutions that are familiar, with long historical roots, have a quite reasonable pull on human affections (as any follower of Edmund Burke would argue) and may have qualities for coping with very complex circumstances that purely rationalistic models cannot uncover. Nevertheless, public finance and institutional economics do provide a conceptual apparatus that permits some discussion of the problem of the assignment of competences between layers of government.

## Public goods and interjurisdictional spillovers

### Public goods

A convenient starting point for a discussion of how competences are assigned between levels of government is the idea that one of the state's basic roles is the provision of public goods. Hume (1740) gave the example of draining land, something that might involve thousands of people in a collective endeavour, the benefits of which would be experienced in common. Each individual would have an incentive to avoid paying and to free ride on the efforts of others, so securing agreement and organising the work would be very difficult, if not impossible. Political society is the solution to this public goods problem – forcing citizens to pay through the tax mechanism and, in democratic states, inducing them (imperfectly) to reveal their preferences in a voting process.

25

Indeed, defence against foreign invasion as well as protection from violence and the provision of security and justice at home are the classical public goods and underlie the economic theory of the state (Baumol 1952).

In the case of pure public goods, all individual people experience the same level of service, and an increase in the population would not cause any reduction in its quality. A larger state in the sense of a bigger population of taxpayers is clearly advantageous in that a given level of public good supply can be achieved at a lower cost per taxpayer. Similarly, there would be an advantage to extending the state by means of joining a federation for the purposes of producing this pure kind of public good. A standard argument, therefore, is that we would expect federal jurisdiction over public goods that have a range that spans the full geographical extent of a federation.

This classical conception is clearly reflected in the US Constitution, which emphasises 'common defence', specifically empowers the US to raise armies and maintain a navy, and forbids to the states the power of making treaties or forming alliances.[6] In contrast, the consolidated treaties of the EU reflect an awareness of the lack of a sufficiently developed sense of common European interest. There is an aspiration 'to define and implement a common foreign and security policy, including the progressive framing of a common defence policy'.[7] This, however, must be seen in the context of a clear statement that 'the essential state functions' of 'ensuring territorial integrity, maintaining law and order and safeguarding national security' are respected by the Union. 'In particular, national security remains the sole responsibility of each Member State'.[8] A common defence will occur only 'when the European Council, acting unanimously, so decides'.[9]

---

6   US Constitution, Article I, Sections 8 and 10.

7   Part 1, Title 1, Article 2(4), Treaty on the Functioning of the European Union.

8   Title 1, Article 4(2) 'Consolidated Treaties'.

9   Title V, Chapter 2, Article 42(2) 'Consolidated Treaties'.

It seems, therefore, that even the case of defence is more complicated than its simplistic classification as a federal public good would suggest. In the first place, any more realistic assessment of defence as a collective good might begin to question the degree of purity that is generally involved. As a federation expands to incorporate more states within its territory, it is not obvious that the new members simply lower the price per unit rather than impose new defence requirements. Neither is it obvious that all states would necessarily consider themselves equally defended by the forces of the federation. Different states might face differing threats requiring differing diplomatic, technical and military responses. If a particular state of a Union suspects that the Union is likely to be unreliable in defence of the state's interests, or to put a relatively low priority on its security concerns, it would be expected to prefer to preserve a significant level of local control over defence expenditure in spite of the possible economies that could in principle be realised through integration.

## Regional and local public goods

If public goods usually depart considerably from the non-rivalness condition of the pure case, it is also true that the geographical range of the benefits conferred by a public good can be restricted. Indeed, the case for 'fiscal federalism' and the existence of devolved governments with powers to determine public goods provision has traditionally depended on local public goods. Street lights confer benefits on passing travellers, no doubt, but primarily they benefit those who live in a given neighbourhood. Flood defences will depend upon the management of particular water courses and will not be of such concern to those who live away from a flood plain. Police forces will often face rather different problems in different cities or regions. There is a strong case here for devolved decision-making on the grounds that local preferences will vary and that knowledge of particular local circumstances will be more likely to influence decisions. Central decisions that impose standard levels of local or even national public goods provision across a federation will not reflect differences in social costs and benefits. They are thus less likely to be efficient in the sense of maximising the possible net social gains available.

Where the mobility of a population between the states in a federation is considerable, and where cultural and linguistic barriers are low, the case for more centralised intervention in the provision of local public goods can be made on the grounds that potential migrants might be prepared to pay for better services. Those who might seek employment or retirement opportunities in neighbouring states could be considered to have an interest in the standards of public services available there, which the federal jurisdiction represents. The introduction of minimum centrally determined standards can then be seen as a (somewhat crude) response to this problem and a way of taking account of the option value of the local services to residents of other states. More commonly, Federal intervention is justified on the grounds of reducing regional disparities of income or wealth; hence the resulting disparities in the ability to finance public goods. If income distribution were the principal concern, then lump sum transfers to poorer states would be predicted – or indeed income transfers to poorer individuals irrespective of state residence. However, interstate fiscal transfers are often earmarked for specific purposes or take the form of matching grants, which suggests that relaxing the constraint of the local tax base is not the main consideration. The matching grants are also supposed to allow for interjurisdictional spillovers in specific areas, and they are therefore a centralised response to a perceived efficiency problem.

### Interjurisdictional spillovers

The idea that interjurisdictional spillovers must inevitably buttress the case for greater centralised (federal-level) collective decision-making is a conclusion that seems to arise naturally from the textbook analysis of market failure and public policy. If central decision makers are informed and benevolent, they will take into account the existence of beneficial or harmful spillovers, and the associated activities will be suitably increased or curtailed. Disinterested and well-informed federal public officials would implement optimal policies. In practice, however, the required information on the preferences of the people affected and the technical opportunities available for mitigating external harm or for taking advantage of spillover benefits will not necessarily be available. Collective decision processes at the centre may reflect the interests of powerful pressure groups or the influence of states that are only very distantly affected.

Institutionally, the situation is analogous to the problem of whether firms should merge to take advantage of mutual spillovers or whether the potential gains can be achieved through contract. As is well known, relatively high transactions costs in the market will favour merger and internal governance, while, conversely, relatively high costs of incentive and control within the firm will favour a contractual solution. If we can regard individual states as equivalent to firms, the choice between growth through merger and growth through the extension of market contracts is mirrored in the state's choice of accession to a federation and the extension of individual treaty arrangements. Just as bee-keepers and apple growers might decide to merge their operations in order to internalise the mutual external benefits that each confers on the other, states might similarly opt for joint decision-making when close, mutual interdependence is the norm. However, some external effects might be relatively straightforward to handle through market contract, in the case of firms, or international treaty, in the case of states.

The important point to note here is that the case for the assignment of a particular competence to a particular level of government cannot be regarded as a matter entirely determined by the existence and extent of spillovers. The important matter is the more complex one of determining the relative bargaining costs, agency costs and effectiveness of different collective decision-making processes. Decisions in the EU made by qualified majority, for example, are capable of imposing high costs on a dissenting state. However, a unanimity rule (required in some areas) might be expected greatly to increase bargaining costs and to reduce the chances of achieving many potentially advantageous agreements. Each state has to determine whether the cost of unwelcome legislation is or is not outweighed by the benefits of Europe-wide agreements that would otherwise not be achievable.

## Competition between jurisdictions

The discussion thus far has concerned the dilemmas that arise when public goods and interstate spillovers give rise to possible gains from cooperation, and states confront the choice of entering formal Union or federal mechanisms to resolve these problems or to remain outside and negotiate treaties on a state-to-state basis. The only general conclusion that can be derived is that the more interdependent the states (the more 'pure' a public good) and the greater the number of states involved (the higher the costs of bargaining), the more potentially advantageous a federal competency in the area will be. Even here, however, reinforced majorities will be required to reassure states that collective outcomes will not result in net losses if interstate income levels or preferences differ greatly. Local public goods, in contrast, are more likely to be allocated efficiently by lower level governments.

The final statement of the previous paragraph has so far been justified by reference to better local information, but it has by no means been fully demonstrated. The median voter theorem is often invoked to predict the provision of local public goods, but this is not guaranteed to be efficient.[10] Furthermore, where voting involves choice over packages of policies rather than single issues, or where powerful local interests (political and bureaucratic) play a decisive role, local collective choices will be distorted, and the greater efficiency of local outcomes is hardly assured. What is required is some mechanism for forcing voters to reveal their valuations of local public goods and for taming the power of local interest groups.

It was Tiebout (1956) who first advanced the idea that the migration of population between jurisdictions could be seen as a decentralised market mechanism for introducing competition and revealing people's willingness to pay for local public goods. A person who regarded an existing level of provision as either excessive or inadequate (at the prevailing tax price in the relevant community) could simply move to another jurisdiction that matched his or her preferences more accurately. In this way, the residents of a jurisdiction become consumers exercising their choice over tax and public goods packages. The classical 'revelation of preferences' problem in the case of public goods is circumvented because the goods are local and consumption requires the voluntary decision to locate at a certain place and pay the tax price. The ability to 'exit' and purchase elsewhere makes the situation comparable to the decision to join a club or purchase any jointly consumed service where exclusion is possible.

The conditions required for this process to work perfectly (in the sense of ensuring the ideal provision of local public goods across jurisdictions) turn out to be extremely demanding. People must be able to set up any number of new jurisdictions, mobility costs must be zero and there is should be a single local public good. With a fixed number of communities, heterogeneous individuals and multiple local public goods, it is not surprising

---

10 The median voter theorem is extensively discussed in public choice theory: see Mueller (2003).

that the Tiebout process cannot be relied upon to ensure an allocation of resources that is efficient (see, for example, Atkinson and Stiglitz 1980: 519–56). Nevertheless, the existence of mobile resources will limit the ability of a local political process to generate results that are massively inefficient or exploitative. From the point of view of the implementation of optimal policy by fully informed officials, these constraints on policy can be seen as highly disadvantageous. But in a world where information is incomplete and dispersed, and where monopoly of political power is a continuing danger, the Tiebout model is a reminder of the potential value of the competitive process, even in the realm of jointly consumed goods.

A similar conceptual framework that has been used to discuss local public goods is the 'Theory of Clubs' in Buchanan (1965). This theory considers the class of services that are consumed jointly by club members but which are also subject to quality deterioration through crowding as the membership expands for any given capacity of the club's resources. New members lower the entry fee per member and spread the costs over a larger number of people, but they also, after a certain point, cause a deterioration in quality. Clearly there will be an optimal membership size for any given scale of output. Similarly, there will be an optimal level of output for any given size of club membership. The members of the club will compare the benefits of reduced crowding with the additional fees required to finance it. Efficiency requires that each club has optimal membership size for its collective output and optimal collective output for its membership size.

As a model of local public good provision, there are again some notable disadvantages. Clubs, as with Tiebout's local jurisdictions, will tend to attract people with similar preferences and incomes. Diversity of membership is unlikely to be a characteristic of a club equilibrium. Further, clubs are financed by fees that are the same for all members, just as Tiebout's local public goods are assumed to be financed by a lump sum tax on each person.

As a representation of the way state or local governments are in fact financed in federal or devolved systems, therefore, these models are not descriptively accurate. However, descriptive realism is not their purpose. Their focus is on the provision of local public goods as a category and the possible use of mobility as a demand-revealing mechanism. Given the rather pure assumptions that people are perfectly mobile and have no local dependency or affections, it is hardly surprising that the results do not reflect actual institutional arrangements. In particular, of course, models such as these make very clear the limited effectiveness of assigning an income redistribution objective to local jurisdictions when factors of production are very mobile.

## The race to the bottom

One of the main objections to competition between jurisdictions is that, if conditions are not suitable, the competitive process will result in lower standards of public services than would be recommended by a social cost–benefit analysis.[11] This, of course, directly contradicts the Tiebout hypothesis and derives from differences in the analytical context. As has been pointed out, Tiebout jurisdictions finance local public goods by lump sum taxes and will tend to attract a homogeneous population. If, instead, we start the analysis by assuming that local jurisdictions (or states in a federation) finance their activities through proportional or progressive income or expenditure taxes, it is clear that high income people will pay a higher tax price per unit of the public good produced than low income people. These high income people could then be enticed away to other jurisdictions offering marginally better terms. Tax competition will mean that jurisdictions with a varied population by income will be unable

---

11  Sinn (2003) presents an extended analysis of 'systems competition' and the circumstances in which it can be expected to function destructively or in a beneficial way.

to charge differential tax prices, and the ability to finance public goods in a progressive way will be impaired.

In general, owners of mobile resources will find themselves subject to lower rates of taxation than those of immobile resources. Owners of financial capital, highly skilled labour and people with rights to profits from footloose corporations will be at an advantage compared with those who are relatively immobile or who own fixed property or land. From a pure efficiency point of view, this is not all bad news. The deadweight losses associated with taxes on labour and capital are substantial (as people adapt their work effort and investment strategies) compared with those on land or natural resources (Tideman and Plassmann 1998; Tideman et al. 2002). Indeed, there are strong ethical and efficiency arguments in favour of a tax structure that targets economic rent (i.e. pure surplus) over other forms of income. For communities of variable population size but with a given quantity of available 'land', it is even possible to show that the public collection of rent is capable of precisely financing an optimal supply of a single local public good.[12]

Nevertheless, the extensive list of shared competences in the EU testifies to the existence of a high level of suspicion of competition between the states. The 'approximation of legislation'[13] is a major objective of the treaties in areas such as health, safety and environmental protection. In general, the assumption is that to leave states solely responsible for these areas would lead to the erosion of standards and the undermining of the 'single market'. The regulation of interstate commerce is a fundamental federal responsibility, but just as the commerce clause has been used historically to extend central authority in the US, the EU has extended its remit in order to ensure the harmonisation of regulations and hence a level playing field. This can be seen clearly in the case of the

---

12  Stiglitz (1977) refers to this as the 'Henry George' theorem.
13  Title VII, Treaty on the Functioning of the European Union.

CAP, where the judgement from the earliest days of the EEC was that the power of the farming interests in each state was too great ever to permit the development of free trade in agricultural goods without centralised intervention to control subsidies. To the extent that health, safety or environmental costs and benefits are truly local, however, harmonisation actually undermines interstate trade. Trade confers benefits when the relative marginal social costs of goods or services differ between states. Regulation that tries to smooth out real cost differences artificially is actually trade-destroying rather than trade-creating. The fear that drives the policy of harmonisation, however, is twofold. First, that, left to themselves, states might impose regulations that act as barriers to trade by protecting local producers. Second, that, faced with a highly competitive commercial environment, states might be unduly reluctant to introduce suitable regulations to correct for genuine, local market failures for fear of putting their domestic firms at a disadvantage. These two concerns push in opposite directions of course. In the first case, the state would be imposing regulations on importers that local producers could somehow circumvent. In the second case, a state would be considering and failing to introduce regulations within its jurisdiction because other states deemed them to be unnecessary. The similarity between the cases is that they both imply the danger of a mercantilist and protectionist policy bias in member states.

In a competitive jurisdictions system, however, it is necessary for regulation to be imposed on a destination basis rather than harmonised across member states. That is, each state should control the regulatory framework within its geographical area and should not discriminate against goods and services imported from other states. Under these circumstances, each state competes for mobile resources by providing local public goods and a suitable fiscal and regulatory environment within its area. The important requirement is that a court of law such as the ECJ is capable of adjudicating in the case of disputes, and is able to pronounce on whether regulations or other measures are acting like non-tariff barriers or are simply reflecting a state's reasonable response to a perceived social harm. This will not always be easy, but similar judgements – for example, about whether commercial agreements are in restraint of trade – are regularly required in the area of competition policy.

Where a state's fiscal and regulatory interventions are tailored to its own circumstances in this way, a reluctance to introduce potentially socially beneficial measures because of foreign competition could only be explained by reference to the power of adversely affected special interests or other imperfections in local political processes. To a significant extent, therefore, the case for more centralisation is based on a lack of confidence in the ability of local political decision-making to reflect the interests of the local population as a whole. Assigning competence in these areas to a central authority is a way of constraining local politicians and interests. However, centralised decision-making processes, as has been noted, open the door to other even more powerful interests. This is because they operate across the entire Union and are less constrained by the force of interjurisdictional competition.

## Conclusion

Economics provides plenty of powerful mechanisms for analysing federal systems – for example, the theory of public goods, public choice, interjurisdictional spillovers, the Theory of Clubs and interjurisdictional competition. It is evident, however, that the complexity of collective choice problems in federations means that simple rules about the assignment of competences are not easily derived.

The least controversial proposition is that local public goods should be supplied by local governments. Here, the economic argument is simply that local decisions are more likely to reflect local preferences and supply conditions, and that local responsibility will also permit a degree of competition to take place (either through Tiebout-style migration or through the ability to compare performance between states). These efficiency considerations seem at first glance to be supported by the political principle of subsidiarity, which appears as one of the founding principles governing the limits of Union competences set out in the Consolidated Treaties of the European Union.[14] The mechanisms to support this principle, however, depend upon 'reasoned opinions' from National Parliaments to draft legislative acts[15] attracting sufficient support from across the Union. The tendency towards greater centralised intervention is unlikely to be much inhibited by this mechanism. Far from leaving undelegated powers with the states, the 'sharing' of competences requires continual (and costly) resistance to incursions on the part of the states. Furthermore, this resistance cannot appeal to clear principles of law but is forced to address the much vaguer question of whether 'the objectives' of a proposed action are or are not 'better achieved at Union level'.[16]

Spillovers between states and public goods that span a group of states as a whole favour more integrated decision-making. States clearly need to come together to agree on mutually advantageous measures. This might normally suggest the assignment of these matters to federal or Union decision-making mechanisms. Even here, however, we cannot conclude that it will be in the interests of every state to accept such an assignment. Centralisation does not ensure efficiency or even that every state will be better off (unless unanimity is the decision rule). The nature of the spillovers (whether uniform across states or skewed in the direction of other

---

14  Title 1, Article 5(3) 'Consolidated Treaties'.

15  Protocol (Number 2) 'Consolidated Treaties'.

16  Title 1, Article 5(3) 'Consolidated Treaties'.

particular states) and the details of the political processes involved would all be expected to determine the political outcome. The most contentious areas concern policies aimed at redistributing income. With mobile factors of production, it is clear that local jurisdictions can be thwarted in their policies of redistribution. The literature on fiscal federalism, therefore, normally assigns welfare policy to the federal level. From the point of view of public choice theory, however, the case is much less clear cut. The tendency for government policies to be directed towards powerful special interests and for the relatively poor to vote for redistributive regulations and tax policies has been likened to the tragedy of the commons (see, for example, McGuire and Olson 1996). Voters and pressure groups in their self-regarding use of the political system do not take account of the effects on the economy as a whole. This can lead to an over-extended state sector (in the sense that everyone could, in principle, be made better off with a smaller one), as people try to use it to redistribute income in their favour. Rent seeking is, in other words, facilitated by democratic centralisation, while interjurisdictional competition will restrict it by giving the power of exit to politically vulnerable groups. Those with confidence in political processes and in favour of highly redistributive systems, therefore, will favour central assignment of competences related to welfare payments and related policies. Those who wish to restrict the redistributive zeal of governments prefer that the responsibility is retained at state rather than Union level.[17]

---

17 Sinn (2003: 78–81) proposes the 'home country principle' as an alternative to harmonisation or the existing 'inclusion principle', under which an immigrant is subject to the taxes and welfare benefits of the host country. This principle 'states that the country in which a person was born remains responsible for the welfare aid this person receives and the redistributive taxes he or she pays' (ibid.: 79–80). The legal, political and administrative problems of such a system cannot be reviewed here, but clearly it would in principle prevent migration from undermining welfare systems while placing constraints on the form that such systems might take. The state as a 'social insurance club' would not be subject to competition from other states because 'exit' would be restricted in this particular area.

# References

Atkinson, A. B. and Stiglitz, J. E. (1980) *Lectures on Public Economics.* London: McGraw-Hill.

Baumol, W. J. (1952) *Welfare Economics and the Theory of the State.* Cambridge, MA: Harvard University Press.

Brennan, G. and Hamlin, A. (1998) Fiscal federalism. In *The New Palgrave Dictionary of Economics and the Law* (ed. P. Newman). London: Macmillan Reference Limited.

Buchanan, J. M. (1965) An economic theory of clubs. *Economica* 32: 1–14.

Hume, D. (1740/1978) *Treatise of Human Nature* (ed. P. H. Nidditch). Oxford: Clarendon Press.

McGuire, M. and Olson, M. (1996) The economics of autocracy and majority rule: the invisible hand and the use of force. *Journal of Economic Literature* 34: 72–96.

Mueller, D. C. (2003) *Public Choice III.* Cambridge University Press.

Oates, W. E. (1972) *Fiscal Federalism.* New York: Harcourt Brace.

Sinn, H.-W. (2003) *The New Systems Competition.* Oxford: Blackwell.

Stiglitz, J. E. (1977) The theory of local public goods. In *The Economics of Public Services* (ed. M. S. Feldstein and R. P. Inman). London: Macmillan.

Tideman, N. and Plassmann, F. (1998) Taxed out of work and wealth: the costs of taxing labor and capital. In *The Losses of Nations: Deadweight Politics Versus Public Rent Dividends* (ed. F. Harrison). London: Othila Press.

Tideman, N., Akobundu, E., Johns, A. and Wutthicharoen, P. (2002) The avoidable excess burden of broad-based U.S. taxes. *Public Finance Review* 30(5): 416–41.

Tiebout, C. M. (1956) A pure theory of local expenditure. *Journal of Political Economy* 64: 416–24.

# 3 INSTITUTIONS FOR EUROPEAN COOPERATION

Roland Vaubel

## The renegotiation

In this chapter, I shall contrast the real, existing EU with the ideal institutions for European cooperation. The British renegotiation will not bring about this ideal, but it may bring the EU nearer to it. The basic choice facing the UK is between opt-outs and reform of the EU institutions. Clearly, general institutional reform is more valuable for Europe and more attractive for Britain than special treatment of an outlier.

Which reforms should the British government aim at? Obviously, they ought to be important for Britain. At the same time, however, they ought to be unimportant or even attractive for the other governments.

Restraining immigration and access to welfare benefits is an example of what cannot be achieved by amending the treaties or adding a protocol. The East Europeans would object. Another example is the demand to abolish the Strasbourg sessions of the European Parliament. The French government would never agree to that.

However, all EU governments share a common interest in curbing the centralising powers of the EU institutions: the Commission, the Parliament and the Court. The British wish-list has to be targeted on the EU institutions, not on other member states.

The EU institution most in need of reform is the Court of Justice. Very few people realise this. The Court is the lynchpin of the system. Without its protection, the Commission and the EU Parliament could not (mis)interpret the treaties in the centralising way they do. As I have shown elsewhere (Vaubel 2014), the rule of law has effectively broken down at the EU level with the open or tacit approval of the Court. Most of these breaches concern the euro zone. However, the UK is also severely affected by the Court's misjudgements on financial and labour market regulation. The Court has upheld the use of Article 114 of the Treaty on the Functioning of the European Union (TFEU) as a basis for financial regulation, even though international differences in process regulations – as Fahey (2011) and others have pointed out – are perfectly consistent with the free movement of capital.[1] Article 114 of the TFEU is about protectionist product regulations, not about process regulations. Process regulations cannot serve as instruments of protection. Margaret Thatcher, in agreeing to the predecessor of Article 114 of the TFEU (Article 100a of the Treaty Establishing the European Community, TEC) in the Single European Act, did not sign up to European regulation of the City. As for labour market regulation, the Court rejected the British complaint against the Working Time Directive, for example. This set the stage for the dozens of EU labour market regulations that followed (Vaubel 2009a).

The Court supports the Commission in 69 per cent of cases against the member states (Sweet and Brunell 2010: 28). It has a vested interest in centralisation. The more powers it transfers to the EU level, the more important and interesting are the cases that the judges will be entitled to decide. The problem can be solved by establishing an additional court – call it the 'Court of Review' – which decides all cases affecting the distribution of powers between the EU and the member states. It would be charged to apply the principles of subsidiarity and proportionality. All other cases would remain with the Court as it stands. The

---

1   I shall explain this in more detail in Section 4.

judges of this subsidiarity court would not be chosen by national governments but delegated by the highest courts of the member states, and they would be required to have judicial experience, which, at present, most of them lack. This reform would be in the common interest of all EU governments.

The reform of the Commission has to deal with its monopoly of legislative initiative. The Commission will not propose legislation if it expects that the resulting legal act will reduce its power. Therefore, EU legislation is a one-way street in the direction of EU centralisation. The Commission's right of legislative initiative is also incompatible with the principle of the separation of powers. The right of legislative initiative belongs to the EU Parliament and the Council. Moreover, the legislative majority requirement in the Council should not depend on the opinion of the Commission as it does at present (Article 294, Section 9 TFEU). Finally, the Commission ought to be stripped of all its non-executive functions (infringement procedures, competition policy, the so-called anti-dumping policy, etc.) as Wolfgang Schäuble, the German Minister of Finance, has suggested.

The EU Parliament has a vested interest in EU centralisation for the same reasons. By transferring powers to the EU level, it increases its own influence. Moreover, there is a problem of self-selection: a euromantic is more likely to run for the EU Parliament than a eurosceptic. Comparative opinion polls by several survey institutions have demonstrated that the members of the EU parliament are far more centralisation-minded than the public at large (see Vaubel 2009a). The required reform is analogous to the reform of the court: the creation of an additional chamber. The second chamber of the EU Parliament would be in charge when – and only when – the legislation concerns the distribution of power between the EU and the member states. The members of the second chamber would be delegated from the national parliaments, as before 1979. To avoid self-selection, the members would be selected by lot from the party groups of the national parliaments. The second chamber could not only veto new centralising legislation, but also – together with a majority of the Council – annul previous centralising legislation. The size of the first chamber could be halved.

The alternative is to strengthen the role of the national parliaments, possibly giving them veto power ('red card') if a certain quorum is reached. Several EU governments support this reform. But it would be less effective than the second chamber because it is more difficult to mobilise a majority of parliaments in a large number of member states.

Apart from these institutional reforms, the governments share a common interest in repatriating EU powers that have failed the test of history. The repatriation must not make any member state worse off. For example, the member states may spend the structural funds and the agricultural subsidies to which they are currently entitled as they think fit.

Where interests and opinions diverge among EU governments, the UK should demand opt-outs. There are various ways of institutionalising them. Most likely, they would cover whole policy fields – say, labour and financial market regulation. Would the right of opt-out be confined to new legislation, or would it also cover the whole body of existing legislation in the policy field? Would the UK be free to opt in for specific pieces of legislation on a case by case basis, or would such opt-ins have to be agreed among the UK and the remaining EU? This might require a permanent liaison committee. If the UK opts in for a specific piece of legislation, would it subject itself to the jurisdiction of the EU Court of Justice with regard to those policies? Would it be free to withdraw again, and under what conditions? All these issues have to be clarified in the negotiations.

The British Prime Minister is trying to exploit the fact that some members of the euro zone (Germany, Italy, Spain, etc.) advocate treaty amendments to introduce additional institutions and powers for the euro zone. The UK would have to assent to those changes. But it is most unfortunate that Cameron and Osborne also actively advocate the political centralisation of the euro zone. This is not necessary to obtain a better deal for Britain.

If the outcome of the negotiations is rejected by British voters in the referendum, the British government may either notify the Council of its intention to withdraw, according to Article 50 of the Treaty on European Union (TEU), or it may try to negotiate the withdrawal by amending the treaties. By directly amending the treaties, it could circumvent the European Parliament and the Commission. This is also in the interest of the other governments.

However, if, for some reason, one of the other governments refused to negotiate a British withdrawal by direct treaty amendment, Article 50 of the TEU would be the only legal avenue for withdrawal. According to this article, the notification of withdrawal would have to be followed by negotiations. The negotiations would not be about whether but how the UK would withdraw. There would be a period of notice of two years, but this could be extended indefinitely by mutual consent.

I assume that the other member states prefer to keep the UK in the EU on present terms as long as possible for at least two reasons. First, the UK is a net contributor. Second, the other member states can outvote the UK on most issues, i.e. they can impose their level of regulation on the UK so as to improve their competitiveness. Thus, they may not negotiate in earnest unless the UK, in its notification, rules out any extension of the negotiations. An extension beyond the two years could also be precluded by the referendum question.

## Which institutions does European cooperation require? A summary

In the following analysis I shall try to show that four types of institutions may be needed for international cooperation:

1.  international courts or arbitration tribunals (enforcing freedom of trade and capital movements, the rules of competition, commitments regarding ocean fishing, defence, development aid and international networks);
2.  international public prosecutors, who monitor compliance in these fields;
3.  international fora, in which these commitments can be negotiated; and
4.  an independent international competition authority.

There ought to be separate institutions for each policy field so as to facilitate specialisation and avoid an undue agglomeration of power and dubious deals across policy fields. With the exception of North Sea fishing and trans-European networks, international cooperation in all these policy fields should ideally be organised at the global level or, if this is not feasible, among all like-minded industrial countries (OECD, NATO). Only if additional partners cannot be found is the EU an optimal area of cooperation.

## Cooperation – for what?

The optimal design of international institutions depends on their purpose. International cooperation among governments may be required for four reasons.

First, the national barriers to international market trans-actions ought to be removed. In principle, it is possible and desirable to do this on a unilateral basis. But politically the liberalisation of trade and capital movements is more easily achieved by reciprocal international agreement – ideally far beyond the EU.

Second, a common market may benefit from a common or coordinated competition policy that prohibits international cartels, international mergers establishing dominant positions and national subsidies to national champions.

45

Third, international cooperation may concern cross-border non-market externalities. These may be positive, as in the case of defence, development aid or research, or they may be negative, e.g. with regard to pollution or ocean fishing. By contrast, if the international spillovers operate through competitive markets, i.e. the price mechanism, and if governments do not commit the mistake of pursuing more targets than they have instruments to pursue, there is no need for international coordination. For instance, national monetary and fiscal policies affecting interest rates in the rest of the world through the market do not require international negotiations, but merely an exchange of information. Indeed, monetary policy collusion and tax cartels are harmful because they lead to inflation and excessive taxation. International interdependence through the market is not a problem but a precondition for efficiency.

Fourth, there may be international economies of scale in the production of national public goods or networks such as roads, railways and pipelines. In most of these cases, however, bilateral cooperation is sufficient.

While the first two justifications require negative action (the prohibition of restrictions of competition), the third and fourth call for positive action – the coordinated provision by governments of certain goods, services and policies.

Negative and positive actions differ with regard to cost. The removal of restrictions of competition has only advantages. It improves the division of labour and strengthens competition. It increases both efficiency and freedom. By contrast, policies dealing with international externalities and economies of scale are costly. Harmonisation ignores the international differences in preferences, and while market integration strengthens competition among governments, political integration weakens it. International collusion and centralisation give politicians more power over the people. Political decision-making in international organisations is far removed from the people and leaves them little choice. Both freedom and democracy suffer. Thus, the cost of positive action may easily exceed the benefit.

Liberalisation and joint intervention not only differ with respect to costs, they also require different institutions. The institutions of a common market ought to be separated from the institutions of collective policymaking. Moreover, collective policymaking should not be centralised in one monolithic institution. A large bureaucracy and an agglomeration of power are to be avoided. An efficient division of labour requires specialised agencies.

## The institutions of a common market

Does the removal of barriers to trade and capital movements necessitate common institutions at all? A treaty without institutions may be sufficient. If the government of a signatory state violates the treaty, those who are adversely affected may complain with a court of that state. Are the courts impartial and sufficiently independent of the government in all 28 EU member states? If not, the Treaty ought to provide for an international tribunal or court.

Should its decisions be binding or not? The history of the General Agreement on Tariffs and Trade (GATT) and the World Trade Organization (WTO) has shown that non-binding arbitration makes a difference. Usually, the losing government alters its policy – but frequently not enough. The Court of Justice of the European Union issues binding judgements. However dissatisfied one may be with its centralising adjudication, its record on trade liberalisation is impeccable. However, it is far too slow, and the chamber in charge should not include judges appointed by the plaintiff or the defendant.

When exporters sue a protectionist government, they generate positive external effects for other exporters. That is why, sometimes, groups of exporters file a joint complaint. However, if joining is costly, there may be a case for appointing a public prosecutor in addition. In the EU, the Commission acts as a 'guardian of the treaties'. It is quite active in this role. There are more than 800 infringement cases pending with the Court – many of them concerning the common market. If the guardian of the treaty is involved in various other dealings with the governments of the member states, there is a danger that the guardian will accept protectionist national policies in exchange for concessions elsewhere. Thus, the Commission as presently constituted is not an appropriate guardian of the treaties. If there is a public prosecutor in charge of the Common Market, he or she should not have any other competencies than this.

Protectionism is not only about tariffs and quantitative restrictions. National regulation of product quality may protect domestic producers against foreign competitors as well. Indeed, there are so many potentially protectionist product regulations that it is very difficult, if not impossible, to outlaw all of them in a treaty. They have to be dealt with one by one. Thus, the Court, in its Cassis de Dijon judgement (1979), opened the door for individual complaints against protectionist national product regulations.

However, the governments and parliaments of the member states have taken a different line. Instead of prohibiting the protectionist national product regulations one by one, they have facilitated the adoption of EU product regulations replacing the national product regulations. They have admitted qualified majority decisions about common internal market regulations. This was Article 100a of the TEC, as introduced by the Single European Act in 1987.

Article 100a TEC had two disastrous consequences. First, a spate of common product regulations poured out from Brussels. As one would expect from a regulatory cartel, they were highly restrictive. Second, the ECJ in 1989 extended Article 100a of the TEC to include the regulation of production processes, i.e. labour, environmental and most financial regulations. This was against the Treaty and deserves to be spelt out.

Article 100a, Section 1 of the TEC (now Article 114, Section 1 of the TFEU) limited qualified majority voting to 'the objectives set out in Article 8a'. Article 8a of the TEC (now Article 26 of the TFEU) contained only one aim, that of 'progressively establishing the internal market', and it defined the internal market as 'an area without internal frontiers in which the free movement of goods, persons, services and capital is ensured in accordance with the provisions of this Treaty'. Since the free movement of goods, persons, services and capital can be obstructed by national product regulations but not national process regulations, Article 100a of the TEC did not permit qualified majority decisions about process regulations.

Two years later, the ECJ in its 'Titandioxide decision' (ECJ Case C-300/89) declared that 'by virtue of Articles 2 and 3 of the Treaty, a precondition for such a market [i.e. an internal market] is the existence of conditions of competition which are not distorted' (nr. 14). This was a clear breach of the Treaty, because Article 100a of the TEC expressly referred to Article 8a and not to Articles 2 and 3. Before the Treaty of Maastricht (1993), Articles 2 and 3 did not even contain the term 'internal market'. (They used the term 'common market', which had never included national product or process regulations.) Even though national process regulations are perfectly compatible with the free movement of goods, persons, services and capital, they were now subject to qualified majority voting because they may affect competition. The door was wide open for qualified majority decisions about EU labour and financial regulations. The UK has challenged several of these decisions, but the Court has always reasserted its position.

When the Treaty of Lisbon was signed in December 2007, Gordon Brown agreed to legalising the Court's breach of the Treaty. He accepted a 'Protocol on the Internal Market and Competition', which reads: 'The internal market as set out in Article 3 of the

Treaty on European Union includes a system ensuring that competition is not distorted.' He formally agreed to the City being regulated by a qualified majority of the EU member states. Commission, Council and European Parliament have based all their process regulations of financial markets on Article 114 of the TFEU. The last British complaint against this was turned down by the Court in January 2014 in the European Securities and Markets Authority (ESMA) case (C-270/12).

The lesson is clear. The institutions of a common market must not include a body empowered to impose common regulations. This holds regardless of whether the regulations are product or process regulations and whether they are adopted by qualified majority or unanimity. The harmonisation of regulations ignores differences in preferences and leads to a higher level of government regulation because it raises the cost of escaping excessive regulation and reduces the voters' scope for comparison. The institutions of a common market – e.g. its court – ought to be confined to preventing national product regulations from protecting domestic producers against foreign competitors. National regulations would continue to bind domestic producers, and imported products that did not conform with these regulations would have to be clearly labeled. In a common market, consumers have more choice – also in quality. Of course, each government is free to adopt the regulations of other countries.

International competition is restricted not only by barriers to trade and capital movements but also by cartels. Domestic cartels can be taken care of by national competition policies. The national authorities have the strongest incentive and the best information to deal with domestic collusion. It is sometimes argued that they may not be sufficiently strict because they ignore the foreign benefits of their actions, but there is no evidence to support this claim. However, cross-border cartels and mergers raise problems of jurisdiction. The simplest solution is to agree on a rule determining which national competition authority is to be in charge. The Closer Economic Relations Agreement between Australia and New Zealand is an excellent example of such a solution. If joint decision-making is desired, the member states may set up a common competition authority that is politically independent. Unfortunately, the current competition policy of the EU is neither confined to cross-border cartels and mergers nor conducted by an independent institution. Power rests with a simple majority of the Commissioners, most of whom know nothing about the case at hand.

The prohibition of national subsidies to national champions can be left to a specialised court. Once more, a public prosecutor would be useful.

## Institutions for joint policies regarding external and scale economies

Negative cross-border external effects are incompatible with the classical concept of liberty. In John Stuart Mill's (1859/1962: Chapter 1, Paragraph 9) words, '... power can be rightfully exercised over any member of a civilised community against his will ... to prevent harm to others'. In an international context, the different nations must be prevented from harming each other. This can be achieved by setting up a supranational authority or, as Ronald Coase (1960) has taught us, by negotiated compensation. A supranational authority is dangerous because it may abuse its power. It is more likely to do so than a national government because it is exposed to less competition. Freedom is better protected if the nation states unanimously agree on rules of compensation. However, the rules have to be enforced. This requires some mechanism of arbitration or a court. Moreover, a guardian of the treaty may be helpful. Let us consider some examples.

One of the most pressing problems of negative externality is cross-border pollution. It has been tackled by agreement – the Kyoto Agreement – under the auspices of the United Nations

(UN). The European states have agreed on an Emissions Trading System, which seems to work (although see Chapter 14).

Another example is Lake Constance. The countries bordering on the lake – i.e. Germany, Austria and Switzerland, or rather the provinces concerned – have established a joint commission for cooperation.

These examples show that problems of pollution are more likely to be global or local than exactly EU-wide. But there is also a common pool problem especially affecting a group of EU member states: North Sea fishing. The fishery fleet of one state inflicts negative non-market effects on the others, and each has an incentive to do so. As a result, the member states have defined some national waters, and they have agreed on national fishing quota for the rest. This is not the most efficient solution – auctioning fishing permits would be better – but it is feasible and better than nothing. Unfortunately, monitoring the quota is mostly left to the national authorities. Compliance among Spanish fishermen, for example, is said to be poor (see Chapter 10).

As these examples indicate, international agreements limiting negative cross-border externalities are practicable and to some degree effective. Decisions about the rules and the enforcement mechanism must be unanimous, but decisions within the enforcement procedure must not. Enforcement requires supranational monitoring as well as compensation and penalties to be imposed by a majority of the contracting states.

The EU deals with positive rather than negative cross-border externalities. The most important cases are defence, development aid and research. When a member state spends more on defence against potential external aggressors, the others are likely to benefit as well. When a member state increases its development aid to third countries, the other EU members will be relieved as well. If more money is spent on research in one country – be it by the government or the private sector, the fruits will sooner or later become available to all. In all three instances, however, the positive external effects extend far beyond the borders of the EU.

The EU boasts a Common Foreign and Security Policy, including a Common Security and Defence Policy (Articles 23–46 of the TFEU). However, the external benefits of national defence are not confined to the EU. They extend to all like-minded nations – notably the US. Thus, a more encompassing defence alliance such as NATO is more efficient. Indeed, there is a danger that the EU Security and Defence Policy weakens NATO. It is meant to reduce American involvement in Europe.[2] As long as NATO works well, there is no need for EU institutions in defence.

Development aid is of concern to all potential donors. It is a matter for all industrial countries (OECD) or even the UN. At the UN level, we have the World Bank Group, and the OECD has set up a Development Assistance Committee. The available research suggests that UN organisations tend to be less efficient than the other international organisations and that the OECD in particular is more efficient.[3] There may be diseconomies of scale that outweigh the gains from encompassing additional external effects. If that is so, there is a case for decentralising development aid – at the EU level or, even better, at the national level. Clare Short, a former UK Secretary of International Development and a member of the Labour Party, once declared in Parliament that 'the Commission is the worst development agency in the world. The poor quality and reputation of its aid brings Europe into disrepute'.[4] In these circumstances, the EU's role in development aid has to be reconsidered. Rather than administering development

---

2  See the section on 'The disintegration of NATO' in Vaubel (1999).

3  An econometric analysis by Vaubel et al. (2007: Table 5) shows that UN organisations employ significantly more staff (taking account of the number of member states, their tasks and so on). Artis (1988) and Vaubel (2009b) demonstrate that the International Monetary Fund is the least accurate forecaster of GDP growth and that the OECD performs much better.

4  The UK Parliament, Select Committee on International Development (2000), Ninth Report, Paragraph 73.

projects, the EU ought to provide a forum for mutual aid commitments conditional on the commitments of the other member states. A commitment procedure would be sufficient to internalise the positive external effects. If tied aid is banned, each nation could be free to spend the committed amounts as they see fit.

Subsidies to research account for approximately 9 per cent of the EU's budget. There is a Commissioner for Research, Innovation and Science. The Commission appoints a committee of scientists, the European Research Council, which invites applications, nominates referees and decides the allocation of funds. To the extent to which these subsidies generate additional research and inventions, all producers who are capable of using these inventions will benefit once the patents have expired. Since the positive externalities extend to all industrial countries, the subsidisation of research is better transferred to the OECD.

Within the member states, positive external effects from agriculture and the preservation of cultural heritage may justify government subsidies. But these benefits accrue overwhelmingly to domestic residents rather than foreign tourists. There is no reason to assume that the national authorities, ignoring the benefits to foreign tourists, pay too little in subsidies. Indeed, the national authorities have a much stronger incentive to pay the optimal amount of subsidy than have the majority of governments or parliamentarians of the member states.

Networks generate both economies of scale and positive externalities. If foreigners link to a national network, they raise its value to domestic users. Such external benefits may justify subsidies for additional users both at home and abroad. The EU does not pay such subsidies, however. If each member state has its own network, each has an incentive to link it with the others. The incentive is strongest among neighbours; it leads to bilateral coordination. To the extent to which there are substantial network externalities from non-neighbouring countries, a forum for negotiations and commitments may be required. There is no need for supranational policymaking. However, once more a tribunal of arbitration or a court may be helpful to ensure that the international commitments are honoured.

## Institutions for redistribution among member countries

Redistribution among the member states accounts for about one quarter of the EU budget.[5] Most of it is implicit, resulting from policies designed to raise efficiency. However, efficient redistribution is explicit and voluntary. In the EU, revenue decisions require unanimity among the member states, but spending decisions are subject to majority voting in the Council and the European Parliament. Ultimately, the cost of redistribution is borne by taxpayers. According to one proposal by the European Constitutional Group (Bernholz et al. 2004), any increase in the EU budget relative to EU GDP ought to require a referendum in each of the net payer countries.

## Conclusion

Why do the EU institutions differ so much from the ideal?

First, the founding fathers of the EEC were centralisers. They used the common market as a stepping-stone to 'political integration'. They intentionally set up institutions that went far beyond what was necessary to abolish the national barriers to trade and capital movements. Their institutions, quite predictably, developed a centralising dynamic of their own.

But there is a second mechanism that they may not have foreseen. Market integration reduces the autonomy of national governments in regulation and taxation. In a common market, a national government that introduces new regulations or raises

---

5 This is the sum of the negative balances of the net payer states divided by the budget.

taxes faces a strong adverse reaction in trade and capital flows. This explains why most national governments, after adopting the internal market programme in 1987, were ready to agree to a plethora of new union-wide regulations in the years to follow.

Third, also unexpectedly, in 1990 Germany achieved unification at the price of losing its currency and monetary autonomy. The malfunctioning of the European monetary union in the wake of the financial crisis has led to further centralising measures – especially in the euro zone. As Wolfgang Schäuble told the *New York Times*, 'we can only achieve a political union if we have a crisis' (18 November 2011).

In the absence of a fundamental institutional reform, the EU will continue on its path towards 'ever-closer union', regardless of whether this aim continues to be invoked in the treaties. The British renegotiation will reveal whether the evils of the current set-up can be overcome. I am afraid they are incurable.

## References

Artis, M. (1988) How accurate is the World Economic Outlook? In *Staff Studies for the World Economic Outlook*. Washington, DC: International Monetary Fund.

Bernholz, P., Schneider, F., Vaubel, R. and Vibert, F. (2004) An alternative constitutional treaty for the European Union. *Public Choice* 118: 451–68.

Coase, R. (1960) The problem of social cost. *Journal of Law and Economics* 3: 1–44.

Fahey, E. (2011) Does the emperor have financial crisis clothes? Reflections on the legal basis of the European Banking Authority. *The Modern Law Review* 74: 581–95.

Mill, J. S. (1859/1962) On liberty. In *Utilitarianism, On Liberty, Essay on Bentham (by John Stuart Mill)* (ed. M. Warnock). London; Glasgow: The Fontana Library.

Sweet, A. S. and Brunell, T. (2010) How the European Union's legal system works – and does not work: response to Carruba, Gabel and Hankla. Faculty Scholarship Series Paper 68, Yale Law School.

Vaubel, R. (1999) Europe in the year 2000: three pitfalls ahead. *Economic Affairs* 19: 22–5.

Vaubel, R. (2009a) *The European Institutions as an Interest Group*. Hobart Paper 167. London: Institute of Economic Affairs.

Vaubel, R. (2009b) Lessons from the financial crisis: the international dimension. *Economic Affairs* 29: 22–6.

Vaubel, R. (2014) The breakdown of the rule of law at the EU level: implications for the reform of the EU Court of Justice. *Festschrift zu Ehren von Christian Kirchner* (ed. W. A. Kaal, M. Schmidt and A. Schwartze), pp. 1353–68. Tuebingen: Mohr Siebeck.

Vaubel, R., Dreher, A. and Soylu, U. (2007) Staff growth in international organizations: a principal–agent problem? An empirical analysis. *Public Choice* 133: 275–95.

# 4 BEYOND THE GHOSTS: DOES EU MEMBERSHIP NOURISH OR CONSUME BRITAIN'S INTERESTS AND GLOBAL INFLUENCE?

Gwythian Prins

## Economic measurements are insufficient to judge this question

The most familiar scales used to weigh the value to Britain of participation in the project of European Union ('The Project') are those calibrated for economic costs versus benefits. They have been the longest in service. Although, over 40 years ago, Edward Heath suggested that amplification of foreign policy influence was another leading benefit of joining, today the preferred test of those promoting continuation of British participation is, often exclusively, one of economics.

Quantified in hard figures, economic cost–benefit is relatively easier to weigh than the metrics that matter most for judging national influence and interests worldwide. There are some technical tests that can be applied to the processes of diplomacy, and results are reviewed towards the end of this chapter. But they are not the most important tests. So, most of what follows discusses the deeper, less tangible, logically prior and decisive considerations.

## How best to nourish British interests: two paradoxes

This chapter explores two paradoxes. It will suggest that, where our interests coincide, which they do sometimes but not always, close British engagement with European nations on security, defence and foreign policy is greatly in the British national interest. It has always been so, and it is especially so in today's menacing world. Transnational cooperation is vital both in combatting the pan-European threat of unconditional Islamism, which is both physically violent and culturally corrosive, and in facing the resurgent malevolence of Putin's demographically and economically stricken Russia.

Ironically, because of the one-way ratchet gearing that was built into The Project from its conception (as will be explained below), and which therefore includes the EU's Common Foreign and Security Policy (CFSP) and the European External Action Service (EEAS) machine that is being rapidly expanded to deliver it, this cooperation cannot occur under the *status quo* of the Lisbon Treaty or anything other than fundamental amendment of it that removes the ratchet. This is the first paradox.

The ratchet is why French politicians often repeat, correctly, that there cannot be a 'Europe à la carte.' It is also why Prime Minister Cameron's 2015 negotiation tactic appears to have been back to front. He appears to have asked what was the most with which the others could live. That tactic cannot deliver Britain's minimum requirements. The starting position with a body constituted as the EU should have been to declare an intention to leave unless Britain recovers full sovereignty by negotiated agreement and basic treaty change. Safe cooperation can only be safely achieved once Britain has *either* been totally released from the CFSP/EEAS by European agreement – and, given the nature of the machine, totally must be totally – *or* removed from that power by the referendum vote of its people.

The 'European idea' died a decade ago for most Europeans, especially south of the Alps. So, firm negotiating should be much easier than before the euro began to poison The Project. By being uncompromising, a second, virtuous paradox appears: in forcing general abandonment of the goal and political trappings of 'ever-closer union' to save itself, British success might also save the free trade area for others too: something that might otherwise be lost in the current crumbling of The Project.

If Prime Minister Cameron were to achieve this, Britain would once again have helped to save Europe from itself, and it would be an act of statesmanship that would be on a par with those of Prime Ministers Churchill or Salisbury, or of Foreign Secretary Castlereagh.

## Why the EU and its fears are older than you think

The current Project was conceived in the horrors of the battlefield of Verdun, had its first flowering and shrivelling in the 1920s and became a political reality in the wake of World War II. Therefore, it is scarred to its core by the European Civil War (1914–45) that gave birth to it. In 1950, it seemed reasonable, even imperative, to neuter the nations of Europe.

The French *eminence grise* of The Project, Jean Monnet (1888–1979), was a bureaucrat, inspired by that vision of a united Europe that Tennyson had expressed in words cherished by generations of world federalists: 'Till the war-drum throbb'd no longer, and the battle-flags were furl'd/In the Parliament of man, the Federation of the world.'[1] Also working at the League of Nations was the Englishman Arthur Salter, his friend and colleague, who wrote *The United States of Europe* in 1931, a book that sets out that shared vision in detail. Another close collaborator was Walter Hallstein, a German technocratic academic who believed in international jurisdiction as the morally superior successor to the laws of the nation states; and his priority is inscribed in the constitution for the ECJ, prescribing travel towards ever-closer union. Monnet, Salter and Hallstein were joined by Altiero Spinelli, a romantic communist who advocated a United States of Europe legitimised

---

1    Alfred Lord Tennyson, *Locksley Hall* (1835).

by a democratically elected European Parliament. In form, but not substance, that also has come into being, albeit with tepid and cooling public support. Such people were not isolated enthusiasts, but they shared a sentiment widespread among the inter-war European elites. Its animator was the leader of the *Pan Europa* movement, Count Richard Coudenhove-Kalergi.

The culmination of frank Utopian federalism came in the form of French Foreign Minister Aristide Briand's proposal for a European Federal Union, which in May 1930 went the same way as the 1928 Kellogg–Briand Pact proposal to outlaw war. The rebuff caused Monnet and his friends to reassess in a less innocent spirit. They chose creeping federalism (the covert acquisition of ever more power without consent). By playing a constitutional game of Grandmother's Footsteps[2] with the unenlightened *canaille*, approaching the goal of federal union obliquely and enticing electorates with tasty a-political morsels at first, it could become – *pouf!* – an irrevocable *fait accompli*. This functional tactic is known as the Monnet Method. Irrevocability is the heartbeat of the process that expands the *acquis communautaire*: the unrepealable 'Community inheritance' of accumulating laws, policies and practices. They sought and obtained the support of popular political leaders such as Konrad Adenauer, Robert Schuman and Alcide De Gasperi to translate the Monnet Method into concrete political forms. One of Coudenhove's ideas from the 1920s was to create a European coal and steel community. In 1952, as 'the Schuman Plan', this became the initial step. Why the reckless sense of mission that justified playing such a game? Because they trusted no one but themselves, and least of all the common people.

---

2   An English children's game. One person ('grandmother') walks in front of a group of others who try to catch up with her to touch her without her seeing them coming. If 'grandmother' turns around, everyone freezes. Anyone caught moving by 'grandmother' is out. In the EU version, the people are 'grandmother' and the federal enthusiasts are trying to catch her without being noticed in time. For a more charitable assessment of such games, see Carls and Naughton (2002).

The Monnet generation was devastated by the Great War. It held the emperors, monarchs, autocrats and diplomats (the sleepwalkers), and the states that they ruled, responsible. Their bungling, they believed, had smashed the long peace for insufficient cause; and we might see why they felt that way.[3] They surveyed the wreckage of Eurasia's multinational imperial states. So, too, did Lenin and Rosa Luxembourg and an assortment of Balkan, Turkish and eastern European nationalists. All agreed that, given their gigantic inequalities, their autocratic rule and their unreformability, the breaking of these empires was deserved, and we too might understand why they thought so. All agreed (as Rousseau once wrote) that 'what can make authority legitimate?' is the axiomatic question in politics; and certainly we should entirely concur with that.[4]

However, they came to wildly different conclusions about what should come next: from democidal communist revolution via national cultural revival to Utopian cosmopolitanism.[5] The USSR (deceased in 1991 after one human lifespan) was the product of the first reaction. Today's ailing EU is the product of the third. Across the century, all that specific diversity and fear boiled down in the brains of the founding fathers into a generalised critique of the nation state as pathological in principle, which it certainly is not. The success of the British nation state both in itself and as a global role model must not be tarred with the transcontinental failures of Austria-Hungary, Russia, the Balkan states, imperial and later Nazi Germany – or France.[6]

3   In light, most prominently and persuasively among the centenary books, of Clark (2012).

4   First quoted as his compass in Kissinger (1957: 3–4), in subsequent books and most recently repeated in Kissinger (2014).

5   'Democide' is death at the hands of one's own government. On the grim calculations of Professor Rudi Rummel (1994), it killed more people by human agency in the twentieth century than any other means.

6   The matter is discussed from many angles by the contributors to Möhring and Prins (2013). Essays from across the political spectrum, in particular by Michael Gove

## 'With Europe but not of it … linked but not compromised'

To play Grandmother's Footsteps with such momentous matters is to play with fire. Just such tactics threatened breakdown of trust in the anti-Napoleonic league, observed the British Foreign Secretary – one of our greatest – in 1820:

> In this Alliance [for which, today, read EU], as in all other human arrangements, nothing is more likely to impair, or even to destroy its real utility, than any attempt to push its duties and its obligations beyond the Sphere which its original conception and understood Principles will warrant … it never was … intended as an Union for the Government of the World, *or for the Superintendence of the Internal Affairs of other States* [emphasis added] … It was never so explained to Parliament; if it had, most assuredly the sanction of Parliament would never have been given to it.[7]

In Castlereagh's words, that is the nub of the British people's complaint about the EU: having from the outset been led up the garden path about the federal purpose and one-way direction of the European project by ghost-haunted and eventually self-confessed federalist Edward Heath, and colleagues, who thereby poisoned the wells of trust in our politics.

Each further step of European integration has advanced on the same principle, unidirectionally and steadily removing power from the nations and banking it in Brussels under the lock of the

---

and Frank Field, by Michael Ignatieff and Daniel Hannan, and by Roger Scruton and Julian Lindley-French, explore and refute the accusation that the nation state in any form is ineradicably 'pathological'. The case for the prosecution is best made by the Foreign and Commonwealth Office's (FCO's) licensed thinker at that time, Robert Cooper. Cooper's view that it is in Britain's interest to depart from its successful 400-year strategy for dealing with the Continent (Cooper 2003: 52–3; 138–51) is once more at the heart of the debate with which this chapter is concerned.

7 Viscount Castlereagh, Confidential State Paper, 5 May 1820, reproduced in Ward and Gooch (1923: 622–33).

*acquis communautaire*, and interpreting 'subsidiarity' to mean that Brussels decides what powers shall remain with the nations. This is the opposite of the usual meaning. The *passerelle* or 'footbridge' clause of the Maastricht Treaty increased the Council's power to accelerate one-way transfers of power to Brussels. The meshing of this ratchet gearing (*engrenage*) is expressed in the goal of 'ever-closer union' and cannot be disengaged without exploding the Monnet project and mechanism. It applies to all areas. In foreign policy, it has been under vigorous acceleration since the creation of the EU foreign policy (CFSP) and External Action Service by the thinly disguised EU Constitution (now known as the Lisbon Treaty, signed in December 2007). The New Labour government objected to both the CFSP and EEAS during negotiations on the draft constitutional treaty, only to be brushed aside and then to capitulate (Open Europe 2007: 10–11).

In short, either the EU must change its very nature, or the British must leave The Project and revert to the script of Lord Castlereagh's great Confidential State Paper of 5 May 1820, which served British foreign policy well for over a century. Winston Churchill memorably condensed its essential message in 1930, writing that, 'we are with Europe but not of it. We are linked but not compromised'.[8] In 1820, Castlereagh spelled out our objection in words that are exactly applicable to Britain today:

> The fact is that we do not, and cannot feel alike upon all subjects. Our position, our institutions, the habits of thinking, and the prejudice of our people, render us essentially different. We cannot in all matters reason and feel alike; we should lose the confidence of our respective nations if we did, and the very affectation of such an impossibility would soon render the Alliance [for which now read the EU] an object of odium and distrust ... We must admit ourselves to be ... a Power that must take our

---

8    Cited in Leach (2004: 25). Churchill was commenting on the rebuffed Briand plan.

Principle of action, and our scale of acting, not merely from the Expediency of the Case, but from those Maxims which a System of Government strongly popular and national in its Character, has imposed upon us: We shall be found in our place when actual Danger menaces the System of Europe, but this Country cannot and will not act upon abstract and speculative Principles.[9]

Only Palmerstonian coalitions of the willing – that is to say, since nations do not have permanent friends but do have permanent interests, coalitions of sovereign nations that share material interests in a concrete issue – are worth having.[10]

## The transforming consequences of the euro

Enthusiasts for The Project dislike and rarely discuss this history. If confronted with it (although the history is what it is), they like to denigrate it as conspiracy theory. Nowadays that is harder to do, because, during its short life, the rolling economic and social disaster of the hubristically named euro has lurched and barged its way to the centre of European affairs. Too hastily promoted by the French elite to counterbalance the crisis (for them) of German reunification, which meant that the sturdy German horse was threatening to unseat the skilful French rider (the phrase is General de Gaulle's), the single currency experiment culminated in the Greek crisis of July 2015.

In September 2015, at the time of writing, the July crisis is following Jean Monnet's prescription that 'people only accept

9   Historians have sometimes described Castlereagh as 'non-interventionist' in contrast to his successors; whereas this passage and Canning's own words confirm a continuity that expresses Britain's rooted geopolitical interests to this day. This historiographic point is further discussed by Castlereagh's most recent biographer in Bew (2011: 481–2).

10  There is nothing insular or introspective about resumption of our historical norm, as Andrew Roberts also stresses in his essay 'British engagement with the continent of Europe' (Abulafia 2015: 29–33).

change when they are faced with necessity and only recognise necessity when a crisis is upon them.' The so-called Five Presidents' Report of 22 June 2015 is plainly a massive attempt in the Monnet mode to use this euro crisis to push for greater fiscal and hence political integration.[11] So, it will probably produce a temporary 'success' for The Project by following the pattern of all previous EU crises: namely, on the German plan, a ruthless subordination of Greek sovereignty to the General Will, ignoring the result of the Greek referendum of 5 July and accepting the consequent fury and further declining public assent for The Project.[12] This looks like a pyrrhic victory. In *Leviathan*, Thomas Hobbes lists 'the insatiable appetite, or bulimia, of enlarging Dominion' as one of the 'diseases of a Commonwealth'. The EU is still only a regulatory machine and has patently not become a state of mind for Europeans (which is why, by the way, it is no more likely to exceed a human lifespan from foundation than did the USSR). The legal philosopher Philip Allott mordantly observes that 'bulimia plus bureaucracy is a reliable recipe for the decline and fall of empires'.[13]

The July crisis of 2015 has gutted the currency experiment; and the debauching of Greek sovereignty by German paymasters, trying to treat a state like a busted factory, is indeed a dirty fall for the whole Project. It has had two further consequences. The humiliation of Syriza was clearly intended to be a deterrent,

---

11  Juncker (Commission), Tusk (Council), Dijsselbloem (Eurogroup), Draghi (ECB), Schulz (EuroParliament), European Commission (2015).

12  In the course of research for the LSE Mackinder Programme project on European integration following the 2005 French and Dutch referenda, an eminent Belgian interviewee happily confirmed Monnet's view that federalists never waste a good crisis, and indeed welcome them, with the charming, informative (and, to any horseman, dangerously inaccurate) analogy that 'you have to frighten a horse to get it to jump a big hedge'. Prins and Möhring (2008), preamble and passim. A frightened horse is an unreliable horse that will one day buck you off.

13  'Of those things that weaken, or tend to the Dissolution of a Commonwealth', Hobbes (1651, 1985 edition: Chapter 29, 375); Allott (2002: 175; on the 'unimagined community' of the EU, 229–62).

but it may have produced the opposite effect, alienating The Project's natural supporters on the Left. In Britain, the new Labour Party leader Jeremy Corbyn has hinted as much. Worse, the attempted criminalisation of the former Greek finance minister Varoufakis for having dared to draw up secret contingency plans for a return to the drachma has inflamed the confrontation (Evans-Pritchard 2015). The British electorate will not have failed to notice all this.

Allott (2002) presciently remarked that the crisis facing the EU is fundamentally one of social philosophy. Matters of personal and political culture have been the least common framing of the question of cost and benefit. Yet they are of the very essence when judging the national interest. In the British case, the Magna Carta concerns are pre-eminent: for the sovereignty of the monarch in Parliament, the distinctiveness of the Common Law, the rights of property, of *habeas corpus* and of a British citizen's freedom under the law, which was Britain's gift to the world.[14]

## The flaw in Europeanism

Recent decades in continental Europe have witnessed a growing rebellion against a fake and forced European identity. This makes British people less eccentric among the peoples of Europe; but it is intensely threatening to the world-view and sense of entitlement of the EU elite, because it strikes at the heart of the foundation myth of Europeanism. It deepens the gulf between rulers and subjects, who now wish to be citizens and not

---

14 A story freshly and readably retold from beginning to end in Hannan (2013). The initial trigger to a vigorous re-examination of why and how British society diverged from that of the continent was Macfarlane (1978). Scruton (2000) elaborates clearly how the essential enduring features grow from these foundations to become the great oak tree that shelters the 'little platoons' of English society, which are the first principle of public affection leading to patriotism (Burke 1790, 1968 edition: 135). The shallower eighteenth-century overlay described by Colley (1992), and what is happening to it, must not be confused with these foundations.

just atoms in 'civil society.' Larry Siedentop famously applied Alexis de Tocqueville's four tests of democratic legitimation formed from his observations of America, to Europe. Siedentop argued that Europe failed the tests essentially because there is no culture of consent or the ingredients to make one (which makes this a basic reason why Britain should maintain sea-room from the continental lee shore).[15] Why this long-standing deficit in Europe?

We must look well before the double disasters of the European Civil War that seared the minds of Monnet and his friends in order to understand that. France has struggled to the present via fifteen further constitutions from its 'stock-jobbing constitution' of 1789 ('...the display of inconsiderate and presumptuous be-cause unresisted and irresistible authority' in Burke's contemporary description). Germany and Italy are established little more than a century, and state identities (let alone democracies) across southern and eastern Europe are more fragile and newer still. In such company, Britain is unusual as an old country, which once successfully ran the world's largest empire and has three times saved Europe from itself since 1815.

However, there is a more fundamental cultural difference between Britain and all those large European countries created 'from above'. Edmund Burke pointed towards it, observing that British liberties are asserted as an *entailed inheritance* from our forefathers, rather than grabbed as *abstract rights*. Robert Tombs mentions a valuable consequence arising, writing that 'it is hard to think of any major improvement since Magna Carta brought about in England by violence'. Continental historical experience, utterly alien to Britain, has, in contrast and repeated ferment, brewed up 'vanguard myths' that morally justify despotic rule in the imposition of identities on people and that validate a

---

15  Siedentop (2000). De Tocqueville's tests were: the habit of local self-government, a common language, an open political culture dominated by lawyers and some shared moral beliefs.

determinist view of history. It is this same concoction that set Burke's nostrils aquiver in 1790:

> The worst of these politics of revolution is this; they temper and harden the breast ... so taken up with their theories about the rights of man, that they have totally forgot his nature.[16]

This type of Europeanism has no interest in a culture of consent nor any serious interest in who people are. Why? Because they are not necessary. A self-justified act of ruling from above simply imparts information and delivers instructions. It is not a new tendency. In 1714 (1970 edition: 77), Bernard Mandeville introduced his ever-topical explanation of human nature by observing that 'One of the greatest Reasons why so few People understand themselves, is, that most Writers are always teaching Men what they should be, and hardly ever trouble their heads with telling them who they really are'. It has been a feature of earlier 'European ideas', too, notably those of the 1930s; and, of course, belief in the false consciousness of the masses makes it the basic conceit of all Marxists, including today's resurgent pan-European hard Left.[17] Sleight of hand is also a common feature, as Bismarck remarked in 1871: 'I have always found the word "Europe" on the lips of those who wanted something from other powers which they dared not demand in their own name', and as General de Gaulle affirmed in 1962: 'Europe is the way for France to become what she has ceased to be since Waterloo'.

---

16 Burke (1790, 1968 edition: 119; 127; 156); Tombs (2014: 886; 2015: 26). Human rights are not a valid expropriating trump card, even when so played. The dark side of human rights is seen when attempts to enforce claim rights as normative dishearten or prevent performance of services by obligation-bearers so that everyone is worse off. Dazzled admirers of abstract liberty rights do not see the dark side. The darkness is compounded by muddled allocation of obligations to rights by the Universal Declaration of 1948, which has infected EU derivatives; so it is rather important to understand today. Human rights need to be rescued from the human rights movement. See O'Neill (2005).

17 The 'European idea', Leach (2004: 92–6).

## What the ghosts did

Ghosts haunt each side. Shocked by President Eisenhower's brutal undermining of Franco-British military success in the 1956 Suez operation, forcing ignominious withdrawal, the British ruling class lives in a generalised fear and presumption of decline from former power that still haunts Whitehall. Sir Anthony Nutting observed at the time that Suez was 'no end of a lesson'; and the lesson was that if the Americans could not be trusted, and with them that whole implicit confidence in the anglosphere as Britain's multiplier of influence, then it would be better to try to join the club of jaunty foreigners, next door. The Commonwealth was treated atrociously. It is one of the queen's greatest gifts to her people that her skilful, quiet and steadfast commitment over 40 years has preserved a possibility of renewal such that 'the UK could use [the Commonwealth] as a power multiplier, like the EU but without the assimilation costs'. Given how Commonwealth economies are thriving in contrast to the troubled or waning economies of the euro zone, Business for Britain and Tim Hewish argue that therefore Britain's relationship with the Commonwealth requires a major rethink and mutually beneficial amplification and realignment.[18]

The Continental ghost already examined is fear of recurrent war. It has dangerously perverse effects. It skews history by suggesting that it was The Project that has somehow prevented European war since 1945, whereas this was more plausibly the work of the Marshall Plan followed by the American-led NATO alliance. Furthermore, it blinds believers to the dangers of ramming 'vanguard' Europeanism, which, as in the Greek July crisis, shreds fragile democracies and summons dark shadows of both Left and Right extremism, as Donald Tusk, President of the Council, correctly identifies: 'It is always the same game before the biggest

---

18  Elliott and Moynihan (2015: 271) and Hewish (2014) passim, but especially pp. 50–73. Hewish handily enumerates the ties that bind the English-speaking peoples.

tragedies in our European history' (Evans-Pritchard 2015). The Project was supposed to banish them forever. Therefore, to answer our exam question productively, we must go beyond the ghosts. We cannot do this unless we understand who they were, what they did to get us where we now are, and how, if they are denied or ignored, they can control us still.

David Cameron was correct to observe in his Bloomberg speech in January 2013 that 'there is not, in my view, a single European demos'. In fact, Jean Monnet's expectation that generation by generation a new European identity would, like dye into wool, seep into people through force of historical inevitability has been inverted. An admittedly crude measure comes from Spinelli's European Parliament. Its elections document how, across the continent, the people have been drifting away for years. Participation levels only rose for the first time since its inception at the last election, which returned more eurosceptic Members of European Parliament than ever before.

## To the July crisis: the hollowing out of European politics

Determinist Europeanism, the Monnet Method and fear of their ghosts mean that the European political elite neither values nor respects (nor fears) the concerns of the electorates. A decade ago, rulers and the ruled took different pathways that have collided in the July 2015 Greek crisis.[19] Divergence began in 2005 with the French and Dutch referenda rejections of Giscard d'Estaing's self-amending European Constitution, which was the next planned milestone on the road to open federal union.[20] In the Dutch case, rejection

---

19  The origins and now realised potentialities of the euro were discussed at that time in Prins (2005) and placed in context by Leach (2004: 70–5).

20  The definitive insider account of how Giscard and his aide Sir John (now Lord) Kerr (formerly Permanent Secretary of the FCO) wrote this extraordinary document and attempted to foist it first on the Praesidium and then on electors is by Stuart (2003).

was by two-thirds of two-thirds of one of the most mature democracies on the continent, and the only well-functioning one to have signed the Treaty of Rome.[21] Yet, recklessly, the verdicts were evaded by repackaging the constitution as the Lisbon Treaty.[22] Then came the third 'no' – the Irish referendum of 12 June 2008 on the Lisbon Treaty. The Irish gave the 'wrong' answer, so they were obliged to correct their mistaken verdict in another referendum, as also happened to the Danes. These results already suggested that two internally consistent but mutually irreconcilable visions of Europe were in collision.[23]

More recently, and in quick succession, opinion polls and political classes did not see three momentous results coming: the Scottish majority to remain in the UK in the 2014 referendum; the British General Election result of May 2015, which returned a majority Conservative government; and the 60 per cent Greek 'no' on 5 July 2015, which was instantly ignored. In these three cases, it is possible that electors simply lied about their intentions to the pollsters, which, if so, further etches the widening gulf between rulers and the ruled, and begs the question why.

The recent emergence of anti-austerity parties backed by younger, well-educated voters in Greece or Spain (Syriza and Podemos) may be especially evident in the southern European countries that are most grievously victims of the social mayhem

---

21  The Dutch association of inherent political freedom with skill in reclaiming land from water goes back to the thirteenth century (Pye 2014:172).

22  The definitive documentation of this deliberate deceit is Open Europe (2007). Of salutary shock are Annex 1, which lists areas where the national veto was lost, and Annex 3, which provides a concordance matching the Constitution with the Treaty clause by clause.

23  As a contribution to the same debate that this volume also seeks to enter, and inspired by the example of The Federalist Papers of 1787 written by 'Publius' (James Madison, Alexander Hamilton and John Jay) in order, as 'Publius' did in the American case, to force clarity and thereby assist informed discussion, Ms Möhring and I have placed the two contending views systematically in the mouths of two imaginary friends, 'Publia' and 'Lydia', using quotations from an extensive series of interviews that she conducted across the continent (Prins and Möhring 2008).

created by the euro; but it is in fact an aspect of a general hollowing of European politics that has been most fully documented by Peter Mair (2013).

Mair's data document a trend across all European democracies since 1990 for voters to cease to vote, or if they do vote to be increasingly likely to switch preferences from one election to the next. This, he argues, is because of growing public recognition of depoliticised, technocratic forms of decision-making. The response has been a politics of protest (fertile and familiar ground for the hard Left) via judicial or quasi-judicial methods; by media, especially modern social media campaigns; or in the streets, rather than by appeal at the redundant ballot box. Insofar as voting is popular, referenda are favoured, short-circuiting the untrusted political class.

Mair concludes that the modern state is viewed increasingly as regulatory and decreasingly as participatory. His fascinating finding that across all European democracies established political party membership has declined, on average, by 50 per cent, with a range from –66 to –27, since 1980, supports this (Mair 2013: Table 4). But what matters for present purposes is that Mair emphasises the role played by the character of the EU in the hollowing out of European democracy, which has caused it to construct '...a protected sphere in which policymaking can evade the constraints imposed by representative government' (ibid.: 99). He too believes that this has aggravated the general trend, because the EU elite's contempt for the electorate is reciprocated.

Therefore, it is not surprising to see a two-pronged countervailing response. On the one hand, there is the current, rapid growth of 'anti-party' politics in most EU countries, especially core countries; on the other is the growth of fierce, romantic nationalist parties in Scotland, Catalonia, Northern Italy and elsewhere. The unpredicted enthusiasm for Jeremy Corbyn in the British Labour Party after its crushing defeat in May 2015 shows that starry-eyed young British voters, like young Greeks or

Spaniards, are not yet deterred by the trampling of Syriza. It may also show that the potential for a revival of anarcho-syndicalist street politics in Europe is greater than democrats credit.

On this evidence, it would be wise for the political and academic elites to acknowledge that deeply embedded and deeply felt but usually inchoate issues of personal and national culture are likely to be decisive in the forthcoming British referendum. That is why this chapter has attended mainly to them.

## Gulliver and the balance of competences

It is notable that in the preferred metric of federalists, British self-interest increasingly favours resumption of sovereign independence in global markets. That is not simply because in quality, in match to British strengths or in size relative to growing markets the troubled EU market diminishes while the Commonwealth, the anglosphere and emerging markets increase, but because of the many regulatory cords with which the EU ties the British Gulliver down. Because of Qualified Majority Voting (QMV) and the unidirectional *engrenage* of the *acquis communautaire*, they make a negotiated release on terms acceptable to the British electorate most unlikely.

Therefore, turning to the practical mechanics of exerting worldwide diplomatic and especially 'soft power' influence, we may see that, for the same 'Gulliver' reasons, the balance of cost and benefit also tilts sharply against British participation in this part of a project of union, should we remain under the ever-expanding powers of the EU External Action Service, particularly if (when?) planned extensions of QMV occur.

In July 2013, the Foreign and Commonwealth Office published a report on the 'Balance of competences' between Britain and the EU. A Venn diagram (Figure 1) reminds us of the range of special British advantages compared with any other EU member, showing our many institutional memberships, especially the

Figure 1   UK membership of international bodies

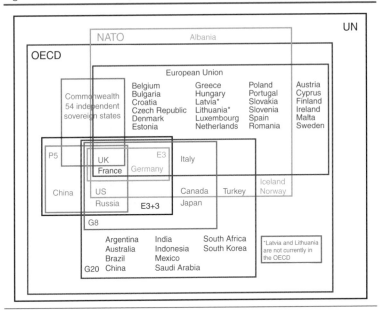

Commonwealth. Alone in Europe, Britain holds a royal flush (HM Government (2013: Paragraph 1.4, Figure 1)).

The report is revealingly conflicted. The FCO authors gamely make as good a fist as they can of the standard Whitehall case. In a different context than the EU, it sounds reasonable: that, by being inside, we can shape and lead, that we gain 'increased impact from acting in concert with 27 other countries' and that outside we would be diminished. However, the evidence does not support this.

The record of Baroness Ashton, Mr Brown's appointee as first High Representative, and the evidence within their report of dismal EU performance as a foreign policy actor, overwhelmingly run against this. Yet momentum increases. They admit frankly that the weight of money, posts and driving ambition to expand the influence of the EEAS cannot but crowd out the underfunded and shrinking FCO. Much more deadly to the case for staying inside is the FCO's own assessment of how the ratchet works. It deserves full quotation:

> when EU law gives the institutions power to act internally in order to attain EU objectives, the EU *implicitly* also has the power to enter into international obligations 'necessary' for the attainment of that objective, *even when there is no express provision allowing it to do so* [emphases added]. In construing 'necessary' in the case law, the [ECJ] only asks whether the external action in question pursues an objective of the Treaties, rather than whether external action is indispensible to the attainment of that objective. (HM Government 2013: 21)

The most thorough independent analysis of the 'Balance of competences' report has been published by Business for Britain in *Change or Go*, to which the reader is referred. It also quotes the passage above in arguing that 'representation creep' is insidious and quotes the FCO authors in further support: 'The EU has over many years sought, in one way or another, to increase its role and present itself as a "single voice" ... put simply, the UK sees a risk that representation comes to equate to competence.' [24] And Whitehall actually knows our strengths.

The authors of *Change or Go* realised that, under pressure from a different crisis, and one year after 'Balance of competences', Whitehall made a much more generous assessment of British power and potential. Therefore, they cite the analysis produced when it seemed that the Union was about to be lost. The Scotland analysis noted how little Britain requires the duplicating services of the EEAS 'to win new business, attract inward investment and

---

24  Chapter 8, 'Foreign Policy,' in Elliott and Moynihan (2015). 'Representation creep' is discussed on pp. 278–9.

champion the reputation of the UK economy'. It enumerated the influence multipliers located in our network of Embassies and High Commissions and rightly presented Britain as a 'soft power superpower' (HM Government 2014: 41–49; Elliott and Moynihan 2015: 269–70).

*Change or Go* also highlights two other powerful but second-order technical reasons why Britain's national interest to engage its European neighbours effectively in alliance is blocked by our subordination to the Lisbon Treaty. The first is that, as a function of being crowded out in the international institutions, the EU constitutes 'a direct and growing threat to British influence' so that 'in these terms, the EU is not a force multiplier for British diplomacy but an inhibitor.' Like a mosquito, it also carries a hidden further risk. The more that the EEAS enters the career stream for high-flying British diplomats on secondment, the more personnel 'go native' and the fewer are left for national duties (Elliott and Moynihan 2015: 256; 280; 286).

The second is the danger to a vital national interest entangled in the EU's current attempt to switch from energy policies designed to support 'climate action' to policies designed to protect the more traditional and comprehensible goal of energy security. Energy is an 'EU competence', and, as *Change or Go* writes correctly, 'energy security is one of the weakest links in EU joint action'. The story is complex, intriguing and little known. It is told elsewhere in full, but, in brief, the arrival of the Juncker Commission led to some brutal internal power-politics in Brussels (ibid.: 273).[25]

While preserving an appearance of continuity of commitment, during 2014–15 'climate action' rapidly dropped in importance as the resurgence of Putin's Russia in the context of the endless euro zone crisis prompted a strong initiative to proof the EU

---

25 The full story of the EU's ongoing attempt to switch from a 'climate action' to an energy security priority is given in Prins (2015).

gas supply system against Russian energy blackmail (which, of course, is what Helmut Schmidt's policy of pipeline entanglement with Russia was supposed to prevent). As with fisheries, Britain could find itself under pressure to provide access to national strategic reserves, as well as at a competitive disadvantage from its obedient gold-plated application of environmental energy measures that other less law-abiding countries ignore in this volatile context. It is all made more tense by the progressive poisoning of the German economy by very high electricity costs and loss of national reserve capacity resulting from the *energiewende* policy to prioritise high cost, subsidy-dependent and non-dispatchable generators.[26] Mr Obama has not helped. His windy rhetoric on 'climate action' via Executive Powers will in any event be snarled up in the courts and Congress. US shale gas has already materially reduced US carbon intensity, although Mr Obama's plan, if effected, will hobble it and, with it, current US economic vitality.

## Successful negotiation requires informed statesmanship

These technical arguments from diplomacy for withdrawal from the power of the Lisbon Treaty are weighty in their own terms; but together they are more than the sum of the parts, as *Change or Go* crisply summarised:

> The problem is circular from a UK perspective for as long as it remains joined to the CFSP. The European diplomatic cadre is a hindrance if it remains ineffective and dangerous if it becomes competent. Withdrawal from the CFSP removes both threats. (Elliott and Moynihan 2015: 265)

---

26 Why the *energiewende* poisons the German economy is explained from first principles in Constable (2014).

Added to the deeper reasons analysed in this chapter, the removal of Britain from the spider's web of the *acquis communautaire* is the prerequisite for the reconstruction of mature and healthy relations with our neighbours and renovation of alliances of interests. It traps axiomatic issues of national identity, interests and security with peculiar tenacity. If this change cannot be achieved by negotiation and revision of the EU Treaties – and there is no historical evidence whatsoever to believe that an adequate renegotiation can be achieved, but rather the evidence of the July 2015 Greek crisis that is before our eyes – then in the forthcoming referendum the course of action for an electorate that speaks for Britain is quite clear.

Our worldwide interests steadily outweigh our continental ones. In pursuing both, our subordination to the instruments of the Lisbon Treaty does more harm than good. As Prime Minister Salisbury would remind us, only when we are no longer under their power can we work safely with our European allies once more. The wheels have finally come off the latest Project for European integration; so it is primarily important for the sake of our national interest to be liberated from that power. But it is also important for our friends. Once more, we may need to be found in our place to help when actual danger once more menaces the System of Europe as the EU, which is reaching the natural lifespan of any political apparatus without a 'demos', now does.

## References

Abulafia, D. (ed.) (2015) *European Demos: A Historical Myth?* London: Historians for Britain.

Allott, P. (2002) *The Health of Nations: Society and Law Beyond the State.* Cambridge University Press.

Bew, J. (2011) *Castlereagh: Enlightenment, War and Tyranny.* London: Quercus.

Burke, E. (1790/1968) *Reflections on the Revolution in France*. Penguin.

Carls, A.-C. and Naughton, M. (2002) Functionalism and federalism in the European Union. *Public Justice Report* 2. http://www.cpjustice.org/public/page/content/functionalism_and_federalism_e (accessed 14 September 2015).

Clark, C. (2012) *The Sleepwalkers: How Europe Went to War in 1914*. Penguin.

Colley, L. (1992) *Britons: Forging the Nation, 1707–1837*. New Haven, CT: Yale University Press.

Constable, J. (2014) Thermo-economics: energy, entropy and wealth. *Economic Research Council* 44(2): 3–14.

Cooper, R. (2003) *The Breaking of Nations: Order and Chaos in the 21st Century*. London: Atlantic.

Elliott, M. and Moynihan, J. (eds) (2015) *Change or Go*. London: Business for Britain.

European Commission, Completing Europe's Economic & Monetary Union, June 2015, http://ec.europa.eu/priorities/economic-monetary-union/docs/5-presidents-report_en.pdf

Evans-Pritchard, A. (2015) Monetary chaos has created the perfect recipe for European civil war. *The Daily Telegraph*, 30 July.

Hannan, D. (2013) *How We Invented Freedom and Why It Matters*. London: Head of Zeus.

Hewish, T. (2014) Old friends, new deals: the route to the UK's global prosperity through international networks. Research Paper, IEA, London. Brexit Prize Finalist.

HM Government (2013) *Review of the Balance of Competences Between the United Kingdom and the European Union Foreign Policy*. London: HMSO.

HM Government (2014) *Scotland Analysis: EU and International Issues*. London: HMSO.

Hobbes, T. (1651/1985) *Leviathan: or The Matter, Form, and Power of a Commonwealth, Ecclesiastical and Civil*. London: Penguin.

Kissinger, H. (1957) *A World Restored: Metternich, Castlereagh and the Problems of Peace 1812–22*. London: Weidenfeld & Nicholson.

Kissinger, H. (2014) *World Order*. New York: Penguin.

Leach, R. (2004) *Europe: A Concise Encyclopedia of the European Union*, 4th edn. London: Profile.

Macfarlane, A. (1978) *The Origins of English Individualism: The Family, Property and Social Transition*. Oxford: Blackwell.

Mair, P. (2013) *Ruling the Void: the Hollowing of Western Democracy*. London: Verso.

Mandeville, B. (1714/1970) *The Fable of the Bees*. Penguin.

Möhring, J. and Prins, G. (eds) (2013) *Sail On, O Ship of State*. London: Notting Hill Editions.

Open Europe (2007) *A Guide to the Constitutional Treaty*. London: Open Europe.

Prins, G. (2005) The end of the European Union. *Open Democracy*, 25 May. https://www.opendemocracy.net/democracy-europe_constitution/ EUconstitution_2542.jsp (accessed 2 September 2015).

Prins, G. (2015) Changing priorities on 'climate action' and energy policy in Europe as they have emerged during 2014: a strategic assessment. *Institute of Energy Economics of Japan*, April. http://eneken.ieej. or.jp/data/6034.pdf (accessed 2 September 2015).

Prins, G. and Möhring, J. (2008) *Another Europe? After the Third No*. Dublin: Lilliput Press.

Pye, M. (2014) *The Edge of the World: How the North Sea Made Us Who We Are*. London: Penguin.

Rummel, R. J. (1994) *Death by Government*. Brunswick, NY: Transaction.

Salter, A. (1931) *The United States of Europe*. London: George Allen & Unwin.

Scruton, R. (2000) *England: An Elegy*. London: Chatto and Windus.

Siedentop, L. (2000) *Democracy in Europe*. Penguin.

Stuart, G. (2003) *The Making of the European Constitution*. London: Fabian Society.

Tombs, R. (2014) *The English and Their History*. London: Allen Lane.

Ward, A. W. and Gooch, G. P. (1923) *Cambridge History of British Foreign Policy, Volume II (1815–1866)*. Cambridge University Press.

# 5 TRANSFORMING THE UK'S RELATIONSHIP WITH THE EU: THE LEGAL FRAMEWORK[1]

Martin Howe

## How to transform our relationship with the EU

Transforming the UK's relationship with the EU can come about, at least in theory, in two ways. Either the terms of our existing membership could be changed, while we still remain a member state; or we can cease to be a member state of the EU but relate to it under an external treaty.

Our relationship with the EU is governed by law, economics and, of course, by politics. As I am a lawyer, my contribution seeks to explain the practical consequences of treaty law and practice on the process of undertaking a transformation of our relationship with the EU, and on the practicalities from a legal and treaty point of view of some different possible models of re-negotiated relationships. It is only by understanding what can realistically be done – and how it can be done – as a matter of EU law and under the European and international treaty framework that it is possible to choose and work towards the best political and economic solutions.

Before returning to the content and strategy of renegotiation from within EU membership, I shall look first and in detail at the mechanism for UK withdrawal from the EU and how it would work out if it were implemented.

---

1 This contribution is based on Howe (2014).

## How UK withdrawal from the EU would work

There is a great deal of ignorance, misunderstanding, misinformation and, indeed, in some quarters, outright hysteria about this subject. But it is not possible to have any form of rational discussion about the costs and benefits of EU membership without having a clear idea about how the UK would operate outside the EU, both vis-à-vis the world at large and vis-à-vis the EU. In order to appreciate the likely scenarios, it is necessary to understand the mechanics of the process by which the UK would get from A to B.

### The withdrawal process under Article 50 TEU

First, the actual exit of the UK from the EU is straightforward in legal terms. The Lisbon Treaty provides a clear and unconditional right for any member state to withdraw from the EU.

Under Article 50[2] of the TEU (which was inserted by the Treaty of Lisbon), the State concerned notifies the European Council of its intention to withdraw. Negotiations then take place on an agreement covering the arrangements for withdrawal. It is envisaged that the agreement will cover transitional arrangements and the future relationship of the withdrawing State with the EU. That relationship might, for example, consist of a free-trade association agreement.

But Article 50 is clear that, even if such an agreement is not reached, the State will cease to be bound by the treaties, and in consequence its EU membership will cease, two years[3] after the date of notification. Thus *it is not possible for the other EU members to block withdrawal or to delay it for longer than the two-year period.*

---

2   For the treaty text see http://eur-lex.europa.eu/collection/eu-law/treaties.html (accessed 14 September 2015).

3   Unless extended by *mutual* consent.

Although Article 50 contemplates that the two-year period will be used to negotiate an agreement on transitional and continuing arrangements, it does not mandate what form such an agreement will take. There is no guarantee that the terms offered will be palatable or even acceptable to the UK. Therefore, *if the UK takes this course, it should be prepared to contemplate a scenario in which it leaves the EU and there is no agreement in place.* In fact, the UK has a strong hand to negotiate a mutually beneficial free-trading relationship, but in order to achieve that objective it would be necessary for it to be prepared to walk away with no agreement if necessary.

In this scenario, the absence of an agreement on the *transitional* (as opposed to continuing) arrangements would be messy but would not be a vast problem. The transitional arrangements would to a large extent be dealt with under domestic law, principally by amendments to the European Communities Act 1972.

Of more significance would be the absence of an agreement covering our future trading relationship with the remaining EU. This would mean that trade between us and other EU members would revert to the multilateral WTO framework. In particular, tariffs on trade in goods would be reintroduced.[4]

The other 'freedoms' of the EU single market would also cease to apply, namely free movement of services, capital and persons. In theory, the UK would be free to require the large EU migrant worker population here to return home, and EU states could require British citizens to leave, although it seems unlikely that either side would want to take the drastic step of expelling established residents.

Because the negotiation and conclusion of an agreement with the EU would be time consuming and the outcome of negotiations

---

4   I have heard it suggested in some quarters either that the UK would retain its membership of the European Economic Area (EEA) after EU exit or that it would revert to the European Free Trade Area (EFTA) membership it enjoyed before joining the EEC in 1973. Both of these are misconceptions without any legal foundation.

might be uncertain up to the last minute of the two-year period under Article 50, in practice it would be necessary for the UK to be getting on with other aspects of the withdrawal process on a unilateral basis, and to be setting up alternative international and regional treaty arrangements that do not involve the EU or require its consent.

## Amending UK domestic law in preparation for withdrawal

After over 40 years of membership, there is a vast existing body of laws within the UK that either directly stem from the EU, or were passed because of EU obligations, or at least are affected by the EU.

First, there are directly applicable EU laws – EU regulations and parts of the EU treaties – that form part of the internal law of the UK, via the gateway of Section 2(1) of the European Communities Act 1972. These would all automatically lapse and cease to be part of the law as from the date of withdrawal. However, in many instances it would not be acceptable to leave a vacuum in the law, and it would be necessary to have a new domestic law in place to cover the subject matter.[5]

Second, there are many Acts of Parliament that implement EU directives or other obligations. These would need to be repealed, kept in force or amended, on a case-by-case basis – it would not be possible to deal with them all with a single global rule.

Third, numerous UK regulations have been made under Section 2(2) of the European Communities Act 1972 in order to implement directives. Many of these regulations amend Acts of Parliament under the sweeping 'Henry VIII' powers[6] of Section 2(2).

---

5   For example, it would not be acceptable to have a vacuum in the law on the licensing of medicines if the UK ceases to be covered by Regulation (EC) No 726/2004 on the authorisation and supervision of medicinal products by the European Medicines Agency.

6   This is a power that gives ministers the right to repeal or amend Acts of Parliament. It is named a 'Henry VIII' power after the Statute of Proclamations 1539, which gave that King power to legislate by proclamation without recourse to Parliament.

These could not just be allowed to lapse automatically on exit. It would be necessary to go through them and decide to revoke, keep or amend them, case by case.

Reviewing these three categories of EU laws and deciding what if anything to put in their place would be a major exercise and would have to be carried out rapidly. The best solution would be simply to press into service the existing regulation-making power under Section 2(2) of the 1972 Act. This could be done by extending it to authorise existing Acts and regulations that implement EU obligations to be repealed in an orderly way, and replaced or amended as appropriate to reflect the new external trade environment of the UK.

Thus, these sweeping 'Henry VIII' powers, which have been used so effectively to implement the incoming tide of EU law, would be used rapidly to unravel EU law. The advantage of using this existing well-oiled machinery would be that there is an existing system for making these regulations by the appropriate government department, or by the devolved legislatures where the regulations fall within devolved areas of law.[7]

There are further changes to UK law that would be essential or at least desirable. The Section 2(2) power should also be extended to allow EU laws to be disapplied within the UK in advance of exit if this proves necessary: for example, if there were an attempt to impose damaging or discriminatory measures during the two-year transition period, or where it is advantageous to dismantle EU regulations before actual exit.

It would be important to clarify the legal position on exit. The ECJ or EU institutions might argue that they should still have power after exit to take decisions or adjudicate on matters that happened before exit, for example, by giving judgement after exit on ECJ cases that are still pending at the date of exit. Article 50,

---

7  It would also be necessary to review areas of competence returned by the EU on exit and decide whether those areas of competence should be exercised by Westminster or outside England by the devolved legislatures.

unlike some other treaty withdrawal clauses,[8] does not provide for any continuing right of the ECJ or other institutions to adjudicate on matters that happened before withdrawal. It would be wholly unacceptable if this were to occur, so the 1972 Act should be amended to ensure that acts of the EU institutions taking place after withdrawal are accorded no legal recognition in the UK.

Since there might well be disagreement over the UK's final years' membership subscription (the budget contribution and 'own resources' payments), it would also be prudent to repeal with immediate effect Section 2(3) of the 1972 Act, which provides for the payment of these sums by officials without the authority of Parliament.

The task of amending UK domestic law in preparation for exit is substantial but achievable, given the two-year period for the necessary work to be carried out. It should also be viewed positively in terms of what can be achieved.

In the process of review of UK law, priority should be given to reforming or sweeping away EU-based laws that interfere with the competitiveness and efficiency of the UK economy. Obvious candidates for scrapping are the Working Time and Agency Workers' Directives, and sex equality workplace laws should be reformed to reverse some of the stranger ECJ rulings.

Reforming financial services regulation would also be a priority, in view of the recent torrent of EU regulatory actions, many of which are felt to be ill-conceived or damaging. Environmental laws should be extensively reformed to eliminate obligations imposed by EU directives that involve high costs with little environmental benefit.

Freed from harmonising directives, significant reforms could be made to intellectual property laws to extend exemptions, to

---

8   For example, Article 58(2) of the European Convention on Human Rights provides that the Convention continues to apply to withdrawing states in relation to acts taking place before withdrawal.

restrict scope and terms of protection that confer no economic benefits, and to simplify areas of the law that are unnecessarily complex[9] thanks to EU interventions. The EU's insistence that rights owners should be allowed to prevent 'parallel imports' of their own goods from outside the EU could be ended with enormous economic benefits.[10]

Once freed from the CAP, as a net food-importing nation, the UK could dismantle the protectionist barriers that keep food prices in the UK higher than world market prices. The UK would regain control over fishing rights off its coast up to international limits, and would need to replace the Common Fisheries Policy (CFP) with a sensible conservation-based national fisheries policy.

The UK would regain control of migration from other EU states. EU citizens who are settled and productively working here should not be put in fear of being sent home, nor would we wish to damage our economy by excluding highly paid or highly skilled workers, such as French bankers in the City. But the inflow of low-skilled workers could be restricted in the same way as it is from non-member states, and much firmer measures could be taken against benefit or health tourists. The UK would certainly want to take more robust measures than are now permitted by EU law to exclude or remove persons engaged in criminal activities.

## International agreements

The UK's external relations now involve many matters in which we have arrangements with other EU members, or arrangements

---

9   For example, the law of designs where EU interventions now mean that there are no less than five different legal rights that apply to the design of goods.

10  Case C-415/99 *Levi Strauss & Co versus Tesco Stores*, where the ECJ ruled that Tesco infringed Levi Strauss's trade mark in the UK by buying genuine Levi Strauss jeans in North America and importing them. The effect of such restrictions is that multinational companies can milk the UK consumer for higher prices than they sell identical goods for in other markets.

with non-EU countries, which are conducted partly or wholly through the EU. For example, in tariff matters, agreements are concluded under the EU's common commercial policy between the EU itself and non-member states. In these cases, upon exit the UK would cease to be part of such agreements and would need to renegotiate any replacement arrangement with the counterparty states concerned.

Many other treaties, however, fall within areas of 'mixed competence' and are concluded both by the member states and by the EU. The most important examples of this category are the WTO Agreements.[11] Under such treaties, the EU and the member states are responsible vis-à-vis non-member states for matters within their respective competences. But if the EU competence disappears on exit, the UK will automatically take on the treaty rights and obligations across the board. The basic categories of agreements are the following.

- International agreements, where the UK's status is unaffected by EU exit, e.g. UN membership and Security Council membership under the UN Charter. We would simply continue as members, but freed of obligations to act in 'solidarity' with EU member states under the Common Foreign and Security Policy.
- Mixed competence agreements, where both the UK and the EU are parties. Under such agreements, the EU is responsible to third states for matters falling within its competence, and the UK is responsible vis-à-vis third states for matters outside EU competence. Such agreements will continue on exit, and the UK's competence will simply expand when EU competence disappears. The most important agreements in this category are the WTO Agreements, including GATT.

---

11  The ECJ ruled on the status of the WTO Agreements in Opinion 3/94 *Re: the Uruguay Round Trade Agreements*.

- International agreements with third states, where only the EU is party, or where member states are also parties *but in their capacity as such.* This category includes not only agreements with third states under the EU Common Foreign and Security Policy, but also numerous trade and association agreements, including the EEA Agreement. The UK would cease to be a party to these agreements on EU exit, so it would need to review them and consider whether to enter into replacement arrangements.

The general review of the UK's external relations would identify many instances where, after EU exit, international arrangements would automatically slot into place to replace existing EU arrangements. For example, the UK would cease to be part of the European Arrest Warrant system, but the European Convention on Extradition (a Council of Europe Convention covering both EU and other states) would then automatically govern extradition arrangements between the UK and the EU states, who are all members of the Convention.

In the field of intellectual property, the UK would remain a member of the European system for centralised examination and granting of patents, since this comes under the European Patent Convention, which is not an EU treaty. Nor does the UK need to be a member of the EU for British-based rights holders to exercise rights within the EU, since non-discriminatory protection must be given under TRIPs[12] and other international agreements.

Even where there is no automatic replacement, there are many existing international or European regional[13] conventions that

---

12 The Agreement on Trade-Related Aspects of Intellectual Property, one of the WTO Agreements.

13 Particularly the numerous conventions on many subject matters which are open to signature by members of the Council of Europe. Exit from the EU would not affect the UK's membership of the Council of Europe which is a wider body with currently 47 member states.

cover similar subject matter to EU arrangements. For example, the Lugano Convention on the mutual recognition and enforcement of judgements in civil and commercial matters is open to non-EU states. It has similar rules to the Brussels Regulation, which applies as between EU members.

In many instances, arrangements that are presently conducted through the EU could be replaced by satisfactory non-EU international arrangements, in which case there is no merit in involving the EU further. The UK needs to sort out its wider international relationships first, before negotiating with the EU. But, where special arrangements with the EU would be of significant benefit, these should be added to the agenda of the negotiations with the EU.

## International trade relations

Before turning to the question of trade relations with the EU after exit, it is worth considering trade relations with the wider world. The majority of the UK's exports are now to non-EU countries, and these exports are rising at a faster rate, so the EU's share of our exports is continuously falling.

The UK was a founder member of the European Free Trade Association (EFTA) until it joined the EEC in 1973. The free-trade relationship between the UK and the EFTA states was preserved, and indeed extended to the rest of the EEC, under agreements between those states and the EEC. The UK's membership of EFTA ceased in 1973, but there seems no reason why the current EFTA states (Switzerland, Norway, Iceland and Liechtenstein) should not welcome the UK back to EFTA in order to preserve the UK's existing free-trade relations with them.

By joining EFTA, the UK would not only secure the continuation of free-trade arrangements between itself and the four EFTA states, but would also be able to join in with EFTA's free-trade arrangements with third countries. There has been much misleading recent propaganda to the effect that it is necessary to be a member of a big trade bloc such as the EU in order to negotiate free-trade arrangements with other countries. This is the reverse of the truth. EFTA has been notably more successful than the EU in negotiating free-trade agreements largely because (unlike the EU) it is not hampered by unreasonable protectionist demands from some of its members.[14] By this means, there is every reason to believe that the UK could secure rapid access to a wider range of free-trade arrangements with third countries than is possible for it as an EU member.

## Post-exit trade relations with the EU

A key objective of the UK would be to secure continued access for exports to the EU market without tariffs on goods and without increased non-tariff barriers on goods and services. Any such arrangement would, of course, be mutual and so provide corresponding benefits for the EU.

The UK's exports of goods to the rest of the EU in 2012 were £147.7 billion; however, the EU's goods exports to the UK for the same period were £226.5 billion.[15] Although the balance of trade in services is not quite so dramatically one-sided, EU exporters would benefit markedly more than UK exporters from continued free trade arrangements. On any rational appraisal of the strength of its bargaining position, the UK should be able to use its position as the EU's major buyer of export goods to negotiate both continued free trade in goods and continued unhindered access to important service sectors, most notably financial services.

---

14  Such as the French desire to shield its film industry from international competition, or unreasonable protectionist demands and fears rather hysterically articulated within the European Parliament, which are holding up the TTIP agreement between the EU and US.

15  Source: Office for National Statistics *Pink Book*.

The financial services aspect of such negotiations would be very important. Under our existing EU membership, we suffer from the problem that unwelcome directives and regulations can be imposed on the City under QMV by a majority of member states, who may be either indifferent to or actually hostile toward the interests of the City. For example, the euro zone states acting together can drive through measures against the UK's opposition. The government is currently seeking to address this issue as part of its renegotiation exercise by way of seeking an interpretative agreement aimed at strengthening the position of non-euro-zone states. How successful this renegotiation exercise will prove in this regard will need careful evaluation of the terms agreed.

The starting point of an external negotiation with the EU would be that the City would escape from this kind of regulatory interference from the EU or euro zone with regard to UK-based transactions and the export of financial services around the world. However, it clearly would be beneficial to negotiate mutual access of financial services between the EU and UK on a basis that respects the UK's regulatory independence. Any attempt to make access to the EU market dependent upon mirroring EU regulatory regimes should be firmly rejected. Given the huge disparity in exports of goods noted above, the UK is in a strong position to negotiate good terms for access for its financial services into the EU market as a condition for allowing continued tariff-free access for the EU's exports of goods into the UK market.

## Possible models for trade relations with the EU after exit

The above represent basic or core terms that it is likely the UK would seek to negotiate after exit, and which, on the face of it, the EU would have every incentive to agree to in its own interests. However, virtually the whole of the continent of Europe as well as other states outside it are in free-trade relations with the EU. There are many free-trading agreements between the EU and other countries, which vary in their structures, although most extend to services as well as goods.

Those that have been most mooted as possible models for a UK/EU post-membership agreement are Norway and Switzerland. In fact, these agreements are radically different from each other.

The EEA members, Norway, Iceland and Liechtenstein, are within the single market for the purposes of the 'four freedoms'.[16] In addition, they are required to apply the regulatory aspects of the single market internally as a condition of continued access to the single market and effectively to follow the interpretation given to EU measures by the ECJ. For this purpose, 'single market' measures include EU health and safety, labour law and equality measures, for example, the Working Time Directive.

Switzerland is a member of the EFTA (as are the EEA states), and it has a large number of bilateral agreements with the EU. In addition to providing for the 'four freedoms' (the freedom of movement of goods, services, capital and labour) of the single market, many of these bilateral agreements facilitate access by Swiss goods and services to the EU single market, as well as (obviously) permitting access in the opposite direction. Many of these agreements effectively flank intra-EU measures. However, the key difference between Switzerland and the EEA states is that Switzerland has an effective choice over whether it is in its interests to sign up to particular arrangements rather than have them imposed on it across the board.

Norway's relationship with the EU under the EEA is not a good model for the UK. This is because the EEA states are effectively obliged to implement the burdensome regulatory requirements of the EU single market but have no vote on framing them. This means not merely existing legislation but future legislation would be passed by legislative process in which the UK would have no

16 Except for agricultural goods and fisheries.

vote at all, but just a consultation right. To leave the EU to escape from its regulatory strictures, from social and employment laws, and from the ECJ's case law, and then to sign up to this sort of arrangement that would keep us subject to all those constraints, but with even less say in them, would be irrational.

By contrast, the Swiss relationship involves the application of the general rules of the EU single market on free movement of goods, services and capital, together with numerous individually negotiated bilateral agreements on subjects including mutual recognition of standards in goods and services and home country certification. Switzerland is landlocked by the EU and conducts a very high proportion of its trade with the EU.

The more Atlantic and global stance of the UK suggests that we would not need to negotiate an arrangement with the EU as detailed and intense as the Swiss one. Indeed, there would be every reason not to do so, and to avoid the commitment that the Swiss have assumed to free movement of persons. Nonetheless, the Swiss/EU agreements[17] provide a detailed checklist of matters for potential agreement with the EU.

## Customs union or free-trade agreement?

One key question is whether the UK should seek to negotiate a *free-trade* agreement with the EU, or continued membership of the *customs union*.[18] This seemingly technical question is of great importance.

In a customs union, no formalities need be applied when goods cross internal borders in the union. In a free-trade area, goods are checked at the internal borders, and only goods that *originate within* the free-trade area are entitled to proceed tariff free.

---

17  Listed (in English) at http://www.europa.admin.ch/themen/00500/index.htm l?lang=en (accessed 21 September 2015).

18  Turkey is a member of the EU customs union even though it is not an EU member.

However, members of a customs union have no freedom to set their own external tariffs and cannot negotiate separate free-trade agreements with countries outside the customs union. In practice if not in theory, a customs union normally entails a requirement to share the revenue derived from external tariffs,[19] and this would be highly disadvantageous to the UK because of its international trade pattern.

After exit, the UK's freedom to negotiate free-trade arrangements with other countries independently of the EU would be of great importance, as would its ability to decide upon its own external tariffs.[20] These considerations bolster the argument against remaining generally in the EU customs union, but we should consider maintaining a customs union covering certain highly integrated industrial sectors[21] to assist the continued free flow of goods (in both directions, to the UK and EU's mutual benefit) without 'rules of origin' formalities.

The UK should hold its nerve when negotiating these arrangements – which are of clear benefit to the EU – and should not be willing to pay an additional price by making concessions elsewhere, or by allowing a mutually beneficial free-trading agreement to be subject to conditions about additional matters or linkages to agreements on other subjects. While it would be disadvantageous (for both parties) if such arrangements cannot be negotiated, this should be kept in context. If no agreement is reached, the total tariffs payable on UK exports, assuming the EU's average weighted external tariff came into force against UK

---

19  This is because goods will enter and bear tariffs in the ports of one country and will then circulate and be consumed in other countries within the union.

20  Some commentators have argued convincingly that adhering to the EU's external tariffs imposes a major cost on the UK because the tariffs are borne by consumers in the UK; but the tariffs mainly protect industries in sectors where the UK no longer has much industry of its own: see, for example, Minford et al. (2005).

21  Such as the car industry.

exports, would be around £6 billion.[22] While trade within the EU may be more heavily weighted to goods that would bear higher tariffs than its external trade, this gives an order-of-magnitude feel. The total amount is *almost certainly less than the UK's current gross contribution to the EU budget.*

The UK could use its savings from the EU budget, and its revenue from levying tariffs on the much larger imports into the UK from the EU, to reduce taxes on its exporting industries, thus mitigating any damaging effects from the imposition of tariffs on exports into the UK. But it should not come to that. With firmness and determination, mutual self-interest should lead to concluding a satisfactory agreement with the EU.

## Renegotiation from within

The basic problem of renegotiating our relationship with the EU from the inside is that the starting point is the vast mass of treaty obligations and EU legislation to which we are subject – the *acquis*. As outlined above, it will all go if we exit the EU, and we can seek to negotiate back only those core elements that are of positive benefit. By contrast, renegotiation from within involves raising a list of specific issues and trying the change the *acquis* on each one. Each and every specific issue that is raised is likely to give rise to its own difficulties, both in securing agreement to it and in implementing any resulting change in a durable and effective form.

To take but one example, a reform of EU employment law to reduce the costs of the present EU laws to the British economy would need an amendment to the EU treaties in order to be permanent and effective. It is hard to see why those member states who support the EU engaging in this area of legislation would

---

22  4 per cent – figure for 2010 (latest available). Source: World Bank, Most Favoured Nation Tariff Rate.

agree to the EU losing its competence in this field. So, the treaty amendment would need to be in the form of a special opt-out protocol relating to the UK, such as the Maastricht social chapter opt-out, but widened in order to prevent circumvention by the use of other treaty articles to impose measures on the UK (as was done with the Working Time Directive).

Such a treaty amendment would need to be agreed unanimously by the governments of all member states. Even if agreed by all governments, it would then need to be 'ratified' or 'approved'[23] by all member states in accordance with their respective constitutional requirements.

The problem with this approach is that there is a strong view in some member states that these types of social and employment laws are an integral part of the European single market. France, notably, believes (across the political spectrum) that it is necessary to protect its high-cost social welfare model by making sure that employers in other member states bear the same high costs as French employers. However irrational such an approach is in an open global economy, where European businesses have to compete with businesses in other parts of the world who are not subject to such burdens, it is a deeply held view, and it would be extremely difficult to persuade France or other similarly minded countries to agree to a treaty change.

The alternative but much less satisfactory and permanent approach would be to try to implement a relaxation of employment laws affecting the UK via amendments to the laws themselves, rather than by treaty change. Theoretically this might be slightly easier than a treaty change, because the amendments could be repealed or amended by QMV rather than unanimity. However, the approval of the European Parliament would be needed to pass the repealing or amending measures, and that approval

---

23 Depending on whether the treaty amendment takes place under the 'ordinary' or 'simplified' procedure in Article 48 of the TEU.

could well not be forthcoming even if sufficient agreement could be reached at a governmental level.

It can be seen that this one renegotiation issue alone raises formidable difficulties. Each and every other specific issue is likely to raise problems of comparable difficulty, if different in kind. Increased restrictions on the free movement of workers are likely to encounter serious opposition from the East European member states. Special measures to protect the UK's financial services from the effects of caballing by the euro-zone states will raise serious difficulties of their own.

The longer the list of specific demands, the longer the list of difficulties that will have to be faced, and the larger the coalition of member states that could be built up in opposition to agreeing with the UK's demands. Even if (hypothetically) all EU governments could somehow be persuaded to accommodate a list of UK demands, the processes of national ratification or approval of the necessary treaty amendments would be likely to take years and could well be derailed by opposition in one or more countries.

The second possible approach to renegotiation is to start at the other end. Instead of attempting to seek specific changes to the vast existing framework (the so-called *acquis*), this approach starts from looking at where we would stand if we were to exercise our right to withdraw under Article 50 of the Lisbon Treaty, and then asking what specific arrangements between the UK and other EU members would be in the mutual interests of the UK and those other members. While still retaining its formal status as a member state, the UK's rights and obligations would be reduced to a limited core under an opt-out protocol, similar in principle to but much wider in scope than the existing protocols, which exclude the UK and certain other countries from aspects of the EU treaties. This is the zero-plus approach to renegotiation.

Renegotiation is a once-in-a-generation opportunity to make changes in our relationship that *solve* the severe tensions over self-government and other matters, which have arisen within the UK and between the UK and other EU states. It is a chance to put the future on a sounder and more harmonious footing. We should not waste this opportunity. We should negotiate for a sheep rather than a lamb.

## References

Howe, M. (2014) *Zero-Plus: The Principles of EU Renegotiation*. London: Politeia.

Minford, P., Mahambare, V. and Nowell, E. (2005) *Should Britain Leave the EU? An Economic Analysis of a Troubled Relationship*. Cheltenham: Edward Elgar; London: Institute of Economic Affairs.

# 6 FREEDOM OF MOVEMENT

Philippe Legrain

Freedom of movement is a fundamentally important freedom. Imagine how limited your life would be if you were born in a village somewhere in Britain and were not allowed to move anywhere else. You would have to go to the local school, good or bad. You could not go to university. Your work options would be few and, quite likely, unrewarding. Your choice of whom to share your life with would likewise be slim. How you might wish you had been born in London, with all the opportunities that it offers. That may sound like an extreme example. But in many respects, it is less extreme than the situation faced by people born in a poor country and denied the right to move to a richer one. Born in a British village, your possibilities would be restricted, but you would still enjoy a high standard of living by global standards, the protection of property rights and the rule of law more generally, decent healthcare and so on. Born in an African village, your prospects would be much bleaker. Indeed, even a bright, industrious and enterprising woman born in Africa would most likely end up leading a worse life than a lazy dimwit born in Europe. The world is anything but flat.

Even in reasonably sized rich countries such as Britain, people place a very high value on freedom of movement. Asked what the EU means to them personally, Britons' top answer by far is the freedom to travel, study and work anywhere in the EU (European

Commission 2014).[1] Some 1.8 million Britons live elsewhere in the EU – nearly as many as the 2.34 million other Europeans who reside in Britain – and many more spent part of their year abroad.[2]

Freedom of movement – liberation from being tied to the land where you happen to have been born – is not just intrinsically important. It is key to unlocking other vital freedoms. In order to trade, people often need to move. To export tourism services, for example, Britain needs to welcome foreigners for a period of time. To seek treatment from a foreign surgeon, people also need to move. If a British patient goes abroad to have an operation, this is generally classified as trade, whereas if the surgeon comes to Britain, it is classified as migration – yet the operations are analogous. Where services have to be delivered locally – old people cannot be cared for from afar; offices and hotel rooms have to be cleaned on the spot; food and drink have to be served face to face – international trade is only possible with labour mobility. So, if the free movement of goods and services is considered to be beneficial, then surely so too is the movement of the people who produce them.

This introduction may seem like an extended diversion from the topic of this chapter: what would an ideal, free-market migration policy for Britain look like, and what kind of feasible relationship with the EU is best suited to delivering it? But in fact, it goes to the heart of the matter. Because whereas there is almost universal agreement among supporters of free markets that free trade is a good thing, the free movement of people is unfortunately much more contested – including, ostensibly, on economic grounds.

---

1   37 per cent of Britons say freedom of movement is the thing they most associate with the EU.

2   EU migrants moving to UK balanced by Britons living abroad. *Financial Times*, 10 February 2014. http://www.ft.com/cms/s/0/5cd640f6-9025-11e3-a776-00144feab-7de.html (accessed 2 September 2015).

This chapter will make the case that Britain ought to allow people to move freely, as indeed it did in the nineteenth century.[3] It will further argue that Britain's current position as a member of the EU offers an almost ideal policy mix: freedom of movement within the EU (with the exception of the transitional controls on citizens of Croatia, which joined the EU in July 2013), with no constraints on Britain's migration policy towards non-EU citizens. While Britain ought to be more open to the rest of the world (and drop the restrictions on Croatian migrants), the barriers to this lie in domestic politics, not EU law. Since the status quo in relation to labour mobility – remaining in the EU with the existing terms of membership – is optimal, alternative options, such as renegotiating the terms of Britain's membership, leaving the EU and joining the EEA, or leaving the EU and negotiating bilateral agreements with the EU, could not improve on it.

## Why freedom of movement is the right policy

Migration is an essential element of economic development. People often need to move to where the jobs are. And by coming together in diverse cities, dynamic people create new ideas and businesses. In our globalising world, where the economy is forever changing and opportunities no longer stop at national borders, it is increasingly important for people – be they British businesspeople or Polish plumbers – to move freely, not just within a country but also internationally. Just as it is a good thing for people to move from Liverpool to London if their labour is in demand there, so too from Lisbon or Lithuania. So governments should allow people to move as freely as politically possible.

---

3   For instance, in 1872, the then Foreign Secretary, Lord Granville, declared that 'by the existing law of Great Britain all foreigners have the unrestricted right of entrance and residence in this country'.

The emerging pan-European labour market is encouraging the allocation of labour to its most efficient use. It enables Britain to specialise in what it does best; reap economies of scale; foster dynamic clusters; and improve the variety, quality and cost of local products and services. Increased mobility also makes the economy more flexible, allowing it to adapt more readily to change. Last but not least, foreigners' dynamism and diversity boost competition, innovation and enterprise, raising long-term productivity growth and living standards.

It is impossible to make an exact estimate of the economic benefits of freedom of movement within the EU. However, they are certainly much greater than generally assumed. Political debate tends to assert, wrongly, that migrants harms locals' job prospects and are a burden on the welfare state. Economic studies often suggest that the benefits of migration to the existing British population are relatively small. But those studies are misleadingly incomplete. The economic models used are often partial: analyses of migrants' impact on the labour market or public finances ignore their impact on the economy as a whole (which, in turn, also affects locals' wages and employment, as well as taxes and spending). They are usually static: broader general equilibrium models analyse the impact of immigration in an artificial world without economic growth, where migrants' dynamic impact on investment and productivity growth, and, hence, on future living standards, is ignored. And even dynamic models generally define away migrants' contribution to innovation and enterprise, because they assume that new technologies fall like manna from heaven and ignore the role of institutions and individual entrepreneurs altogether. In a neo-classical growth model, which fails to explain technological progress and ignores the role of Schumpeterian waves of creative destruction, Albert Einstein, Sergey Brin, EasyJet or the City of London simply do not exist.

To grow fast, dynamic economies need to generate lots of genuinely new – and often disruptive – ideas and then deploy them across the economy. Such ideas sometimes arrive from individual geniuses coming up with incredible insights in isolation – and those exceptional people seem disproportionately to be migrants. Globally, around 30 per cent of Nobel laureates were living outside their country of birth at the time of their award. For example, Venkatraman Ramakrishnan of the University of Cambridge's Laboratory of Molecular Biology, who became President of the Royal Society in November 2015, is an Indian-born and US-educated biologist who determined the structure of the ribosome. Other examples include Andre Geim, a Russian-born scientist who developed a revolutionary supermaterial called graphene at the University of Manchester, and Christopher Pissarides, a Cypriot-born economist at the London School of Economics. But new ideas mostly emerge from creative collisions between people. For those interactions to be fruitful, people need to bring something extra to the party. The saying 'two heads are better than one' is true only if they think differently.

Since I first wrote about this (Legrain 2007), plenty of research has backed up my case that both immigrants individually and the interaction between diverse people more generally generate new ideas. As Scott Page (Professor of Complex Systems, Political Science and Economics at the University of Michigan, Ann Arbor) explains, groups that display a range of perspectives outperform groups of like-minded experts. His research shows that 'organisations, firms and universities that solve problems should seek out people with diverse experiences, training and identities that translate into diverse perspectives and heuristics' (Page 2007). That diversity dividend can be large, because an ever-increasing share of our prosperity comes from solving problems – such as developing new medicines, computer games and environmentally friendly technologies; designing innovative products and policies; and providing original management advice. Empirical evidence bears this out. Diversity in general and immigration in particular are associated with increased patenting as well as higher productivity, as I detail in my latest book (Legrain 2014: Chapter 11).

As well as helping to generate new ideas, migrants help deploy them across the economy through their entrepreneurial dynamism. Britain's most valuable technology company, ARM Holdings, which designs the chips in most smartphones, was established with the help of Austrian-born Herman Hauser. Europe's most profitable airline, EasyJet, was founded by a Greek entrepreneur in Britain, Stelios Haji-Ioannou. Many of the entrepreneurs in Tech City, a hub for technology start-ups in East London, are foreign. For example, two Estonians set up TransferWise, a peer-to-peer currency exchange that enables people to send money abroad without paying the extortionate fees charged by banks. Overall, immigrants in Britain are nearly twice as likely to set up a business as UK-born ones.[4] Contrary to the belief that only some immigrant cultures are entrepreneurial, Global Entrepreneurship Monitor surveys show that in Britain all their categories of immigrant are more entrepreneurial than white UK-born people (Levie and Hart 2009).

Migrants tend to be more enterprising than most because they are a self-selected minority who have taken the risk of uprooting themselves and tend to have a burning desire to get ahead. Like starting a new business, migrating is a risky enterprise, and hard work is needed to make it pay off. Since migrants usually start off without contacts, capital or a conventional career, setting up a business is a natural way to get ahead. And because outsiders tend to see things differently, they may be more aware of opportunities and go out and grab them.

It is often argued that while highly skilled migrants may be beneficial to Britain, less-skilled ones are not – and that the government should admit the former, but not the latter. Yet it is

---

4   Migrants to the UK had a total entrepreneurial activity rate of 16 per cent, compared with 9 per cent among UK-born people (Centre for Entrepreneurs 2014).

impossible to identify in advance how, or how much, anyone will contribute to society, let alone how their children will. Nobody could have guessed, when he arrived in the US as a child refugee from the Soviet Union, that Sergey Brin would go on to co-found Google. Had he been denied entry, America would never have realised the opportunity that had been missed. How many potential Brins does Britain turn away or scare off – and at what cost?

Governments are incapable of picking individual winners, let alone planning an entire economy's ever-changing manpower needs. So, a selective immigration policy cannot possibly determine the correct number and mix of people that Britain needs now, let alone how these will evolve in future. Just think how damaging such policies would be if applied between London and the rest of the country, or between England and Scotland. Why should it be any different between Britain and the rest of the EU, or between Britain and the US? Allowing people to work wherever they want and companies to hire whomever they want would clearly deliver a better outcome.

Indeed, basing a selective immigration policy on the premise that Britain benefits from high-skilled immigration but not from the lower-skilled variety is economically illiterate. It is equivalent to arguing that Britain benefits from importing American software, but not Chinese clothes. In fact, the gains from migration depend largely on the extent to which newcomers' attributes, skills, perspectives and experiences differ from those of existing residents and complement ever-changing local resources, needs and circumstances. Migrants may have skills that not enough locals have, such as medical training or fluency in Mandarin. They may have foreign contacts and knowledge that open up new opportunities for trade and investment. Their diverse perspectives and experiences can help spark new ideas and solve problems better and faster. As risk-taking outsiders with a drive to get ahead, they tend to be more entrepreneurial than most. Having moved once, they tend to be more willing to move again, enabling the job market to cope better with change. And they may be more willing to do less-skilled and less-attractive jobs that most locals with higher living standards, education levels and aspirations no longer want to do, such as pick fruit or care for the elderly.[5] Or they may simply be young and hard-working, a huge bonus to an ageing society with increasing numbers of pensioners to support. Newcomers' taxes can also help service and repay the huge public debt that has been incurred to provide benefits for the existing population.

Critics who counter that Britain could make do without migrant labour may be literally correct – Robinson Crusoe scraped by alone on his island – but autarky would make us all much poorer. While alternatives may exist – paying higher wages may induce a higher local supply of labour, or over time induce people to acquire the skills required for jobs in demand; some jobs can be replaced with machines or computers; some tasks can be performed overseas – closing off one's options clearly has a cost. Without foreign labour, for instance, English strawberries would go unpicked, or be so prohibitively expensive that Spanish ones picked with foreign labour would be imported instead. Like trade barriers, immigration controls reduce Britons' welfare – and by raising the cost of products and services, they harm the poor most.

While Britain's future prosperity depends on developing new high-productivity activities and nurturing existing ones, a large share of future employment will be in low-skill, low-productivity location-specific activities, precisely because such tasks cannot readily be mechanised or imported. The biggest area of employment growth in Europe is not in high-tech industries, but in care for the elderly. Yet retirement homes already cannot find enough suitable local applicants for care-working vacancies, nor

---

5   Indeed, according to the modern trade theory of comparative advantage based on factor endowments, an economy such as Britain, where low-skilled labour is relatively scarce, would benefit more from low-skilled migration than the higher-skilled variety.

can the elderly be properly cared for by a robot or from overseas. Persuading young local people who would rather do something else to work in a retirement home would require a substantial wage hike – and that implies pensioners making do with much less care, big budget cuts elsewhere or large tax rises.

Critics respond by claiming that immigrants impose all sorts of costs, notably harming Britons' job prospects, burdening public finances and causing congestion on a crowded island. Yet study after study shows that such fears are largely unfounded.[6]

Starting with the labour-market impact: immigrants do not take local people's jobs any more than women take those of men, because there is not a fixed number of jobs to go round. As well as filling jobs, they create them when they spend their wages and in complementary lines of work. Critics who argue that immigrants harm the job prospects of European workers implicitly assume that newcomers compete directly with Britons in the labour market – and that the economy never adapts to their arrival. If immigrants were identical to native workers and suddenly arrived in an economy with no vacancies, they would indeed have a temporary negative impact on local workers – but only until investment caught up with the increased supply of workers and higher demand for goods and services.

But immigrants and British workers are not identical. The newcomers, after all, are foreign: they speak English less well; they have fewer contacts and less knowledge of local practices; and low-skilled migrants may have less education and fewer skills than local workers. At most, then, they are imperfect substitutes for local workers, and compete only indirectly with them in the labour market. Some individuals, then, may lose out: an unreliable local builder who does shoddy work may find himself out of work, with a need to up his game or retrain. But even if Polish

---

6  On the fiscal impact, see, for instance, OECD (2013: Chapter 3). On the labour-market impact, see, for instance, Dustmann et al. (2008) and Centre for Research and Analysis of Migration (2014).

builders are willing to work for lower wages than local ones, they do not necessarily deprive local brickies of work: if home repairs are cheaper, more people can afford house improvements, while reliable, established builders may be able to charge richer clients more (and employ Polish workers). Mostly, though, immigrants take jobs that local workers cannot or will not do, and thus do not compete with them at all. On the contrary: immigrants often complement local workers' efforts, raising productivity and thus lifting their wages. A foreign childminder may allow a doctor to return to work, where the latter's productivity is enhanced by hard-working foreign nurses and cleaners.

While Milton Friedman famously said that 'it's just obvious that you can't have free immigration and a welfare state,'[7] he was mistaken, as Britain's experience in the EU shows, and as I explained at length in an earlier pamphlet (Legrain 2008). Contrary to public perception, there is no evidence that Britain's welfare state acts as a 'magnet' for 'benefit tourists'. All 100 million or so people from the ten poorer ex-communist member states that joined the EU in 2004 and 2007 are free to move to Britain, as indeed are the citizens of crisis-hit countries such as Spain, Italy, Portugal, Greece and Ireland. Once they have been in Britain three months and are deemed 'habitually resident', they are eligible for some welfare benefits, albeit only for three months. Yet, of the 440 million or so citizens from other EU countries who could live in Britain, only 2.34 million do, and only 1.1 million of those are from the poorer member states who might conceivably be attracted by Britain's welfare system. Scarcely any are claiming welfare, let alone moving here with that purpose.

That people would be enterprising enough to up sticks to move to Britain in search of a better life and then choose once here to languish on welfare rather than earning more working

---

7    See http://openborders.info/friedman-immigration-welfare-state/ (accessed 2 September 2015).

is scarcely credible – and thanks to Britain's admirably flexible labour market, they do not get trapped in unemployment as they might in countries with insider–outsider labour markets. Indeed, in 2004, when Britain, Ireland and Sweden alone opened their labour markets to citizens of the A8 ex-communist countries that had just joined the EU, very few opted for Sweden, despite its very generous welfare state. Since Britain and Ireland restricted A8 citizens' access to social benefits for the first year, prospective welfare migrants should have opted for Sweden. Yet of the 324,000 Poles who emigrated in 2005, only one in 100 went to Sweden – overwhelmingly to work (OECD 2007: Table 1.2 and Chart 1.7).

Far from being a burden on public finances, EU migrants to Britain are net contributors. Migrants from the EEA (the EU plus Norway, Iceland and Liechtenstein, which are also part of the free-movement area) contributed around 4.5 per cent more in taxes than they received in benefits over the period 2001–11, according to a study by Christian Dustmann and Tommaso Frattini of University College London. Recent EU migrants (those who arrived after 1999) contributed 34 per cent more in taxes than they received in benefits over the same period. In contrast, over the same period, the total of UK natives' tax payments was 11 per cent lower than the transfers they received. Recent EU migrants were more than 50 per cent less likely than natives to receive state benefits or tax credits. They are also far better educated than natives: 32 per cent had a university degree. The comparable figure for UK natives is 21 per cent. The estimated net fiscal contribution of immigrants increases even more if one considers that immigration helps in sharing the cost of fixed public expenditures (which account for over 20 per cent of total public expenditure) among a larger pool of people, thus reducing further the financial burden for UK natives. The main reasons for the large net fiscal contribution of recent EEA immigrants are their higher average labour market participation (compared with natives) and their lower receipt of welfare benefits (Dustmann and Frattini 2013).

It is often said that EU migrants put pressure on public services. But if their taxes more than pay for the services they receive, the real issue is that public services are not flexible enough to cope with change. After all, if a British person moved from Liverpool to London and local services could not cope, who would be blamed? Nor do hotels or Tesco complain that they cannot cope with increased demand for their services.

It is also nonsense to assert that Britain is 'full up'. Three-quarters of the country is agricultural land; even in England the urban reservations that we live in account for only 11 per cent of the surface area. There is plenty of space left: even in London there is still lots of derelict land. The problem is planning restrictions that excessively restrict development, driving up residential land prices to the benefit of large landowners and at the expense of everyone else. Having more people around does not have to be a problem: most people choose to live in cities, not the countryside. The most densely populated place in Britain is Kensington and Chelsea, which is hardly a hell-hole.

The final category of objection is, to put it kindly, cultural: that newcomers will not fit into British society and may harm it in some way. It is odd that some defenders of individual freedom take a communitarian approach, assuming that everyone ought to fit in, a prescription that they would doubtless resist for someone born in Britain. Others speak of a threat to national identity, even though Britishness is increasingly based on civic values not ethnicity. So, while some people with liberal economic views may also have nationalist political views, their nationalist objections scarcely count against the liberal, or free-market, case for freedom of movement. As for the issue of how a liberal society copes with illiberal members, this is posed not only by the admission of some immigrants who are illiberal, but also by the presence of illiberal natives. Liberals must always be vigilant to defend

Britain's liberal institutions – not least against authoritarian governments – but this is scarcely sufficient grounds to restrict freedom of movement within the EU.

## Why EU membership offers the best of both worlds

This chapter has argued that freedom of movement is the first-best policy for Britain, on the basis of liberal values as well as on economic grounds. But what kind of international cooperation is needed to achieve the desired first-best objective? Again, one can make an analogy with trade. The first-best outcome globally is free trade and, independently of what other countries choose, the first-best policy for Britain is unilateral free trade. But there are three reasons why the government might wish to sign an international trade agreement. First, because in the event that unilateral free trade was politically unachievable, the prospect of negotiating better access to foreign markets could help overcome protectionist domestic interests that fear import competition, and thus make it politically possible to lower British trade barriers. Second, as a result, such a trade agreement could give British exports better access to foreign markets, and thus enable Britain to import more. Third, because trade agreements tie governments' hands, raising the political cost of erecting future trade barriers. Ideally, such a trade agreement should be global, or at least as nearly global as possible, that is, with the members of the WTO. Otherwise, a regional or bilateral trade agreement implies a cost: giving privileged access to imports from countries in the agreement at the expense of those from non-signatories.

One can reason similarly with mobility. The first-best outcome globally is freedom of movement and, independent of other governments' policies, the first-best policy for Britain is unilateral openness to foreigners. But insofar as that is not politically possible, greater openness to foreigners may be achievable as part of a treaty that offers Britons the right to move to other countries and raises the political cost of trying to raise future immigration barriers for protectionist and/or nationalist reasons. Ideally, such an agreement would be global, but insofar as this is not possible, a treaty that provides for freedom of movement across the 28 countries of the EU is clearly desirable. Clearly, this does entail a cost: Poles have privileged access to the UK job market compared with Australians. But there is nothing in the terms of EU membership that prevents the UK from offering equally good access to Australians. The divergence is due to British domestic politics, not EU treaty commitments.

There is thus a big difference between Britain's relationship with the EU in trade and that in labour mobility. The EU is a customs union for trade in goods and services, which requires a common external tariff and a single set of trade regulations; but in the case of labour flows, it is simply a free-trade area, with countries free to set their own tariffs and entry requirements for non-EU citizens. Thus, whereas one might argue that Britain should leave the EU in the hope of signing a free-trade agreement offering equivalent access while also being able to sign freer-trade deals with non-EU countries, that flexibility is already available in the UK's current relationship with the EU on labour mobility.

Since EU membership places no restrictions on UK immigration policy towards non-EU countries, this could (and ought to be) much more liberal. The model in this respect is Sweden. In December 2008, Sweden's liberal conservative government introduced radical reforms that allow businesses that cannot find suitable local workers to hire foreign ones of any skill level from anywhere in the world on two-year renewable visas. Insofar as immigration controls are deemed politically necessary, this open, flexible and non-discriminatory policy is greatly preferable to the UK's confused, arbitrary and discriminatory approach.

In terms of welfare policies, all the evidence shows that migrants move to work not to claim benefits, but in any case EU rules do not prevent non-discriminatory welfare reforms, ie, ones that apply equally to all EU citizens, akin to the WTO principle of national treatment in trade. So, the UK is free to restrict welfare benefits as it pleases, providing it does so for all potential recipients. Moreover, the EU's Free Movement Directive makes clear that the right to move and reside freely is not absolute. In theory, after three months an EU national without a job has no right to remain in another EU country unless they have sufficient means not to become an 'unreasonable burden' on the welfare state.

Thus, from a liberal perspective, the combination of freedom of movement and equal treatment within the EU and decentralised, unconstrained national decision-making for non-EU immigration is pretty much ideal: it prevents protectionist and discriminatory policies within the EU and does not prevent liberal policies towards the rest of the world.

The arguments for leaving the EU in order to 'regain control over our borders' and restrict EU migration are illiberal and economically harmful. Economic liberals should have no truck with them.

## References

Centre for Entrepreneurs (2014) *Migrant Entrepreneurs: Building Our Businesses, Creating Our Jobs.* London: Centre for Entrepreneurs.

Centre for Research & Analysis of Migration (2014) What do we know about migration? Informing the debate. Fact Sheet, Centre for Research & Analysis of Migration, London. http://www.cream-migra tion.org/files/Migration-FactSheet.pdf (accessed 2 September 2015).

Dustmann, C. and Frattini, T. (2013) The fiscal effects of immigration to the UK. Discussion Paper 22/13, Centre for Research and Analysis of Migration (CReAM). http://www.cream-migration.org/publ_up loads/CDP_22_13.pdf (accessed 2 September 2015).

Dustmann, C., Glitz, A. and Frattini, T. (2008) The labour market impact of immigration. *Oxford Review of Economic Policy* 24: 477–94.

European Commission (2014) Public opinion in the European Union. Standard Eurobarometer 81, Spring.

Legrain, P. (2007) *Immigrants: Your Country Needs Them.* London: Little, Brown.

Legrain, P. (2008) *Is Free Migration Compatible with a European-Style Welfare State?* Expert Report 11 to Sweden's Globalisation Council.

Legrain, P. (2014) *European Spring: Why Our Economies and Politics Are in a Mess – and How to Put Them Right.* London: CB Books.

Levie, J. and Hart, M. (2009) Global Entrepreneurship Monitor: United Kingdom 2008 monitoring report. Global Entrepreneurship Monitoring Consortium, London.

OECD (2007) *International Migration Outlook 2007.* Paris: OECD Publishing.

OECD (2013) *International Migration Outlook 2013.* Paris: OECD Publishing.

Page, S. (2007) *The Difference: How the Power of Diversity Creates Better Groups, Firms, Schools, and Societies.* Princeton University Press.

# 7 EVALUATING EUROPEAN TRADING ARRANGEMENTS

Patrick Minford

In this contribution, I focus on the net costs to the UK of the EU's CAP and its customs union in manufactures. It is well known that the CAP is expensive for the UK; what is less well known is the cost of the protectionist customs union in manufactures. We are often told by defenders of the EU that the 'single market' is good for jobs and industrial output; however, the single market, supposedly created by a set of regulations, is actually a market where prices are inflated by a substantial protectionist apparatus. I use a computable general equilibrium (CGE) model to estimate the cost of this protectionism and the corresponding gains that might flow from leaving the EU.

## What trade theory has to say about the EU customs union

At the heart of trade theory lies the simplest of models, designed to analyse the long-term effects of trade restrictions. It assumes there is a homogeneous commodity, whose price in the absence of protection would be set domestically at the world price. A tariff or equivalent trade barrier, t, would raise its domestic price above the world price (PW) to PW$(1 + t)$. At this higher price, domestic supply increases, and domestic demand decreases, so imports fall; tariff revenue is levied on the imports (t × imports), and foreign suppliers receive PW. In a customs union, where a group of countries levies the tariff and internal trade is free of protection, the country's supply and demand are the same as in the simple tariff case, the difference being that imports are supplied by customs union partners at the price PW(1 + t), so the government receives no tariff revenue. If the country has any exports, they are diverted away from the world market, where the price is only PW, to the customs union market, where the price is PW(1 + t). Overall, the result for the product is a rise in the price paid by consumers and received by home and rest-of-EU producers to PW(1 + t). In terms of whom a country trades with, the effect is trade diversion: that is, imports from the rest of the world are replaced by imports from the EU, wherever these can be produced at a cost less than PW(1 + t), and exports to the rest of the world at the price PW are replaced by exports to the rest of the EU at the price PW(1 + t).

The government may receive a share of the customs union revenue received on any remaining imports from the rest of the world, according to some formula. However, this revenue accrues to the EU, and any sharing of it with national governments is counted as a component part of the country's net budget contribution – accounted for separately in that country's membership cost. So, in our trade calculations, no revenues are recorded.

Protection of EU output may also be achieved by levying anti-dumping duties, or by physical quotas on imports, or just by the threat of these measures, so that foreign producers raise their prices to avoid them – so-called self-restraint.[1] These measures act like straightforward tariffs to raise prices, again from PW to PW(1 + te), where 'te' is the tariff equivalent. We can therefore treat these measures or the threat of them in just the same way as we treat tariffs in their effect on prices and trade.

---

1   In this case, the EU receives no revenue on any remaining imports; this in turn means that they will ask member governments for more of a fiscal contribution, a cost one must account for elsewhere as part of being in the EU.

The welfare costs to the UK arise because consumers pay higher prices to other EU producers in place of world prices, and they consume less, while extra resources are absorbed from suppliers into the protected industry.

For the price to rise to $PW(1+t)$ as a result of these tariff measures, it is necessary for the customs union as a whole to be a net importer; otherwise the exports diverted to the home EU market will undercut this higher price, since they can only get PW on the world market. To achieve the same protectionist outcome when the EU is a net exporter, the customs union must also pay an export subsidy equal to the tariff so that exporters do not undercut the home market, as they are now getting $PW(1+t)$ on their exports. This problem is most prevalent for agriculture, so under the terms of the CAP export subsidies are payable as well as import tariffs. That means prices are held above world prices for all commodities covered by the CAP.

In the case of traded services, import protection is at the level of the nation state, and there is no customs union. The EU single market has, in general, not yet been applied to services, so they effectively lie outside our analysis here. The reason for the absence in general of a single market in services lies precisely in these national protective systems (other than in the UK, where services are in most cases highly competitive and lightly regulated); national governments have been unwilling to allow their service providers to be undercut by competition from other EU providers.

This model we have been discussing refers to one market alone for a given commodity; the rest of the economy's prices are taken as given, or else some other ad hoc decision is made about how they will vary as this industry expands. However, the model can be extended to explain the general behaviour of all prices and quantities (general equilibrium) by specifying the rest of the economy, calculating the market-clearing prices everywhere in it, and also in the rest of the world. The famous

Heckscher–Ohlin–Samuelson model is attractive to use for the extension. This is because it brings in the ultimate long-run determinants of comparative advantage with a minimum of complication by assuming perfect competition in all markets, as well as production behaviour that has constant returns to scale. We discuss how this CGE model works in more detail below.

## The cost of EU protection

In this section, we use measures of EU protection to estimate its welfare implications for the UK and for the EU. For this, we use a CGE world model from Minford et al. (2015), along the lines just explained, to generate estimates of changes in trade that result from this protection.

It is difficult to get reliable and up-to-date measures of EU protection, because the world is constantly changing. In particular, China's trade costs are moving rapidly in response to its own opening up and also its rapid internal growth of wages and living standards. Furthermore, we cannot obtain direct measures of Chinese prices; our only price measures come from the OECD and cover only OECD members.

To deal with this complex situation, we have decided to use two simplifying devices. First, we gauge the latest trends in protection in agriculture and manufacturing by using broad measures of protection that we have managed to calculate and updating them according to indicators built up by international bodies. The basis of these measures is price comparisons across countries, allowing for transport costs (Bradford 2003). A full account of the method is given in Minford et al. (2015). Comparing prices allows us to calculate the effect of non-tariff measures such as anti-dumping duties and threats to use them, both of which are widespread in today's world.

Thus, for agriculture our estimate of protection is based on Bradford (2003) and his original tariff equivalent for 1990 of

Figure 2    **Level and composition of producer support in OECD countries**

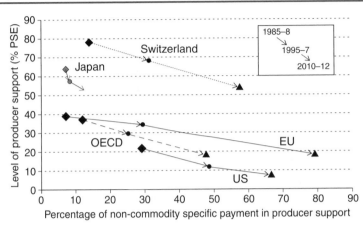

Source: OECD, PSE/CSE database, 2013.

36 per cent. OECD estimates of the producer subsidy equivalent within the EU (PSE, a measure of essentially the same protective margin) are approximately the same for this period, as can be seen from Figure 2. By 2010–12, the estimate has fallen to around half, at about 18 per cent. We take this latest figure to be approximately the current measure. Plainly, change continues as farming adapts; one of the indicators of change is the percentage (shown in Figure 2) of non-commodity support in the total, which has by now reached 80 per cent. What this implies is that farmers are in effect being compensated for not growing food on their land. Presumably it is this type of measure that is gradually reducing the PSE; to project where protection may be in 2020, our target year for this calculation, we take it that it will be reduced further in line with this trend. In the spirit of avoiding spurious apparent accuracy, we put the measure at 10 per cent.

If we turn to manufacturing, the situation is more complex still. It is usually assumed that since the various GATT and WTO rounds have brought manufactured trade tariffs down across the world (including the EU), EU protection is light in this sector. However, in the wake of retreating tariffs, governments have been given wide discretion to reach agreements on trade quotas, to impose anti-dumping duties or to threaten them and negotiate pre-emptive price rises by importers. Furthermore, these processes reinforce the power of cartels to be established and to survive. Thus, what starts as temporary protection against dumping ends as the equivalent of a permanent tariff. Tariffs are transparent; but these measures are hard to monitor. While we know how many duties have been imposed and what trade agreements have been made, we cannot easily find out what pre-emptive measures may have been taken, nor can we tell whether agreements that have notionally lapsed have done so effectively (especially if a cartel of producers has been implicitly allowed to perpetuate it, as noted above). Calculating the tariff equivalent has to be done by looking at the price-raising effect of all the various interventions.

Fortunately, there are data on prices now on a wide scale because of the purchasing power parity calculations being done by international organisations. A pioneering study by Bradford (2003) of the price differentials between major OECD countries and their least-cost OECD supplier suggested that the EU was substantially more protectionist in impact than the US, even though the latter has resorted to a similar number of anti-dumping duties (Bradford 2003). Averaging across the EU countries studied (Germany, the Netherlands, Belgium and the UK), Bradford's figures, which are adjusted for distribution margins, tax and transport costs, are 40 per cent tariff equivalent for the EU against 16 per cent for the US. These percentages are not much different if one looks at 1999 instead of his original 1993 (see Table 1, based on Bradford and Lawrence (2004)).

Le et al. (2009) updated these figures to 2002 and extended the comparison, now that OECD membership has risen, to include Korea in particular. They also covered all EU countries and made

Table 1    Estimates of tariff equivalents on manufactured goods
           resulting from all trade barriers (in per cent)

|             | 1990 | 1996 | 1999 |
|-------------|------|------|------|
| Belgium     | 42   | 65   | 42   |
| Germany     | 39   | 60   | 29   |
| Italy       | 38   | 36   | 21   |
| Netherlands | 42   | 58   | 41   |
| UK          | 41   | 41   | 50   |
| US          | 16   | 14   | 15   |

Note: Data are expenditure-weighted average ratios of imputed producer prices to the landed prices
of goods from the country with the lowest level price in the sample.
Source: Bradford and Lawrence (2004).

an attempt to update the figures relative to China. The figures
for the EU-weighted average against lowest-cost non-EU trade
partners are somewhat lower in 2002; the US and Korea are, between them, the lowest price alternatives. For the EU as a whole,
the 2002 figure comes out at 21 per cent, against 30–40 per cent
on the narrower basis for the 1990s. For the US, which has also
embraced policies of non-tariff protection, the 2002 figure is
6.5 per cent, against middle double-digit percentages in the 1990s.

If one attempts to include China, which is possible, in a crude
way, for 2002, the implied protection estimates become much
larger: 68 per cent for the EU and 48 per cent for the US. These
numbers should be treated cautiously because we do not have
prices in separate commodity categories for China; indeed,
China as yet does not produce for export a whole range of advanced products in competition with Western countries. The estimates rely on the manufacturing wage cost comparisons made
by the US Bureau of Labour Statistics (which estimates China's
manufacturing wage costs per hour at 7 per cent of Korea's);
we also assume that unskilled labour represents 30 per cent of
total costs, a percentage deliberately put on the low, cautious
side. Nevertheless, even these crude estimates indicate just how

China's products are being kept at bay by various means, at least in finished form. Even as protection may be coming down on the products of the more developed emerging market countries such as Korea, we can see that it is rising in response to the penetration of Chinese products.

Summarising these measures, we find that by 2002 EU protection may have come down on our preferred measure, based on OECD price comparisons, from a range of 30–40 per cent in the 1990s to 21 per cent by the early 2000s. On the other hand, China did not enter these numbers, and against China the protection may have been far greater. Nevertheless, China is itself changing fast, and for the sophisticated manufactured products with whose protection the EU is mainly concerned, it has allied itself with Japan and Korea through large supply networks. Thus, 'made in Japan or Korea' may in practice mean 'assembled from largely Chinese components' in these countries. As with agriculture, we notice a downward trend in protection, and, again, to avoid an impression of spurious accuracy, we project a continuation of this trend going on to our target year of 2020, where we set the relevant percentage of manufacturing protection also at 10 per cent.

## The CGE model

We now turn to our CGE model of trade to obtain measures of the cost to the UK and the EU of this protectionist policy. First, we explain in more detail just what a CGE model is, before going on to explain how the model works in outline.

A CGE model of international trade, as used here, is intended to contain the relevant relationships that will hold in economic theory across economies and will determine the pattern of trade and the prices at which it takes place. These relationships are numerical so that we can extract meaningful estimates of the quantitative effects of changing trade policies in the long run.

For this purpose, we cannot aspire to any 'exact realism', but we do want to obtain estimates that (a) are consistent with good, uncontroversial economic theory and (b) give a reasonable idea of potential orders of magnitude for the long run. The way it is done is to construct a baseline set of estimates that correspond to the actual known facts; the model is set up so that it fits these facts. Then, the alternative set of policies is injected into the model to find out what the alternative facts would look like. We are concerned about long-run effects for the obvious reason that these policy changes stay in effect for very long periods; indeed, they can often be permanent. For instance, our joining the EU occurred more than 40 years ago, and if we leave the move will undoubtedly not be reversed in a hurry. Experience shows that large-scale changes in trade arrangements have quite radical effects on the shape of economies; therefore, we need a model that can work out what these effects might be. Table 2 shows the CGE model estimates of leaving the EU, in terms of the percentage effects on a wide range of economic variables.

In this particular CGE model, there is full competition in all products with free entry. There are world markets for three traded goods (agriculture, manufactures and services); world supply and demand fix the relative prices of these goods, hence the two relative prices of agriculture/manufactures and services/manufactures. Tariffs (or equivalent measures) raise home prices in the country, raising them above their world price. For an individual country, therefore, prices of traded goods are set in world markets plus the effect of its own tariffs. In each country there is also a non-traded good, produced under full competition at its long-run average cost.

We now consider what happens in each country to its supplies and costs. Because of competition, all prices equal long-run costs; hence, the prices of skilled and unskilled labour and land, the domestic production inputs entering each commodity, are driven to levels that satisfy this equality. That is, they are priced so that they are competitive, given the traded goods prices set in the world market. There are three traded goods and three prices of factors of production that are set in the country. The price of capital is set worldwide, and capital circulates at this price to wherever it is needed. For simplicity, we set this price as fixed at a constant world real interest rate times a fixed world price of production in manufacturing (of 1). Effectively, we are assuming that, in the long run (the focus of the model), savings are always made available as required at a fixed rate of interest. The wage and land costs, once fixed by traded goods prices, then determine non-traded goods prices.

With all prices set in this way by world prices, tariffs and production technology, we go on to determine how much is produced of each type of good. This is fixed by available supplies of factors of production – assumed to be unskilled and skilled labour. Land, we assume, is provided freely as needed by planners, subject to a restriction placed on agricultural land, such that agricultural production is controlled to a fixed amount. Non-traded production has to be equal to non-traded demand, which depends on total GDP and relative non-traded prices. With these restrictions on agriculture and non-traded output, we can work out the size of each sector that will exactly exhaust available supplies of the two sorts of labour. Then, from that, we can work out how much capital and land is needed by each sector.

So, to summarise, world prices (determined by world demand and supply by all countries, as resulting from their country solutions) plus tariffs fix country prices, and so costs of labour and land. Given these costs and each sector's resulting demands for these factors per unit of output, the sizes of each sector adjust so that the available supplies of the two types of labour are equal to sectoral demands.

So, a tariff on manufactures, for example, acts to raise a country's price of manufactures. Then, because manufactures use a lot of unskilled labour, its expansion drives up unskilled wages.

In order to force other industries to economise on the unskilled labour manufacturing needs for its expansion, the other traded sectors contract. The non-traded sector's size moves close to proportionally with the whole economy, as demand for non-traded goods is related proportionally to total income, apart from any effect of its changing relative costs brought about by the tariff. The rise in tariff raises consumer prices so that consumers are less well off than they would have been buying the manufactures more cheaply from abroad.

It might seem on the face of it that 10 per cent protection in agriculture and manufacturing is not a very large or significant amount. It raises prices in these two sectors by 10 per cent over the world price, while leaving service prices at world levels. For those used to macro models of short-to-medium-run behaviour, relative price movements of different sectors of this order occur regularly; for example, world raw material prices can double or triple and greatly affect retail prices of sectors using those materials. Yet we do not observe huge sectoral output swings in the economy.

The difference here is that we are computing the long run effect of permanent relative price changes of these sectors. The sectors with higher prices pay higher wages to the workers, both skilled and unskilled, they need; they pay more for land and use more capital, whose price is fixed in world markets. What our CGE model shows in Table 2 is that resources are heavily attracted out of the service sector into agriculture and manufacturing. In fact, we assume that output in agriculture is capped (effectively by control on the land that can be used in this sector) in our model by government policy; so, the attraction into this sector is frustrated by rising land prices. However, for manufacturing no such limit exists, and the result is a substantial boost to manufacturing at the expense of services.

Table 2 goes on to show that the effect of raising prices for these two sectors by 10 per cent is first a substantial (7.5 per cent)

Table 2    Effects of UK and EU tariff of 10 per cent on agriculture and manufacturing: percentage changes from base

| % changes | UK | EU | NAFTA | RoW |
|---|---|---|---|---|
| y | −3.71 | −3.39 | 0.22 | 0.16 |
| yA | 0.00 | 0.00 | 0.00 | 0.00 |
| yM | 93.33 | 49.07 | −18.42 | −12.22 |
| yS | −27.02 | −30.91 | 6.97 | 8.20 |
| yD | −3.62 | −3.47 | 0.21 | 0.16 |
| EA | −11.16 | −4.29 | 0.47 | 0.76 |
| EM | −0.56 | −0.57 | 0.03 | 0.19 |
| ES | −5.00 | −4.76 | 0.30 | 0.06 |
| w | 13.25 | 13.25 | −1.16 | −1.16 |
| h | −8.00 | −8.00 | 4.11 | 4.11 |
| l | 48.37 | 48.37 | 0.92 | 0.92 |
| N | 1.25 | 1.25 | −0.12 | −0.12 |
| H | −2.06 | −2.06 | 0.52 | 0.52 |
| L | −28.30 | −28.00 | −0.18 | −0.28 |
| K | 7.08 | 7.75 | 0.50 | 0.37 |
| CPI | 8.18 | 8.15 | 0.79 | 0.76 |
| PA | 10.48 | 10.48 | 0.43 | 0.43 |
| PM | 10.00 | 10.00 | 0.00 | 0.00 |
| PS | 1.89 | 1.89 | 1.89 | 1.89 |
| PwA | 0.43 | 0.43 | 0.43 | 0.43 |
| PwS | 1.89 | 1.89 | 1.89 | 1.89 |
| Welfare | −3.39 | −3.00 | 0.07 | −0.03 |

Glossary: y=output; E=expenditure; w=wages of unskilled; h=wages of skilled; l=rent on land; N=unskilled labour; H=skilled labour; L=land; K=capital; CPI=consumer prices; P=price of commodity. Suffixes: A=agriculture; M=manufacturing; S=services; W=world.

rise in the cost of living. Wages of unskilled workers go up more than this (14 per cent) because they are disproportionately used in manufacturing. But skilled workers' wages fall by 11 per cent, being disproportionately used in service industries. Landowners do well, with land prices soaring 47 per cent. We see in these

figures how the politics of vested interests works; unions representing unskilled workers, farmers and other landowners, and
manufacturing businesses, will clearly support being inside
the EU.

Yet the effect of shifting output into sectors where their
productivity is less than the price paid by consumers is an overall loss of welfare for UK citizens; these citizens would value
more the output lost in services whose production contracts
32 per cent. The loss of welfare, measured by the loss of potential
consumption by UK households, is 3.3 per cent. This potential
consumption change is measured as the change in the value of
all output, deflated by its consumer price cost (i.e. the change in
[nominal GDP/CPI]), minus the change in the value of resources
used to generate it. In other words, the welfare effect is the percentage change in the resources available for consumption to UK
households.

This cost is computed as if the protective measure is a tariff.
However, the customs union acts as a tariff in its effect on out-
puts and consumption; but the equivalent of the 'tariff revenue'
(i.e. the extra cost of imports due to the protection) is disposed of
differently. There is revenue on imports from outside the EU; this
revenue (paid by UK consumers) accrues to the EU itself, but it is
already counted in the UK's net contribution (after rebate and EU
spending on UK projects). There is also revenue accruing to EU
businesses that sell protected goods to the UK, because they can
charge higher prices. This revenue is not counted elsewhere and
is a cost to UK consumers. Our businesses also gain more from
other EU consumers on their exports; so the 'net revenue' paid by
UK consumers to EU consumers is the tariff times the net imports
by the UK. For manufacturing, where we have large net imports
(about 8 per cent of GDP), this net revenue transfer amounts to
0.8 per cent of GDP on the 10 per cent tariff equivalent we have
assumed. This amount is not included in our Table 2 calculation,
so it has to be added to it. For agriculture, the workings of the

CAP on transfers between countries are complex and are already counted in the net UK contribution. So, in sum, the total cost to the UK of the protection of agriculture and manufacturing is 4.1 per cent of GDP.

Some politicians attach totemic significance to manufacturing. We have heard quite a few arguments since the 2010 election that the economy should be 'rebalanced' towards manufacturing. One can see why the vested interests listed above would want this; it is no doubt to appeal to these interests that politicians make these arguments. But there is no economic case for encouraging output in sectors that market forces would contract. For such a case, there would have to be some disparity between social and market values; yet there is no such disparity. Similar arguments were made two centuries ago for preserving agriculture, with a similar lack of basis.

Leaving the EU and eliminating this protection would, according to these figures, raise service output and effectively eliminate manufacturing in the long run. The reason for this is fairly simple: as the UK has developed in the decades since the economy began to be liberalised in 1979, there has been a big rise in the share of skilled labour in the workforce. By now, approximately 50 per cent of university-age people go on to some form of higher education or equivalent. This has favoured the expansion of skill-intensive industries of which the service industries are the principal examples. We can also include in these industries the design element of manufacturing, which is a service industry; 'manufacturing' in the national accounts includes this, inside the manufacturing firms it comprises. So, to the extent that service activity is currently included in manufacturing, this part would not be eliminated, but just reclassified. These workers are engaged in jobs that require the use of their brainpower and associated skills. The actual making of things, manufacturing in the original sense, has contracted hugely in the UK. What the CGE model tells us is that in the absence of EU protection this actual making would largely disappear.

This result should not be regarded as very shocking. The strongly declining share of manufacturing in GDP has been an unremitting trend feature of the UK since the 1980s; it would be intensified by leaving the EU, and eventually we would be left only with those parts of manufacturing that involve design and high-tech skills, as one would expect in a relatively small country heavily endowed with skilled and educated labour.

We note that there is a good demand for unskilled workers in the non-traded service sector (distribution, construction, utilities and so on), which cannot be supplied by bringing in cheaper substitutes from abroad. As this non-traded sector is around half of the economy, one can see that if roughly half the labour force is unskilled it will be fully employed in the non-traded sector, and there will be little of it left over for the manufacturing sector. Plainly, EU protection, as we have seen, raises the wages of unskilled workers; but if there was a case for redistribution to these workers because they were poor, then this would already be done by public redistribution policy. This policy area is extremely active in the UK, as evidenced by the high progressivity of the tax-benefit system. There is no case for using protection to help carry out this policy, since it is clumsily directed at the issue and, as we have seen, creates a big cost for the economy as a whole.

It turns out that the costs to EU citizens of the EU tariff on agriculture and manufacturing are roughly the same as those for the UK. Thus, when the 10 per cent tariff is levied EU-wide, including in the UK, Table 2 more or less replicates in the rest of the EU what happens in the UK. The only difference for the rest of the EU is that there is a small net revenue gain due to the net revenue transfer from UK to rest-of-the-EU consumers. However, as a per cent of the much larger rest-of-the-EU GDP total, it is only 0.15 per cent of their GDP. Thus, the total welfare cost to the rest of the EU is just under 3 per cent of GDP.

## Considerations of 'Brexit'

It might be thought that such estimates are all very well but that if we left the EU there would be a quite separate problem of being 'outside' the EU 'market', as well as 'excluded' from other markets with which the EU has signed free-trade agreements (FTAs). The recent IEA-prize-winning paper on Brexit (Mansfield 2014) recommended that the first activity to be undertaken after Brexit should be a general negotiation of FTAs with Uncle Tom Cobleigh and All. What are we to make of such arguments? Is it true that there are gains in trade terms to be had from leaving the EU and that yet we are vulnerable to problems of 'access' to all such markets?

What we need to understand is that if some other countries set up barriers against our trade, unlikely as that is, it would have no implications for the world prices of the types of products we produce. Those prices are set in all the markets of the world. If our producers faced some extra tariffs in some markets, this would have no effect on the world price of the goods we produce. The UK produces a small fraction of world exports in virtually all product markets. These UK exports will be more expensive in the markets with extra tariffs, but the impact on the overall demand for these products will be negligible. Then what will happen to our exports in the markets where they face these tariffs? They will be diverted to markets where they do not. In the markets where we face tariffs, our competitors will sell the goods we did not sell; we will sell more in their other markets.

Given that world prices will be unaffected, our calculation holds exactly. This calculation estimates the gains of moving from protected EU prices on EU imports and exports to world prices on these. On non-EU exports and imports we get world prices already.

This is not an easy idea to grasp for those not used to international trade theory. Most people think in terms of 'market access' and the bilateral bargaining between producers and the country to which they are selling. But this is not how world trade works – except in the very short run, which is soon over and so not relevant to a long-term shift such as leaving the EU.

This illustrates what is known in international trade theory as the 'importance of being unimportant'; a small supplier in world markets such as the UK, faced with a tariff from country X, would simply divert supply to another market and so keep its price unchanged, passing the tariff on to the consumers in country X. The UK is too small to affect the world price of any product it sells; hence, it is 'unimportant' at the world level.

This powerful argument implies that the calculation of the UK's net trade gains is immune to what third countries decide to do with their trade barriers on UK products. It is explicitly based on the assumption that the EU raises its usual most favoured nation (mfn) barriers on UK products, so that UK export prices in the EU market revert to world prices.

## What about a trade agreement with the EU?

It is sometimes said that we should try to obtain an FTA with the EU. The problem with this is that with free trade the UK would enjoy lower prices on goods that are protected in the EU. If they levy on us the usual EU tariff equivalent, then prices of UK exports to the EU would be brought up to EU levels, so the protection to EU producers would not be undermined. Hence, it is natural to make the assumption that the EU levies its usual (mfn) tariff equivalents on us when we leave. If we ask it not to, then in effect it seems we are asking to remain inside the customs union, and are not leaving at all. However, in FTAs such as NAFTA, different countries can have zero tariffs against third countries, even while enjoying zero tariffs from other FTA partners. It may well be possible for the UK to negotiate such arrangements for particular industries that are highly integrated across the EU.

For example, there are some industries in which competition is heavily restricted – such as aerospace and airlines. In these examples, existing markets are heavily organised between the UK, EU and other producers. In effect, leaving the EU would leave these arrangements intact.

An example of a highly integrated industry is the volume car industry, in which multinational companies have invested heavily on the assumption of a protected EU market. For such cases, the drop to world prices would lead to heavy losses. An arrangement whereby the UK and the EU maintained zero tariffs and tariff equivalents against each other would make a lot of sense for this industry; effectively, the EU market would maintain its existing prices, and UK producers would continue to sell into the EU market at these prices. This is even though UK prices for cars would fall to world levels, so that EU producers would lose their EU price premium in the UK market.

Failing this, given that the UK encouraged these investments, it could reasonably make some compensation when policy changes, on the usual basis that reform requires that losers be, if possible, compensated by gainers (in this case, taxpaying households who enjoy lower consumer prices and other firms that enjoy lower input prices).

Alternatively, the existing arrangements for this industry could be left in place for a transitional period of a decade, allowing the industry time to adjust its capital stock and strategies to the new reality. This would mean that for a decade the current EU customs union protection would be continued by the UK for this industry only. The gain to the economy of this part of the trade regime change would be deferred for this decade – but then it would be reaped like all the rest.

In effect, such agreements with the EU would amount to negotiating a 'Breset' rather than a 'Brexit'– a resetting of our relationship with the EU, rather than a termination of all ties. The EU is, after all, a close neighbour, and we would aim to have friendly and cooperative relationships with such a neighbour, in trade as in so much else.

## Opposing views

There are some studies that argue there would be losses for the UK should it leave the EU customs union. One is by Ottaviano et al. (2014), who estimate that leaving the EU would imply costs of 1–3 per cent of GDP due to the imposition of the EU's common tariff on the UK. This is to be compared with our calculated gain of around 4 per cent of GDP.

As we noted above, we would in practice aim for a new treaty, which would preserve the helpful aspects of our trade relationships, notably good common regulation and bilateral free trade. Thus, the calculations of Ottaviano et al. (2014), which come up with a net loss of UK welfare from leaving the EU, leave out two important elements.

1. They do not factor in the effect of moving to free trade with the rest of the world from existing EU protective measures. Since, in our calculation, the EU levies tariff equivalents on the rest of the world of about 10 per cent, this omission would generate large negative effects if included in their calculation. They appear to assume that the UK would levy the same tariff equivalents on the rest of the world (accounting for around half UK trade), whereas in our view the UK would move to free trade vis-à-vis all countries. Certainly that is the policy we propose on 'Brexit'/'Breset', so it should be costed accurately.

2. They assume that the EU would react by raising trade and regulatory barriers against UK exporters, even though we impose none such on EU exporters to us. As discussed above, this is highly unlikely, because EU industries are closely integrated in many cases with UK industry and the UK market. They would be damaged by difficulties in

accessing UK input products and would fear retaliation by the UK to EU aggression. At the same time, it is possible for UK exporters to have free access to the EU market without undermining the existing prices created by the customs union. While EU businesses would regret the loss of high preferential prices in the UK market, they would be against a vindictive response that would make matters worse for them.

A final concern is how accurate their model can be in assessing a major change in commercial relationships such as leaving a customs union. The multilateral gravity model they use, due to Costinot and Rodrigues-Clare (2013), assesses all countries' bilateral trade according to calculated bilateral elasticities: these effectively 'sum up' the total (general equilibrium) effects of the change. Thus, Costinot and Rodrigues-Clare argue that, if one is prepared to assume some set of 'micro-foundations' (i.e. underlying relationships between consumers and producers, such as the state of competition), one can regard the gravity model as an accurate method to evaluate any shock to trade. At a theoretical level, one can accept that, given a constant elasticity of trade response, an estimate of the effects of a tariff shock would be accurate.

However, the question is whether one can regard such an elasticity as 'structural', that is, invariant to the type of policy shock created. The basic point is a simple one: an elasticity sums up the effect of a tariff on trade via many different channels, some of which reinforce each other, some of which offset each other. These channels will be activated to different degrees by different shocks. Therefore, an elasticity that works when only one thing is disturbed, namely the product tariff, will differ when that disturbance is accompanied by many changes to other tariffs. In the case of a large shock to the structure of trade, such as leaving a customs union, the elasticity will no doubt be quite different again. As Costinot and Rodrigues-Clare point out, the difficulty lies in assessing the elasticities to use. What we would add is that they are likely to vary with the nature of the joint shock imposed on the economy as well as the effects of this on ambient features of the economy, such as consumer prices, wages and supplies of capital and different types of labour.

Our model here, based on four sectors and four major 'countries' can reasonably be criticised as too aggregative to provide highly accurate estimates; yet it does have an explicit theoretical defence of the way it computes the equilibrium structure of industry and consumption. It is, at least, for sure a structural general equilibrium model that can in principle evaluate any shock to the structure of trade or the economy. The gravity model may work well numerically, and be more accurate in detail, for quite general changes in conditions, such as a general drop in transport costs, mirroring globalisation, which is what Costinot and Rodrigues-Clare use it for. The problem with using it for a shock to trade structure such as the UK leaving a customs union is that the responses will certainly not be the same as for a general globalisation shock; indeed, such a shock changes the UK's internal structure substantially, in a way that is not assumed in a gravity model.

## Other costs and benefits

A further argument of Ottaviano et al. (2014), for which they also cite related studies, is that there would be 'dynamic' effects of leaving the EU, from reduced investment, technological diffusion, export learning effects and investment in research and development (R&D). However, all these effects assume that there is no expansion in similar but opposite effects as trade expands with the rest of the world. We see here again the omission of the general rest-of-the-world effects of leaving a customs union. It must also be stressed that estimating these effects is difficult and uncertain; the empirical literature on growth is marked by much elaborate theory but considerable problems in 'identifying' the effects of growth mechanisms in practice.

Probably the most important element for the UK is the extent to which the UK state can establish favourable tax and regulation conditions for competition and entrepreneurship. In this, leaving much of the damaging features of EU intervention would be beneficial, regardless of the structure of trade. Here, recent work (Minford 2015) has shown strong evidence that barriers to business affect UK growth. This is identified in Table 3 as a factor that could lower UK growth by some 0.5 per cent per annum, as a result of the dynamic effects on entrepreneurship of excessive regulation, especially in the labour market.

It is also said that we would no longer influence EU regulations, which is true. But we do not influence the regulations of any country to which we export, and yet our exports are made to conform to them; this is part of our export costs, and our influence in the EU has little if any impact on these costs. By leaving, we avoid the massive cost of these regulations to our own production in general, as is also shown in Table 3. What will happen when we leave is that our exporters will have to continue to observe EU regulations on their products, as they do now, and as they do for all other countries to which they export; this is simply a normal cost of exporting anywhere. Also, under the new

Table 3  **A survey of costs from EU membership**

|  | % of GDP |
| --- | --- |
| Net UK contribution | 0.5 |
| Costs of CAP and of EU protection of manufacturing | 4.0 |
| Regulations | 6–25 |
| Bailout transfers | 2–9 |
| Effects of EU regulations on growth to 2035 | 0.5% p.a. |
| Effect of joining the euro on economic volatility | Doubling of volatility |

Source: Minford et al (2015).

suggested UK–EU treaty, they could agree to continue to implement these regulations on all their production. As for everyone else (over 90 per cent of GDP), EU regulations will cease to be relevant, lifting both a current burden and a future threat.

Table 3 also shows other costs of being in the EU, identifed by Minford et al (2015). These include euro entry (part of 'ever-closer union'), bailout costs and the EU membership fee. They do not include the economic cost/benefit of immigration; however, because the economic effects of immigration on particular but large groups of UK citizens have been highly negative, control of the border is now an issue of great political importance.

Another study is that of Open Europe (2015). This at least considers the case we set out here of moving away from the EU to full free trade. It uses the Global Trade Analysis Project (GTAP), a large CGE model with many sectors, linked by input–output relationships, and generally under imperfect competition. It is, hence, rather similar to the models used by Ottaviano et al. (2014). Such a model suffers from the same criticisms: that it cannot deal properly with a large-scale change in trading regime, such as leaving a customs union for free trade. However, we can get from the Open Europe (2015) study what the effect on welfare would be of such a change; and it appears to be of the order of an improvement by 1 per cent of GDP. This order would be understated in my view by the failure to embody all the long-run effects examined in our model here. But, at least one can see that it points in the same direction of gains from free trade – as, indeed, one would expect and hope such a model to find.

## Conclusions

What we see here is that the EU protects agriculture and manufacturing through its commercial policies, namely its tariffs, its non-tariff barriers and the CAP. By leaving the EU, the UK would be able to abandon the EU's protectionist system in favour of free trade combined with transitional compensation for those hit by the changes. This would raise economic welfare by around 4 per cent (i.e. UK households would be able to consume 4 per cent more goods and services) and enhance the shift of the UK economy away from manufacturing into service industries, which is where UK growth has largely been concentrated in the decades since 1979.

This apparently surprising and shocking result – that leaving the EU customs union would be beneficial and would reorientate our economy towards the service activity at which the UK excels – should not really be such a surprise. There was nothing God-given about the UK joining the EU customs union; indeed, many fine trade theorists, such as the late Harry Johnson, argued strenuously against it, on precisely the grounds of the damage that this paper has now quantified. He visualised the UK instead as part of the free world trading system, and not cooped up in a regional protective union.

It turns out that if the UK decides to leave the EU, it will simply recapture this original role in world trade, much as is the case for some other small countries, such as New Zealand and Singapore. It will sell its products at world prices to those who wish to buy them. It has no need of innumerable trade agreements, nor does it need to join EFTA, NAFTA or any other FTA. It simply needs to rejoin the world trading system, abolish its tariffs and trade restraints with all and sundry and enjoy the resulting dividends of free trade.

## References

Bradford, S. C. (2003) Paying the price: final goods protection in OECD countries. *Review of Economics and Statistics* 85(1): 24–37.

Bradford, S. C. and Lawrence, R. Z. (2004) *Has Globalization Gone Far Enough? The Costs of Fragmented Markets*. Washington DC: Institute for International Economics.

Costinot, A. and Rodriguez-Clare, A. (2013) Trade theory with numbers: quantifying the consequences of globalization. Discussion Paper 9398, March, Centre for Economic and Policy Research, London.

Le, V. P. M., Minford, P. and Nowell, E. (2009) European economic policy: protectionism as an elite strategy. In *The European Union and World Politics* (ed. A. Gamble and D. Lane). London: Palgrave Macmillan.

Mansfield, I. (2014) *A Blueprint for Britain: Openness not Isolation*. London: Institute of Economic Affairs.

Minford, L. (2015) The impact of policy on UK output and productivity growth, 1970–2009: testing an open economy DSGE model. PhD Thesis, Cardiff University.

Minford, P., with Gupta, S., Le, V. P. M., Mahambare, V. and Xu, Y. (2015) *Should Britain Leave the EU? An Economic Analysis of a Troubled Relationship*, 2nd edn. Cheltenham: Edward Elgar; London: Institute of Economic Affairs.

Open Europe (2015) What if...?: The consequences, challenges and opportunities facing Britain outside the EU. http://openeurope.org.uk/intelligence/britain-and-the-eu/what-if-there-were-a-brexit/ (accessed 2 September 2015).

Ottaviano, G., Pessoa, J. P., Sampson, T. and Van Reenen, J. (2014) The costs and benefits of leaving the EU. London School of Economics, Centre for Economic Performance, May 13.

# 8 UK EMPLOYMENT REGULATION IN OR OUT OF THE EU

J. R. Shackleton

## Europe's reach[1]

When in 1973 the UK joined the EEC, later the EU, it only involved committing the country to rather limited elements of employment regulation – most notably the principle of equal pay for men and women, embodied in Article 119 of the Treaty of Rome. As equal pay was already the law in the UK, this might not be thought to be of great significance, but it became clear over time that the European interpretation of the principle was stricter than the original UK legislation had intended. The 1975 Equal Pay Directive and a subsequent ECJ ruling established that it is not only equal pay for the same work that is covered by equality legislation, but also 'work to which equal value is attributed'. The implications of this Directive are still resounding more than 40 years later, with employers obliged to make comparisons between apparently very dissimilar jobs that men and women undertake.[2] Moreover, what is meant by 'pay' was broadened to

---

1  A fuller discussion of the development of EU competence in this area can be found in HM Government (2014).

2  One recent case concerns Birmingham City Council, which is estimated to owe more than £1 billion in back pay following a legal ruling. Thousands of female council workers, such as carers, cleaners and cooks, have come forward with claims after it was ruled they had been discriminated against compared with male roadworkers, male street sweepers and bin men, who had picked up extra pay through regular overtime and other bonuses. See *Birmingham Post* (2014) Council is 'stalling' on equal pay

include occupational pensions, and two European rulings in 1994 subsequently established that the exclusion of part-time workers from employers' schemes was illegal because females were more likely to work part-time than men.

The European Commission's ability to propose employment regulation was limited until the 1990s, although some intervention was possible under health and safety powers. In 1989, however, the Charter of Fundamental Social Rights of Workers set out considerable new areas of European 'competence'. This Charter became part of the Maastricht Treaty. John Major's government opted out of what became known as the 'Social Chapter', but the incoming New Labour government signed the UK up to the full programme in the Treaty of Amsterdam. European influence on UK employment regulation was further entrenched by the Human Rights Act of 1998, which incorporated the European Convention on Human Rights into UK law. However, Labour was more reticent when signing the 2007 Treaty of Lisbon. Together with Poland, it secured an exemption from a further extension of EU powers over employment matters. The Lisbon Treaty's new Charter of Fundamental Rights included 54 provisions over a wide range of matters, including such employment-related elements as the right to strike, the right to collective bargaining, the right to fair working conditions and protection against dismissal. Although the UK's opt-out was regarded at the time as watertight, there have been occasional concerns that European Court rulings may lead to these rights being extended to the UK.[3]

---

settlements, 3 May. http://www.birminghampost.co.uk/news/local-news/birming ham-city-council-stalling-equal-7066029, and *Birmingham Post* (2015) 'Staff died' waiting for Council Pay update, 25 June. http://www.birminghampost.co.uk/news/ regional-affairs/staff-died-waiting-city-council-9521937 (both accessed 15 September 2015).

3   Of course, UK workers already have significant rights in these areas, but they are granted by the UK Parliament and could be amended or scrapped. If they were to become subject to European law, however, this would no longer be the case.

Whether or not these concerns are justified, it is already the case that many areas of UK employment regulation are now required by our European obligations and cannot be unilaterally reformed or scrapped while we remain members of the EU.

Such areas include the (currently highly controversial) freedom of movement between member states; restrictions on working hours; parental leave; pro rata payments for part-time workers; information and consultation requirements (including European Works Councils for large multinationals); consultation over collective redundancies; equal conditions for permanent and agency workers; maintaining conditions for workers transferred between undertakings; and the outlawing of discrimination, not just between men and women, but on grounds of ethnic origin, religion, sexual orientation, disability and age.

It may be easier to point to areas where there is *not*, as yet, a common European approach. One is minimum wages, where there is no compulsion for EU members.[4] Another is unfair dismissal, an important UK concept that does not have exact counterparts in other European countries.[5] A third is collective bargaining, where there are, as yet, no trans-European requirements.

In this chapter, I sketch the contours of European labour law and its intellectual background, drawing a contrast with the UK's traditions as well as the ideas of Anglo-American economists and contemporary classical liberals. I go on, however, to explain how there is now a strong domestic taste for interference in labour markets, which means that exit from the EU,

---

4  Although Jean-Claude Juncker, the new President of the European Commission, is among those who have advocated that a compulsory minimum wage be set by each national authority: http://www.euractiv.com/sections/social-europe-jobs/juncker-calls-minimum-wage-all-eu-countries-303484 (accessed 22 July 2014). See also Schulten (2010).

5  'Unfair dismissal' is a form of employment protection legislation (EPL) that lays down conditions under which contracts can legitimately be terminated. It now only applies to people who have been employed for two years, and it is one of the less strict EPL regimes in the EU (OECD 2013: Chapter 2).

while increasing the potential for deregulation, might initially make less difference than is often assumed. I conclude by outlining a minimum regulatory package, which might form the basis for a 'new start', were a future UK government able and, above all, willing to think seriously about the labour market from first principles.

## European law and the labour market

Our European obligations arise primarily from *Treaties* (for instance, the free movement of labour) and from *Directives* (for instance, limitations on working time). The latter are proposed by the European Commission and must be adopted by the Council of Ministers and the European Parliament. They lay down end results to be achieved in every member state. National governments must adapt their laws to meet these goals, but they are free to decide how to do so. A time limit is set for a Directive to be 'transposed', as the eurojargon has it, into domestic law.

Table 4 lists some of the most important employment Directives. The table shows the most recent relevant Directives, which consolidate and add to earlier Directives. The development of European labour law has moved in one direction only, to greater transnational regulation. The process has never gone into reverse: indeed, it is difficult to see quite how it could be reversed significantly without a fundamental change in approach. Each new member of the EU has to sign up to the whole package, the principle of the *acquis communautaire*. There is no obvious constitutional mechanism to unpick existing Directives: this is one of the problems hindering attempts to renegotiate the terms of the UK's relationship with the EU.[6]

---

6   Although it has been argued that a member state's parliament could in principle alter the way in which it has transposed Directives, removing any 'gold plating' (discussed later in this chapter) accreted in the process of transposition (Sack 2013).

Table 4    **Key European employment directives**

| Area | Main features | Most recent Directive # |
|---|---|---|
| Equal pay | Forbids all gender discrimination in relation to pay, broadly defined. | 2006/54/EC |
| Equal treatment in employment and occupation | Requires equal treatment in employment and membership of certain organisations; no discrimination by gender, age, disability, religion, belief or sexual orientation. | 2006/54/EC |
| Collective redundancies | Requires employers to consult staff representatives and provide information about reasons for redundancy, criteria for selection, etc. | 98/59/EC |
| Transfer of undertakings | Aims to safeguard employment rights, requires consultation with employees when business ownership is transferred. | 2001/23/EC |
| Protection of employees in event of insolvency | Aims to guarantee payment of employees if employer becomes insolvent. | 2008/94/EC |
| Obligation to inform employees of applicable working conditions | Employees must have job specification, information about pay, leave arrangements, etc. | 91/533/EEC |
| Pregnant workers | Mandates fourteen weeks maternity leave, protected employment, avoidance of exposure to risks, time off for antenatal care, etc. | 92/85/EC |
| Posting of workers | Employers' obligations in posting of workers to other member states in the provision of services. | 96/7/EC |
| Working time | Fixes maximum working week, requires rest periods, mandates four weeks annual paid leave. | 2003/88/EC |
| European Works Councils | Employers with 1,000+ employees in EEA must set up a European Works Council. | 2009/38/EC |
| Parental leave* | Mandates four months unpaid time off for each parent of a child aged up to eight. | 2010/18/EU |
| Leave for family reasons* | Rights to unpaid time off for urgent family reasons. | 97/75/EC |
| Part-time working* | Requires comparable treatment to full-time staff on open-ended contracts. | 98/23/EC |

Table 4  **Continued**

| Area | Main features | Most recent Directive # |
|------|---------------|------------------------|
| Fixed-term work* | Fixed-term workers must not be treated less favourably than permanent workers; maximum renewals of short-term contracts mandated. | 99/70/EC |
| Temporary agency work* | Requires equal treatment of agency workers in respect of pay, working time and annual leave. | 2008/104/EC |
| Maritime labour standards | Requires ratification of ILO Maritime Labour Convention. | 99/95/EC |

# Latest directive may consolidate earlier directives or Treaty obligations. Equal pay, for example, dates back to the Treaty of Rome in 1957.
*Under Framework Agreement.
Sources: http://europa.eu/legislation_summaries/employment_and_social_policy/employment_rights_and_work_organisation/index_en.htm (accessed 26 June 2014), Sack (2014).

Another point worth noting in Table 4 is that several Directives have been developed under 'framework agreements' involving what Brussels terms 'European social dialogue'. That is, their content has been agreed following discussion between 'social partners'. For instance, the Fixed-term Work Directive resulted from discussions between three bodies: the private sector UNICE[7] (*Union des confédérations de l'industrie et des employeurs d'Europe*), CEEP (*Centre européen des entreprises à participation publique et des entreprises d'intérêt économique général*, a body representing public sector employers) and ETUC (the European Trade Union Confederation). This corporatist dialogue could be argued seriously to under-represent the interests of smaller businesses and unorganised workers (including the self-employed and unemployed).

In addition to Directives, there are *Regulations*. These are the most direct form of EU law, as once passed (either jointly by the

---

7   Since rebranded as 'BusinessEurope'.

EU Council and the European Parliament or by the Commission alone) they have immediate legal force in every member state. For example, Regulation (EEC) 1408/71 covers the application of social security schemes to people moving between member states. It requires that persons residing in the territory of a member state enjoy the same benefits as the nationals of that state, a provision that has been highly controversial as mobility between EU members with very different living standards has increased in recent years. Regulations have also been used to mandate sectoral provisions relating to Directives. Thus, for instance, Regulations set specific limitations on working time in road transport, railways, civil aviation and seafaring.

There are also *Decisions*, which can come from the EU Council or the Commission, and relate to specific cases. They require individuals or authorities to do something (or else stop doing something).

Finally, the ECJ also has the power to adjudicate in cases of employment law that come before it, and its rulings have been very important in defining, for example, the scope of European legislation on age discrimination and the interpretation of the Working Time Directive. ECJ decisions cannot directly overturn domestic laws, but they may oblige UK governments to alter legislation to make it compatible with EU law.

A recent example of a ruling that, if confirmed, may lead to alterations in UK law is the ECJ Advocate-General's opinion[8] that obesity can amount to a disability, and thus obese individuals should be a protected group in terms of discrimination legislation.

---

8    The verdict concerned the case of a grossly overweight Danish childminder who was sacked because it was claimed that he could no longer fulfil his duties: amongst other things it was said that he needed help to tie children's shoelaces. See *The Guardian* (2014) Obesity can be a disability, EU Court rules, 18 December. http://www.theguardian.com/society/2014/dec/18/obesity-can-be-disability-eu-court-rules (accessed 15 September 2015).

## Why intervention?

No labour markets anywhere escape some regulation, which goes back hundreds of years. There have been a few rigorous advocates of a completely free market, at least where adults are concerned[9] – most notably Richard Epstein (1984, 2003) with his continuing defence of the 'contract at will'. Epstein sees the freedom to engage in employment relationships as analogous to freedom to trade. He points out that the contract at will, which allows employers and employees to end contractual relationships without any repercussions, reduces the complexity of such relationships and consequent litigation, and thus promotes employment. He argues that employment relationships are fundamentally misread if they are assumed to involve inherent inequality between employers and employees, and he asserts that in reality freedom to contract works, in most cases, to the advantage of both parties (Epstein 1984: 953).

Epstein's logic has much to commend it. But many, perhaps most, economists have nevertheless accepted the need for a considerable degree of intervention in labour markets. Where economic reasoning is adduced to support intervention in 'Anglo-Saxon' countries such as Britain and the US, it usually involves an analysis of the ways in which the market for labour services fails to meet the strict assumptions of perfect competition. This model is derived from the neoclassical revolution of the latter part of the nineteenth and first half of the twentieth century, and it has been embodied in standard textbooks ever since as the touchstone of an optimal economic system.

Those adhering to this approach invoke the concept of market failure (Bator 1958) and point to a number of areas where

---

9   The argument for the exclusion of minors from many types of employment dates back to the early nineteenth century, although economists have sometimes queried this (Kis-Katos and Schulze 2005).

labour markets appear to perform badly (Wachter 2012). These include alleged externalities,[10] information asymmetries[11] and imbalances of market power.[12]

Probably a more fundamental argument for intervention in employment, however, does not lie in such quibbles about the assumptions of perfect competition. Rather, it lies in the claim that labour market outcomes are intrinsically *unfair*: they offend against some conception of social justice. Hayek (1976:58) called social justice 'a mirage', on which no two people could ever agree. It is nevertheless a powerful mirage and has led to many attempts to interfere with the workings of labour markets. Very obvious examples in Britain include 30 years of incomes policies from the 1940s to the 1970s, and more recently minimum wages and equal pay legislation.

---

10　These are held to arise where decisions by employers and employees focus on private concerns and do not encompass wider third-party costs or benefits of employment: one example might be the creation of a large number of redundancies in an area where there are currently few alternative sources of employment.

11　These arise where different groups have access to different amounts of information. For instance, suppose an employer knows that a particular production process is hazardous to health, while employees are unaware of this; or suppose that potential private providers of unemployment insurance do not know anything about the level of commitment and motivation of individuals and so face moral hazard problems when offering such insurance. Such dangers are often held to justify government intervention on health and safety matters or to provide unemployment benefits.

12　Whereas the idealised competitive system assumes a large number of buyers and sellers of labour services competing with each other, in practice one or both sides of the market may be in a rather stronger position. This is usually considered to be the employer side: if there is only one (*monopsony*) in a particular geographical or occupational area, wages may be forced down below the level that would prevail in a more competitive market. However, a particular group of workers that can control the supply of labour (perhaps through a trade union, perhaps through a professional body) may exercise some monopoly power to force wages up. Some regulatory intervention might be advocated in either of these circumstances, although Austrian economists point out that positions of market power tend to be undermined over time through innovation (the collapse of union power in the docks with the advent of containerisation is a case in point) and unanticipated ways of doing things.

This is not strictly a market failure in economists' terms; rather, it is a political reaction against labour market outcomes such as extreme inequalities in pay. If this reaction is strong in the UK, it is stronger still in some continental countries: in France, for example, President Hollande came into power to reverse the modest elements of employment deregulation that took place under his predecessor, and to raise taxes on high earners.

What all these rationalisations for government action downplay or ignore, however, is the possibility of 'government failure' (McKean 1965). For government intervention, seductive in theory, is frequently ineffective in reaching its ostensible objectives. First, governments cannot, any more than the private sector, know everything that is relevant to economic decisions, so it is not omnipotent in relation to externalities or information asymmetries. Indeed, private firms may be better placed to gather useful information, as it is in their direct financial interest to do so. So, for example, even a well-intentioned and hard-working government employment agency may be worse at finding you a job than a private agency.

Secondly, intervention will always involve costs, which may be greater than any benefit. A mandated benefit such as paid holidays may lead to reduced employment (if the costs are passed on to the consumer), or it may be offset by a reduction in wages. There can often be knock-on, second- or third-order effects from a decision to intervene: it changes the market and creates incentives for new forms of behaviour, which may be considered worse than those the intervention sought to improve. Imposing a minimum wage may lead employers to worsen other aspects of a worker's job, or may lead to compromising safety to save money or reducing fringe benefits or intensifying shift work. Or it may force workers onto benefits or out into the shadow economy, where wages are lower than legitimate businesses are allowed to pay. And there is evidence that anti-discrimination legislation can lead to reduced pay and/or reduced employment for 'protected groups' such as older workers[13] and those with disabilities.[14]

There are also considerable compliance costs associated with employment regulation. Records must be kept, procedures must be reorganised, training must be provided to everyone, new staff need to be taken on to check and monitor. As many regulations (for instance, in the area of discrimination) are ambiguous and the costs of getting things wrong can be very high, defensive HR departments often impose excessive levels of compliance to reduce risk.[15]

Third, rules and regulations may be unduly influenced by interested parties to secure advantages for themselves at the expense of other firms, workers and consumers – this is known as 'rent seeking'. A suggestion that nursery staff need more training, for example, may be hijacked by training providers, trade unions[16] and other commercial interests with an agenda of their

---

13  In examining the effects of state age protection and age discrimination laws in the US, Joanna Lakey concludes that 'employers ... react to these laws by failing to hire older men who will be more difficult to fire' (Lakey 2008: 458).

14  Acemoglu and Angrist (2001) claim that the Americans with Disabilities Act led to a reduction in the employment of disabled workers. Bambra and Pope (2007) produce some evidence for the Disability Discrimination Act having had the same effect in the UK.

15  There are now over 250,000 employees shown in the Annual Survey of Hours and Earnings as having personnel, industrial relations, training or human resources in their job title, and this ignores junior administrators and a share of the time of general managers and others. On a narrower basis, the Institute of Personnel Management (now the Chartered Institute of Personnel and Development) had 12,000 members in 1979: in 2014, the CIPD had in excess of 135,000.

16  The union movement in the UK used to be very wary of labour market regulation. There was a strong belief in 'free collective bargaining', with unions negotiating with employers to improve the conditions of their members. A national minimum wage was opposed, and Wages Councils were only tolerated in sectors where, for various reasons, unions were weak. The development of employment rights was treated with suspicion, as they might be a means by which governments undermined unions. Indeed, this was part of the reason why the Conservatives introduced unfair dismissal legislation (originally proposed by the Donovan Commission and rejected by the union movement) in the early 1970s. Now, however, a much weaker trade union movement sees government intervention as positive and devotes much campaigning energy to pushing tighter employment regulation.

own, which may not coincide with the perceived problem. As they are a concentrated source of influence, they tend to do better at getting their way than widely dispersed interests such as those of parents and their children. Interested parties always include government regulators, who may try to influence political decisions that favour the expansion of their remit and thus lead, over time, to larger civil service or other budgets and more power.

And, of course, democratic politicians almost inevitably respond to 'the vote motive' (Tullock 2006). They are drawn to policies that appeal to the median voter, even though they may be quite conscious on one level that such policies are likely to be ineffective or even counter-productive – for example, pressuring firms to alter their remuneration systems for executives.[17]. The median voter, in the context of the labour market, is an 'insider' employed in a secure and reasonably well-paid job. He or she tends to favour policies that maintain and enhance that position – improvements to working conditions, restrictions on job entry, employment protection. Less well-placed outsiders (labour market entrants, minority groups), who may lose from such policies, have little political influence.

These factors taken together suggest that we can be excused for having a sceptical attitude towards proposals for government intervention in labour markets in whatever context. But it is also important to emphasise the special factors that impart a bias towards regulation, and regulation of a particularly inefficient kind, in the EU context.

## European political economy

For one thing, emphasis on economic analysis is often seen as an Anglo-Saxon vice, which does not have as strong an appeal

---

17  To be fair, such behaviour may not be as reprehensible as it is often painted, for in a party system it is always necessary for politicians to compromise, accepting some policies that they dislike in return for support over other issues that they consider more important. The recent experience of coalition government in the UK surely drives this home.

in continental Europe, where economics has, in the past, had less influence than jurisprudence. Legal traditions dating back to the Romans, and in modern terms built on Napoleonic and Bismarckian ideas about the role of the state, emphasise government control and regulation, with rights-based ideas rather than the tradition of common law (Siebert 2006).

Political systems support this: in the post-war period, leading parties in Western Europe were either social democratic (particularly strong in Northern Europe) or Christian Democrats (emphasising Catholic traditions of social concern). And, with the expansion of the EU to embrace much of the formerly communist Eastern Europe, a large population was absorbed that had grown up with the expectation of extensive state involvement in the labour market.

Allied to this has been the popularity of systems of proportional representation, which leads to frequent coalitions and an expectation of compromise, particularly in those countries, such as Germany, Italy and Spain, which had been torn apart in the interwar period by extremes of right and left. In parallel with this was the expectation in many countries that compromise should also prevail in the conduct of employment relations. Hence, there is widespread recognition of, and government support for, collective bargaining,[18] and various forms of worker representation[19] in large private sector businesses in Germany, France, the Netherlands and elsewhere. More generally, there is broad sympathy with the idea of social dialogue between representatives of capital and labour.

Indeed, this preference for compromise and deal-making might even have been responsible in the first place for the expansion of EU competence to include employment regulation. Some commentators have argued that the development of the Social

---

18  In France, for example, the results of such bargaining extend to all workers in a sector or industry, even though membership of the bargaining unions is often pitifully low.

19  Works Councils and employee representation on supervisory boards.

Charter in the 1980s was a response to the development of the single market. As this was seen (wrongly) mainly to benefit business interests, the expansion of the social dimension was thought to provide benefits to workers, a kind of *quid pro quo*. The union side of the social partnership saw increasing international competition as threatening workers:

> the expansion of EU labour regulation was born out of a concern
> that the increased competition resulting from the completion of
> the single market in 1992 would lead to a race to the bottom in
> labour standards (ibid.: 3).

This fear of what is termed 'social dumping' is widespread: the European Commission even has an official definition. It describes the practice as a situation 'where foreign service providers can undercut local service providers because their labour standards are lower'.[20] To economists, this looks perilously close to protectionism. And, logically, if EU members are not to be allowed to compete over employment regulation, why should they be allowed to compete over wages? Or even over other advantages, such as transport links, or better training, or higher levels of capital investment?

Finally, the particular form of governance of the EU, with the Commission (a sort of Civil Service) having such an important role in initiating policy[21] – a role found in no nation state – arguably produces a permanent bias towards interference in labour markets.

Moreover, since the EU's budget is currently constrained to a fixed proportion of EU GDP, regulatory solutions to perceived

20 http://www.eurofound.europa.eu/observatories/eurwork/industrial-relations
-dictionary/social-dumping (accessed 19 July 2014).

21 It is important to note that the Commission finances a large number of pressure
groups and charities, which, according to Snowdon (2013), generate apparent public support for the policies it wishes to pursue.

problems are inevitably preferred to financial redistribution. Where economic inequality is an issue, for example, a nation might favour some income-related benefit, which could be targeted at those most in need. A European 'solution' would instead be to mandate employers to provide extended leave, reduced working hours and so forth, even though this might not be the economically most efficient way of helping people,[22] or indeed what the intended 'beneficiaries' necessarily want or value.

## Would repatriation of powers over the labour market make enough of a difference?

The levels of intervention associated with the EU have led many UK-based critics to argue for significant repatriation of government powers over employment regulation as a key element in any renegotiation of the country's relationship with its European neighbours. What would be the impact of success in this endeavour?

Complete withdrawal from the EU would bring some clear benefits. It would, for example, prevent a qualified majority of EU members imposing further employment restrictions on the UK; it would remove the necessity for involvement of 'social partners' in labour market matters; it would remove the powers of the ECJ to add new non-negotiable obligations on British employers. It might be possible, while staying in the EU, to achieve some of these benefits – although it might leave open the possibility of 'back door re-regulation' of the labour market using other means, such as new health and safety obligations and changes to competition and company law.

But what effect would repatriation of some or all powers over employment have? Open Europe (Booth et al. 2011) has

---

22 A bias that is also often found amongst single-issue pressure groups, which prefer mandates (for example, employer adjustments to the needs of disabled people) or prohibitions (for example, smoking bans) to transfers and taxes.

calculated the continuing cost of European regulation of labour markets by adding up the costs shown in government impact assessments conducted at the time legislation was passed. On this basis, it calculated that a 50 per cent cut in the cost of regulation could add £4.3 billion, in 2011 prices, to GDP. On some back-of-the-envelope assumptions about the proportion of such a gain going into productivity increases, it further suggested that the equivalent of 60,000 new jobs could be created.

Seizing on these estimates, the Fresh Start Project (2012; 2013) noted that the bulk of these gains would come from scrapping the Temporary Agency Workers Directive and the Working Time Directive.[23] It put the repeal of this legislation at the centre of its proposals for renegotiation of the UK's European employment commitments.

It is not clear what process might be followed, for remember that all the relevant legislation has been passed by the UK Parliament, and Parliament must repeal it. One approach suggested by Iain Mansfield[24] in the extreme case of a complete UK withdrawal is to pass a 'Great Repeal Act', which would require all European-influenced legislation to be reviewed within three years. While I have a good deal of respect for Mansfield's proposals, such a review (unpicking 40 years of legislation) would be a truly massive task to conduct alongside a normal legislative programme, and some prioritisation would surely be necessary.

Even if legislation could be unpicked relatively easily, it is simplistic to think, as the Fresh Start project seems to assume, that repealing the relevant legislation would necessarily free up significant resources, at least in the short term. For the costs arise through having to develop new procedures (for example, to record working time), taking on extra workers, altering contracts

---

23 According to Open Europe, two-thirds of the costs of European employment regulation are associated with these two Directives.

24 In his winning entry for the Institute of Economic Affairs' 'Brexit' prize (Mansfield 2014).

and shift arrangements and so forth. Companies would find it costly to reverse such changes, and few might initially choose to do so, given that it would mean disruption and cause friction with employees.

Over time, new entrants might take advantage of relaxed regulation, and existing firms might alter their practices, but such innovations could take years to emerge, and they could be overtaken by other labour market changes and new patterns of work (for example, the spread of self-employment and working from home – which, incidentally, may already have mitigated some of the original costs of European regulation).

But, in any case, given the continuing (indeed, growing) predilections of our domestic politicians for regulation, would a domestic review process lead to significant change? It is worth noting the words of Lord Mandelson, admittedly made while he was a European Commissioner:

> Before you accuse Brussels of excessive regulatory zeal, remember that a greater part of the burden on business comes from national measures which go beyond what is required by European legislation.[25]

Mandelson may very well have been correct in his assessment.[26] It is indeed possible that European Directives complained about in public were secretly welcomed by UK administrations. Some certainly seem to have been 'gold-plated': that is, the transposing legislation has added to Directive requirements in various ways, so that regulation goes beyond what is mandated by the EU. Gold-plating, according to Tebbit (n.d.), can occur when the

---

25 http://europa.eu/rapid/press-release_SPEECH-07-365_en.htm (accessed 13 July 2014).

26 Though, as Vaughne Miller (House of Commons Library 2010) shows in his lengthy examination of the issue, it is no easy task to put a figure on the proportion of legislation directly resulting from Brussels.

government extends the scope of its implementing legislation beyond what is required by a Directive, when it fails to take advantage of exemptions allowed by a Directive, when it introduces penalties for employers in its implementing legislation that go beyond the penalties required by a Directive or when it introduces its transposing legislation earlier than required.

One example is the Working Time Directive's requirement for four weeks annual holiday; since the Directive came into force, the Labour government increased this to 5.6 weeks (Department for Business Innovation and Skills 2014: 8). Similarly, the Coalition government added significantly to the parental leave requirements of the 2010 Directive. Sack (2013) provides other examples.

In any case, the recent imposition of pension auto-enrolment, the new Conservative government's National Living Wage, its apprenticeship levy proposals and compulsory pay audits hardly suggest that even centre-right UK politicians are enthusiastic for a large-scale reduction in employment regulation. The Labour Party,[27] the Liberal Democrats and the Green Party all advocate further expansions of employment law.

So, although recovery of domestic powers over employment law may be a *necessary* condition for major deregulation of the labour market, it is very far from being *sufficient*. Those arguing for greater labour market freedom need to change the mindset of our own politicians, and indeed the current beliefs of much of the general public.

It needs patiently to be explained that much employment regulation does very little to benefit employees as a whole. Though

---

27 The recently elected Labour Party leader Jeremy Corbyn wants much more regulation of labour markets, including a higher living wage than the UK's Living Wage Campaign is calling for, a maximum wage fixed as a multiple of the lowest paid and the banning of zero-hours contracts. He has also hinted that, if David Cameron's renegotiations lead to exemptions from EU employment law, he might propose leaving the EU.

it may protect and boost the incomes of some groups of workers, this is often at the expense of other, perhaps more vulnerable, people. It certainly does little to boost economic growth. More fundamentally, it may erode personal freedom and choice in subtle ways and contribute to a culture of dependency.

## A minimum level of regulation?

But it would be unwise to assert that there are no grounds for any restrictions on employment matters at all. Substantial deregulation is certainly needed, but there may still be a core element of regulation that many market liberals would support. Opinions may differ on this, but my suggestions would be as follows.

First, it seems reasonable to place some restrictions on the hours worked and types of jobs undertaken by children and young people.

Second, safety considerations do require some limitations on hours worked in areas such as transport and healthcare, where employees working excessive hours (even if voluntarily) may be a danger to others.

Third, employment contracts need to be enforceable, cheaply and effectively. Where employers irresponsibly breach contracts or fraudulently deprive workers of agreed pay, employees need some cheap and effective mechanism for redress.

Fourth, recognising that dismissal without any notice at all can be very destructive to the well-being of employees and their families, but that excessive employment protection can have adverse effects on job creation, we need a form of no-fault dismissal with some minimum level of compensation.[28]

It is also rather difficult to imagine that in today's world there should not be some form of anti-discrimination legislation,

---

28 Perhaps on the lines suggested in Adrian Beecroft's report to the Department for Business Innovation and Skills (2012). This sensible proposal was vetoed by the Liberal Democrats when they were part of the Coalition.

despite its often perverse effects. However, legislation should be much more tightly drawn, and there should be limits on the compensation that can be claimed.[29]

There may be other elements that could be added to this list, but it is clear that any such list would be a great deal shorter than that covering today's employment legislation. At the moment, there are approaching 100 different areas in which employment law constrains businesses and employees. Whether we are to be in or out of the EU, this needs to change.

## References

Acemoglu, D. and Angrist, J. D. (2001) Consequences of employment protection? The case of the Americans with Disabilities Act. *Journal of Political Economy* 109: 915–57.

Bambra, C. and Pope, D. (2007) What are the effects of anti-discriminatory legislation on socioeconomic inequalities in the employment consequences of ill health and disability? *Journal of Epidemiology and Community Health* 61: 421–6.

Bator, F. M. (1958) The anatomy of market failure. *Quarterly Journal of Economics* 72(3): 351–79.

Booth, S., Persson, M. and Scarpetta, V. (2011) Repatriating EU social policy: the best choice for jobs and growth? Open Europe, London. http://archive.openeurope.org.uk/Content/Documents/Pdfs/2011 EUsocialpolicy.pdf (accessed 10 July 2014).

Department for Business, Innovation and Skills (2012) Report on employment law (Beecroft report).

Epstein, R. A. (1984) In defense of the contract at will. *University of Chicago Law Review* 51: 947–82.

---

29 It is interesting to note that the recent introduction of charges for employment tribunal applications has dramatically reduced claims for unfair dismissal where there is an upper limit on compensation, but claims concerning sex discrimination (where there is no such limit) may have risen. See *The Times* (2014) Sex bias cases are growth industry fuelled by big payouts, 23 July.

Fresh Start Project (2012) Options for change green paper: renegotiating the UK's relationship with the EU. http://www.eufreshstart.org/downloads/fullgreenpaper.pdf (accessed 9 July 2014).

Fresh Start Project (2013) Manifesto for change: a new vision for the UK in Europe. http://www.eufreshstart.org/downloads/manifesto-forchange.pdf (accessed 9 July 2014).

Hayek, F. A. (1976) The atavism of social justice. In *New Studies in Philosophy, Politics, Economics and the History of Ideas.* London: Routledge and Kegan Paul.

HM Government (2014) Review of the balance of competences between the United Kingdom and the European Union: social and employment policy. https://www.gov.uk/government/uploads/system/uploads/attachment_data/file/332524/review-of-the-balance-of-competences-between-the-united-kingdom-and-the-european-union-social-and-employment-policy.pdf (accessed 10 October 2015).

House of Commons Library (2010) How much legislation comes from Europe? Research Paper 10/62. http://www.parliament.uk/business/publications/research/briefing-papers/RP10-62/how-much-legislation-comes-from-europe (accessed 9 July 2014).

Kis-Katos, K. and Schulze, G. G. (2005) Regulation of child labour. *Economic Affairs* 25(3): 24–30.

Lakey, J. (2008) State age protection laws and the Age Discrimination in Employment Act. *Journal of Law and Economics* 51: 433–60.

Mansfield, I. (2014) *A Blueprint For Britain: Openness Not Isolation.* London: Institute of Economic Affairs.

McKean, R. N. (1965) The unseen hand in government. *American Economic Review* 55: 496–506.

OECD (2013) *OECD Employment Outlook 2013.* Paris: OECD Publishing.

Sack, P. (2013) The Midas touch: gold-plating of EU employment directives in UK law. Policy Paper, Institute of Directors, London. http://www.iod.com/influencing/policy-papers/regulation-and-employment/the-midas-touch-goldplating-of-eu-employment-directives-in-uk-law (accessed 9 July 2014).

Schulten, T. (2010) A European minimum wage policy for a more sustainable wage-led growth model. Article. http://www.social-europe.eu/2010/06/a-european-minimum-wage-policy-for-a-more-sustainable-wage-led-growth-model/ (accessed 10 July 2014).

Siebert, W. S. (2006) Labour market regulation in the EU-15: causes and consequences – a survey. Discussion Paper 2430, IZA, Bonn.

Snowdon, C. (2013) Euro puppets: the European Commission's remaking of civil society. Discussion Paper 45, Institute of Economic Affairs, London.

Tebbit, A. (n.d.) Does the government 'gold-plate' EU employment directives? http://bit.ly/1TzszRl (accessed 10 July 2014).

Tullock, G. (2006) *The Vote Motive*. Hobart Paperback 33. London: Institute of Economic Affairs.

Wachter, M. L. (2012) Neoclassical labor economics: its implications for labor and employment law. In *Research Handbook on the Economics of Labor and Employment Law* (ed. C. L. Estland and M. L. Wachter). Northampton, MA: Edward Elgar.

# 9 PROSPECTS FOR A REFORMED AGRICULTURAL POLICY

Séan Rickard

## Introduction

The Common Agricultural Policy (CAP) is not only the EU's[1] most expensive policy – it costs some €58 billion per year and accounts for 40 per cent of the EU budget – but also its most complex and interventionist programme. Yet, despite its many faults and failures, it attracts relatively little attention and criticism outside academic circles. This may reflect its presentation as delivering the benefits of a pleasant countryside and supporting a traditional rural way of life. The CAP has enjoyed an exceptional and prominent position since the founding of the EU; indeed, the promise of a common agricultural policy helped secure ratification of the Treaty of Rome (Parsons 2003). French determination to secure a profitable arrangement for their farmers reinforced a Commission keen to press ahead with at least one ambitious common policy, and none seemed more promising than agriculture (Ludlow 2005). Paradoxically, it was a sector with strong farmers' unions upon which the Commission hoped to build the type of relationship capable of breaking the national mould of European politics (White 2003).

Compared to its current manifestation, the CAP started out with the straightforward intention of holding the domestic prices

---

1   The term 'EU' will be used throughout, even where it would be more historically correct to speak of the EU's predecessors, i.e. the EEC or the European Communities (EC).

of key agricultural commodities at sufficiently high and stable levels to encourage production and provide a reasonable standard of living for farmers. Since its inception in the 1960s, the CAP has undergone several reforms. Each reform has been driven by political disquiet regarding the CAP's cost and effectiveness. Agricultural exceptionalism continues, but the method of support has changed, and the policy's complexity and scope has increased with the addition of new and diverse objectives. Despite the reforms, there is widespread doubt amongst academic critics regarding its ability to achieve its goals (Jambor and Harvey 2010).

The purpose of this chapter is twofold: firstly, to consider the prospects for fundamental reform of the CAP; and secondly, in the event of a 'Brexit', to examine the nature and pace of agricultural policy reform in the UK. Fundamental reform is defined here as ending agricultural exceptionalism and allowing the industry's structure and performance to be determined by unfettered market forces. In order to understand something of the complexity of the CAP and why it has proved so difficult to reduce the level of farm subsidies, I will first briefly outline how the policy has developed. I will also explain the political and industry forces that have successfully protected its exceptional position. Finally, I will consider to what extent the influence of these forces might wane following a Brexit, thereby allowing a fundamental reform of UK agricultural policy.

## A politically driven policy

Perhaps inevitably when reaching agreement between divergent interests, the objectives set for the CAP at its founding were vague. In summary, its five objectives were to (i) increase productivity, (ii) ensure a fair standard of living, (iii) stabilise markets, (iv) assure supplies and (v) deliver 'reasonable' prices for consumers (European Union 2006). The objectives were crafted with the depressed state of agriculture in the 1930s, and the food deprivations of World War II, in mind. Consequently, of the five objectives, ensuring a fair standard of living for farmers – by implication protecting farm incomes and farm numbers – was *primus inter pares*. Based largely on 'price support' involving variable levies, i.e. tariffs to raise import prices to domestic levels, and official intervention buying at predetermined prices, the CAP was spread from grains to other major products during the 1960s. Intervention prices for the coming year were set by the Agricultural Council, which operated *de facto* under an implicit rule of consensus (Hayes-Renshaw et al. 2006). This way of working ensured that as production responded to higher prices, eventually creating structural surpluses, i.e. a permanent state of excess supply, the Agricultural Council's reaction was to increase budgetary expenditure to cover the cost.

Under pressure from national governments and farmers' unions, the Agricultural Council refused to countenance a reduction in support price levels. Instead, as budgetary expenditure rose, it chose the less divisive policies of supply management and export subsidies. Production controls were first introduced for sugar in 1968 and for milk in 1983, to be followed by the voluntary 'set-aside' of productive land for cereals in 1988. But surpluses continued to mount, and the cost of export subsidies rose as the EU increasingly resorted to dumping its surplus agricultural commodities on world markets. These interventionist policies were failing to stem rising budgetary costs, and, moreover, the use of export subsidies was a source of tension with trading partners.

Within the European Council, as CAP expenditure rose to account for around 70 per cent of the EU budget, there was growing recognition that reform was inevitable. This view was reinforced by the launch of the Uruguay GATT Round and mounting anger by the US and Cairns Group[2] at the CAP's trade distorting policies.

---

2  A coalition of 19 agricultural exporting countries which account for over 25 per cent of the world's agricultural exports.

Eventually, these pressures resulted in the 1992 MacSharry[3] reform. The reform transferred the basis of support from farm prices to annual direct payments. In the process, it shifted the burden of support from consumers to taxpayers. By 1992, agricultural production in the EU was in chronic oversupply, so the authorities could not credibly claim that continued support was necessary to protect production. Thus, the payments were defended as 'temporary compensation' for lower market prices, while protection of the environment and rural development were introduced as justifying continued support.

The piecemeal approach to the environment embodied in the 1992 reform reinforced the belief that the objective was primarily to continue to support farm incomes without encouraging production growth. The reform had, however, opened the door to the environmental lobby – which seized the opportunity. The result was the consolidation of environmental objectives in the 2000 reform, which separated CAP expenditure into two tranches: Pillar I and Pillar II. Pillar I accounts for more than 70 per cent of CAP expenditure and is largely used to fund direct farm payments. Pillar II, which is co-financed from national funds, is aimed at improving agricultural competitiveness, the environment and the rural economy, i.e. largely channelled to farm businesses. The introduction of co-financing was implicit recognition that budgetary restraints would constrain future CAP expenditure, but it also marked, albeit on a small scale, the introduction of 'renationalisation'. In other words, under Pillar II national and/or regional authorities can decide, within limits, the objectives and content of rural policies for their regions.

In preparation for the impending eastward enlargement of the EU, the CAP was further reformed in 2003. This reform fully decoupled direct payments from production, i.e. they were to be

---

3   Irish politician Ray MacSharry was Commissioner for Agriculture and Rural Development, 1989–93.

set on an area basis, regardless of historical production. The new decoupled payments added a further dimension to renationalisation by allowing member states to adjust modestly the conditions attached to their receipt and the scope to modulate, i.e. reduce, the payments for larger-scale farms. A bizarre side effect was that it was no longer necessary to grow anything in order to receive payments. In principle, decoupling increased the influence of markets in farmers' decisions, and the 2008 reform continued this trend, most notably by abolishing set-aside and setting 2015 for the phasing out of milk quotas. In 2013, the CAP underwent further reform to make it 'more equitable and greener' and to phase out sugar quotas by 2017. The history of the CAP, the key pressures for reform and its growing complexity are summarised in Figure 3. In contrast to the US, where agricultural reform during the 1990s represented a decisive move towards market liberalism, in the EU the underlying protectionist goals remain intact (Skogstad 1998).

## An inefficient and ineffective policy

According to the European Commission, financial support for farming is necessary to deliver 'viable' food production, the sustainable management of natural resources and balanced development across the EU (European Commission 2014). But the ability of the CAP to protect farm incomes and numbers is weak. At best, direct payments have slowed the long-term decline in the numbers engaged in farming. In practice, 'sustainable management' consists largely of attempts to constrain highly productive, intensive systems. As regards balanced development, direct payments are inequitably distributed, the product of their historical role as compensation for reductions in support prices. Direct payments, per hectare, are smallest in the countries with the lowest per capita incomes and greatest dependence on agriculture, as measured by share of GDP.

Figure 3  **History and reforms of the CAP**

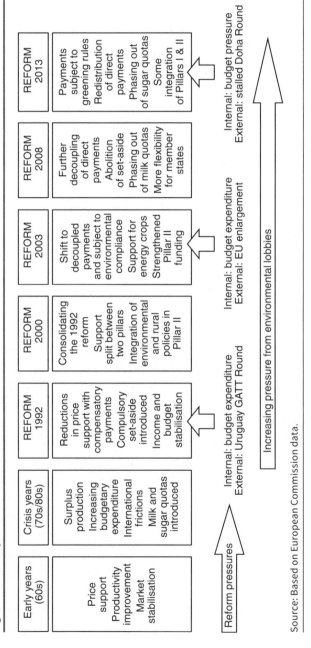

Source: Based on European Commission data.

Since the 1960s, both the number of EU farms and the numbers engaged in farming have declined at an annual rate of 2 per cent. Over the same period, the annual reduction in the utilised agricultural area has been less than 1 per cent. Consequently, there has been a slow but steady concentration of production on larger-scale, more specialised farms (Brouwer 2006). In the absence of decoupled payments, some 80 per cent of EU farms would not break even. If the payments are included in farms' revenue, then this proportion only falls to 65 per cent (European Commission 2010). The growing average size of farms in the EU is evidence of the existence of economies of scale. Larger farms deliver a superior performance in terms of productivity, unit costs and incomes. The average value added per labour unit for the EU's largest farm size group is more than ten times that for the smallest farms group (ibid.).

Figure 4 is a schematic of the relationship between scale and dependency. The diagram shows how economies of scale cause unit costs to decline as farm size increases. In practice, some of the smallest farms are profitable, but most should be described as 'hobby' or 'lifestyle' farms operated on a non-commercial basis. More than one-third are involved in off-farm gainful activity, e.g. they are part-time or have other sources of unearned income (ibid.). Most EU farms are constrained by their small scale; about 70 per cent have an area of less than 5 hectares (European Commission 2013). Few of these farmers are likely ever to be in a position to earn a reasonable living from their land. The logic of Figure 4 is that structural change towards an industry composed of fewer, larger-scale farms would reduce the need for public subsidy. As decoupled payments prolong the life of unprofitable farms, they frustrate evolution to a more efficient industry structure. The Commission argues that decoupled payments improve competitiveness by encouraging farmers to tailor production decisions to market requirements, but the evidence for this is lacking (Rickard and Roberts 2008). Rather, they impact

Figure 4   **Scale and dependency**

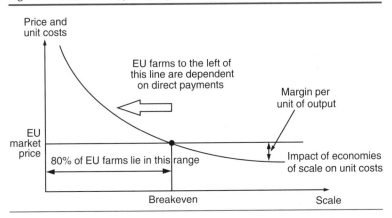

negatively on efficiency (Rizov et al. 2013) by enabling farms to avoid productivity-enhancing change at a time when productivity growth and, most notably, crop yields across the EU display a slowing rate of increase (Lobell et al. 2009).

Besides public expenditure savings, other advantages would follow the removal of decoupled payments. Agricultural support was largely phased out in New Zealand during the 1980s. An OECD study concluded that this had 'enhanced the flexibility of a sector that had been renowned for its inability to respond to change' (Vitalis 2006). What is beyond dispute is the need for EU agriculture greatly to increase current levels of productivity, particularly with respect to natural resources, e.g. land, fresh water, minerals and fossil fuels. The Royal Society (2009) argues that more productive and sustainable agricultural systems – inevitably dubbed 'sustainable intensification' – could be delivered by technological advances. While much scientific research is now focused on scale-neutral biotechnology, engineering advances are now heavily concentrated on scale-biased, precision technologies. Defined as the fusing of agricultural engineering and information technology, precision technologies achieve much greater efficiency in the use of scarce resources, but these benefits can only be realised when adopted at the farm level, and this involves expensive investment.

Decoupled payments may prolong the life of many smaller farms, but the extent to which they augment incomes is not sufficient to generate a surplus to fund performance improving investment (Viaggi 2011). An OECD review of the evidence concluded that 'larger farms are better performers as they can achieve economies of scale' (OECD 2011). As implied in Figure 4, economies of scale not only increase the likelihood that a farm is generating profits but also mean a greater volume of output over which to spread investment costs. Hence, larger-scale farms are better able than their smaller counterparts to invest in productivity and sustainability-enhancing, technological advances. Moreover, there is some evidence that when a scale-invariant advance, e.g. genetically modified (GM) crops, is combined with a scale-enhanced advance, e.g. precision technology, farms gain an additional economy of scope (Fernandez-Cornejo et al. 2001).

## Prospects for radical reform of the CAP

The foregoing indicates that, if the objective is economic efficiency, the priority for future CAP reform should be the phasing out of direct payments. Indeed, the European Commission has acknowledged that such action would not only lead to:

> a more competitive and less diverse sector ... [but also] ... farms which will continue to be economically viable in the new environment will be larger, more open to innovation leading to cost optimisation, productivity growth and less labour-intensive. (European Commission 2011)

But the European Commission and the farmers' unions argue that the objectives of the CAP now embrace more than efficiency and competitiveness. The Commission rejected the phasing out of decoupled payments because it would 'lead to failure of many agricultural holdings and would put additional pressure on the viability of rural areas with higher unemployment and migration', and the concentration of production on larger-scale farms would cause the 'likely intensification of production in fertile areas and the abandonment of production and land in more marginal regions' (European Commission 2011). Significantly, the Commission did not claim that the removal of decoupled payments would be followed by a fall in total EU agricultural output. This reflects the fact that the contribution of smaller-scale farms – those deemed most vulnerable to the removal of support – is proportionally less than their numbers (Martins and Tosstorff 2011).

A modelling exercise by a group of European academics (Renwick 2011) concluded that the overall reduction in EU production following the removal of decoupled payments was likely to be small – around 1 per cent – though the impact for regions and farm types would vary more significantly. The study also identified environmental benefits such as lower overall greenhouse gas emissions and reduced soil erosion. Indeed, the budgetary savings arising from the removal of all payments to farmers under the CAP would create scope for better-targeted and more efficiently funded environmental and rural policies. In the absence of the CAP, national governments would be free to implement environmental and rural policies based on regional rather than agricultural priorities. Moreover, the release of land as less efficient farms exited the industry would provide space to deliver ecosystem services, such as woodlands and habitat conservation, recreation, as well as carbon sequestration (Burgess and Morris 2009).

The CAP's multifunctionalism is an inefficient way to deliver environmental and rural policies, but it serves to deflect attention and criticism from income support. That it remains, despite multiple objectives, primarily a social policy was confirmed by an expert report (Sapir et al. 2003), commissioned by the President of the European Commission. The report concluded that the CAP had become a redistributive policy spreading wealth to farmers instead of an instrument to promote efficiency. Despite its authority, the report was ignored. Born in the era of the postwar welfare state, the CAP's objective of protecting farm incomes has endured – a situation viewed by both the political and wider populations of Europe as legitimate, if no longer open-ended. The fact that in each member state average agricultural earnings are lower than the national average, and that around half of the EU's farms are defined as semi-subsistent (Davidova et al. 2013), is stressed by the farming lobby as the justification for continued income support. And now that the Lisbon Treaty has given the European Parliament greater oversight of the CAP, there is little prospect of a significant reduction in funding for farm payments in the foreseeable future.

Strong political support for 'family farms' and very powerful farmers' lobbies explain why it has proved impossible to undertake any reform of the CAP without the assurance that funding would continue at prevailing nominal levels. The evidence points to another twenty years or more in which there will be periodic reforms of the CAP. But in the absence of some unforeseen external pressure, they will not seriously disturb the course set: the real value of decoupled payments will decline alongside a steady reduction in farm numbers. Future reforms will probably continue the drift towards a greater influence for market forces, the encouragement of sustainable farming practices and partial renationalisation. The farmers' lobbies are bitterly opposed to renationalisation (NFU 2013), and for this reason renationalisation will remain a minor adjunct to the CAP.

# Visualising a reformed UK agricultural policy outside the EU

The relative efficiency of UK agriculture within the EU has featured heavily in the literature – see, for example, Lund and Hill (1979). Compared to other EU farm industries, only the Czech Republic has an average farm size greater than the UK, and, as indicated above, larger-scale farms tend to be more productively efficient. Productivity growth is a good indicator of longer-term survivability, but comparative studies show that since 1960 UK agriculture's total factor productivity (TFP) has grown at a slower rate than comparable countries, e.g. Germany and Denmark. This may indicate that other EU agricultural industries are now far ahead of the UK, or simply that they have been playing catch-up. What is beyond dispute is that all EU farming industries are being hampered by CAP Directives restricting or withdrawing some advanced technologies. GM plant seeds and the recent banning of certain plant protection products are examples of this. These restrictions are the product of the growing influence of non-farm pressure groups, specifically environmentalists. Whatever the merits of their campaigns, the result is that, within the EU, farmers are being required to operate below the technological frontier while increasingly facing international competition from farming industries that are not so constrained.

David Cameron has not, at the time of writing, revealed the areas in which he hopes to negotiate a new relationship with the EU; but the foregoing suggests it would be futile to attempt fundamental reform of the CAP. At best, if he is so minded, he might be able to extend renationalisation to allow national governments to determine what practices and technologies farmers adopt. For example, the EU has recently given governments the power to decide – within limits – whether to plant GM crops. In principle, if the UK voted to leave the EU, fundamental reform would be possible. This, however, raises two questions. First, would the actual pace of reform in the UK be faster? And secondly, what form might it take? In 2005, the Labour government published its 'vision for the CAP' (HM Treasury 2005), in which it argued that the CAP not only imposed substantial costs on consumers and taxpayers but also was out of step with the challenges of globalisation, and a source of international criticism. According to the 'vision document', the solution was the elimination of all market support, including decoupled payments, while retaining 'targeted' payments to maintain the environment and promote sustainable rural development.

Further guidance as to UK agricultural policy in the event of Brexit is provided by the Coalition's submission to the European Commission in advance of the 2013 reform (Defra 2011). On this basis, the UK would reduce public expenditure on farming 'without interfering with the EU level playing field', but funding would continue for environmental and rural payments to farmers. The concern to preserve a level playing field is worrying. This is a key argument used by the National Farmers' Union (NFU) and its fellow lobbyists to justify the continued receipt of direct payments. The devolved administrations in Scotland, Wales and Northern Ireland are also supportive of decoupled payments, as a larger proportion of their farmers would be vulnerable by virtue of their smaller scale and more difficult geography. The erroneous argument that the loss of direct payments for UK farmers would make them less competitive within the EU holds sway with many, who perhaps should know better (House of Commons 2013a). Also, the rapid removal of decoupled payments might be thwarted if the government feared claims for compensation on the basis that investment decisions had been made on the expectation that the payments would continue for many years. That said, it seems likely that, whatever government is in power, decoupled payments would be reduced at a faster pace if the UK was freed of the need to comply with the CAP.

The speed and nature of agricultural policy reform in the UK would be subject to negotiation not only with the devolved administrations but also with the NFU, as the leader among farmers' lobbies, and non-farm pressure groups. The reaction of the environmental lobby to the 'vision document' was more positive than that of the farmers because of the expectation that expenditure on Pillar II-type environmental and rural payments would be increased. The existence of devolved administrations and powerful pressure groups suggests that there would be transitional arrangements spreading a substantial reduction, if not the complete removal, of decoupled payments over a period of years. Furthermore, the overall fall in public spending would be moderated by a significant switch to Pillar II-type measures. These are often criticised as indirect farm income support, but the government might view such expenditure – in principle aimed at improving farm efficiency and productivity – as serving to reduce opposition to cuts in decoupled payments.

In addition to reduced public funding, UK agricultural policy outside the EU would almost certainly involve a greater focus on competitiveness. Successive UK governments have argued for the removal of remaining trade barriers and the liberation of farmers in making decisions regarding their businesses. However, it is far from clear to what extent the government would remove the regulations currently imposed on farm businesses. It is difficult to conceive – particularly given the strength of the UK environmental lobbies – a significant moderation of existing EU Directives regarding pollution, e.g. nitrate and pesticide leaching, water quality, birds, habitats and animal welfare.

A more subtle but potentially significant change would be a more embracing attitude towards the frontiers of science and technology. Freed from the constraints of the CAP's voting rules, a British government is likely to be more accepting of biotechnological advances. These would include GM technology, and both farmers and manufacturers would benefit from the UK's exit from the EU's long, drawn-out, opaque system for approving new pesticide products. There is, however, a question as to how quickly British farmers would take up the more controversial technologies. Consumer attitudes would be a major influence: a recent survey showed that only 14 per cent of UK consumers are strongly opposed to GM foods, while 82 per cent were either undecided or held only mildly positive or negative opinions (IGD 2014). Experience suggests that environmental lobbies would continue to oppose the adoption of GM technologies and, more generally, larger-scale, intensive farms.

Of key importance would be the UK's post exit trade relationship with the EU. There are in principle four trade relationships that the UK could seek with the EU (House of Commons 2013a): a highly integrated option of a European Economic Area (EEA) agreement; a less conditional European Free Trade Area (EFTA) agreement; a UK specific preferential Regional Trade Agreement (RTA); or resort to a WTO most-favoured-nation (MFN) agreement. An EEA agreement would appear to offer the greatest likelihood of equivalence to existing arrangements. However, the House of Commons Foreign Affairs Committee inquiry into the UK's future relationship with the EU concluded:

> we agree with the Government that the current arrangements for relations with the EU which are maintained by Norway, as a member of the European Economic Area, or Switzerland, would not be appropriate for the UK if it were to leave the EU. (House of Commons 2013b: 9)

Agricultural trade is, in principle, excluded from EEA and EFTA agreements. It is instead covered by separate bilateral agreements, which grant limited preferential access to both sides. Presumably, the government's Plan A would be to negotiate a preferential RTA. The out campaigners assert that a satisfactory RTA could be negotiated but they provide no articulation on the details of such an agreement. However, it is doubtful whether the EU would be willing to enter into such an agreement if it did not include the four 'freedoms' involving the movement of goods, capital, services and people. These four freedoms are incorporated in the EU's treaties with the EEA and Switzerland as a member of the EFTA (House of Commons 2013a). Given the uncertainty attached to successfully negotiating a preferential RTA, voters should be clear as to Plan B before an in–out referendum. This presumably would be the adoption of WTO 'most favoured nation' tariffs. To use just one of many examples, UK exports to the EU of cheddar cheese with a minimum fat content of 50 per cent would face a tariff of €167.10 per 100 kg. As the UK has a persistent trade deficit with the EU in food and agricultural products – £16.4 billion in 2014 (Defra 2014) – this suggests that it would be in the EU's interest to reach a negotiated bilateral agreement.

The resort to WTO 'most favoured nation' agreements would leave UK exporters of agricultural products in the position of, say, US exporters today in facing non-tariff barriers of various kinds involving compliance with prevailing CAP regulations. For example, UK exports would continue to be subject to the CAP's regulations concerning maximum pesticide residues. However, in the event of the UK rapidly adopting GM crops, this is unlikely to pose a problem. The CAP's paradoxical approach is an almost complete *de facto* moratorium on growing genetically altered crops, but the same products can be imported from non-EU countries. The removal or reduction of trade barriers arising from regulations and standards lies at the heart of the Transatlantic Trade and Investment Partnership (TTIP) currently being negotiated with the US. Membership of a TTIP agreement should be a priority for an independent UK. Otherwise, regulations, particularly those addressing new products and technologies, are likely increasingly to diverge, creating additional challenges for food producers seeking to be certified as permitted to sell in both the EU and US. Finally, further uncertainty surrounds the web of regional trade agreements that the EU has with many countries. Presumably, the UK would seek to negotiate new regional trade agreements with these countries in order to continue with the EU's tariff preferences. But there might be opposition; for example, Brazil would surely protest if the UK offered tariff concessions on raw sugar to least developed countries as if it were still applying the EU's Economic Partnership Agreements.

## End piece

Following the 2013 reform, the CAP's current multifunctional structure will not change before 2020. Following the adoption by the EU of a seven-year multiannual financial framework, there is little prospect, in the absence of a serious funding crisis, of an overall reduction in the funds devoted to the CAP, specifically to a lessening in the share going to decoupled payments in the following seven years. This implies that the pace of structural change will continue at its lacklustre historic rate. Renationalisation will continue within strict limits, although it is highly probable that the EU's reticence towards biotechnological advances will wane. In the event of Brexit, UK agricultural policy reform is likely to move at a faster pace and also in a direction that gives primacy to productivity and competitiveness. Unfettered access to the single market would be a priority for the food industry in any exit negotiation, but it is impossible at this time to anticipate how successful the UK might be in this endeavour. Finally, those hoping for a rapid reduction in wasteful public expenditure on agriculture are likely to be disappointed, as powerful lobbies will bring their influence to bear to minimise cuts in payments and extend the transitional period.

## References

Brouwer, F. (2006) Main trends in agriculture. Background Note 1, August, LEI Agricultural Economics Research Institute, Wageningen.

Burgess, P. and Morris, J. (2009) Agricultural technology and land use futures: the UK case. *Land Use Policy* 26S: S222–S229.

Davidova, S., Bailey, A., Dwyer, J., Erjavec, E., Gorton, M. and Thomson, K. (2013) Semi-subsistence farming – value and directions of development. Study, April, European Parliament Committee on Agriculture and Rural Development. http://www.europarl.europa.eu/studies (accessed 7 September 2015).

Defra (2011) UK response to the Commission communication and consultation. Report, January, Department for Environment, Food & Rural Affairs, London.

Defra (2014) Overseas trade in food, feed and drink. Statistical Data Set, Department for Environment, Food & Rural Affairs, London. https://www.gov.uk/government/statistical-data-sets/overseas-trade-in-food-feed-and-drink (accessed 7 September 2015).

European Commission (2010) Developments in the income situation of the EU agricultural sector. Report, Directorate-General for Agriculture and Rural Development, European Commission, Brussels. http://ec.europa.eu/agriculture/rica/pdf/hc0301_income.pdf (accessed 7 September 2015).

European Commission (2011) Common Agricultural Policy towards 2020: assessment of alternative policy options. SEC(2011), 1153, Final/2, October, pp. 72–75, European Commission, Brussels.

European Commission (2013) Agricultural census 2010 – main results. Eurostat, European Commission. http://epp.eurostat.ec.europa.eu/statistics_explained/index.php/Agricultural_census_2010_-_main_results#Further_Eurostat_information

European Commission (2014) The Common Agricultural Policy (CAP) and agriculture in Europe – frequently asked questions. Press Release, European Commission. http://ec.europa.eu/agriculture/faq/index_en.htm#4

European Union (2006) Consolidated versions of the Treaty on European Union and of the Treaty establishing the European Community. *Official Journal of the European Union* C321 E/1, December,

Brussels. http://www.ecb.europa.eu/ecb/legal/pdf/ce32120061229
en00010331.pdf (accessed 7 September 2015).

Fernandez-Cornejo, J., Daberkow, S. and McBride, W. (2001) Decomposing the size effect on the adoption of innovations: agrobiotechnology and precision agriculture. *AgBioForum* 4(2): 124–36.

Hayes-Renshaw, F., Van Aken, W. and Wallace, H. (2006) When and why the EU Council of Ministers votes explicitly. *Journal of Common Market Studies* 44(1): 161–94.

HM Treasury (2005) A vision of the Common Agricultural Policy. Report, December, HM Treasury and Department for Environment, Food & Rural Affairs, London.

House of Commons (2013a) Leaving the EU. Library Research Paper 13/42, July, London.

House of Commons (2013b) The future of the European Union: UK government policy. First Report of Session 2013–14, Volume 1, May, Foreign Affairs Committee, London.

IGD (2014) Consumer attitudes to GM foods. Report, Institute of Grocery Distribution. http://www.igd.com/our-expertise/Shopper-Insight/ethics-and-health/4130/Consumer-Attitudes-to-GM-Foods/ (accessed 7 September 2015).

Jambor, A. and Harvey, D. (2010) CAP reform options: a challenge for analysis and synthesis. Discussion Paper Series 28, April, Centre for Rural Economy, University of Newcastle upon Tyne.

Lobell, D., Cassman, K. and Field, C. (2009) Crop yield gaps: their importance, magnitudes, and causes. *Annual Review of Environment and Resources* 34: 179–204.

Ludlow, P. (2005) The making of the CAP: towards a historical analysis of the EU's first major policy. *Contemporary European History* 14(3): 347–71.

Lund, P. and Hill, P. (1979) Farm size, efficiency and economies of size. *Journal of Agricultural Economics* 30(2): 145–58.

Martins, C. and Tosstorff, G. (2011) Large farms in Europe. Eurostat, Statistics in Focus, European Commission. http://epp.eurostat.ec.europa.eu/cache/ITY_OFFPUB/KS-SF-11-018/EN/KS-SF-11-018-EN.PDF

NFU (2013) EU farming unions unite on CAP concerns. Web Article, National Farmers' Union. http://www.nfuonline.com/news/latest -news/eu-farming-unions-unite-on-cap-concerns/

OECD (2011) Fostering productivity and competitiveness. In *Agriculture*. Paris: OECD Publishing. http://dx.doi.org/10.1787/9789264166820-en

Parsons, C. (2003) *A Certain Idea of Europe*. Ithaca, NY: Cornell University Press.

Renwick, A., Jansson, T., Verburg, P., Revoredo-Giha, C., Britz, W., Gocht, A. and McCracken, D. (2011) Policy reform and agricultural land abandonment in the EU. *Land Use Policy* 30: 446–57.

Rickard, S. and Roberts, D. (2008) UK farming post reform: the key marketing challenges. *Journal of Food and Agribusiness Marketing* 20(1): 5–27.

Rizov, M., Pokrivcak, J. and Ciaian, P. (2013) CAP subsidies and productivity of the EU farms. *Journal of Agricultural Economics* 64(3): 537–57.

Royal Society (2009) Reaping the benefits: science and the sustainable intensification of global agriculture. Policy Document RS1608, London.

Sapir, A., Aghion, P., Bertola, G., Hellwig, M., Pisani-Ferry, J., Rosati, D., Viñals, J. and Wallace, H. (2003) An agenda for a growing Europe: making the EU system deliver. Report of an Independent High Level Group, July, Brussels.

Skogstad, G. (1998) Ideas, paradigms and institutions: agricultural exceptionalism in the European Union and the United States. *Governance* 11(4): 463–90.

Viaggi, D., Bartolini, F., Raggi, M., Sardonini, L., Sammeth, F. and Gomez y Paloma, S. (2011) Farm investment behaviour under the CAP reform process. Research Paper JRC 62770, European Commission Joint Research Centre, Brussels.

Vitalis, V. (2006) Subsidy reform in the New Zealand agricultural sector. In *Subsidy Reform and Sustainable Development: Economic, Environmental and Social Aspects*. Paris: OECD Publishing.

White, J. (2003) Theory guiding practice: the neofunctionalists and the Hallstein EEC Commission. *Journal of European Integration History* 9(1): 111–31.

## 10 FREEDOM FOR FISHERIES?

Rachel Tingle

The management of maritime fish stocks and fishing poses considerable problems for policymakers of any country because of the problem long recognised by economists as the tragedy of the commons (Hardin 1968). This arises when resources are accessible to many people ('non-excludable'), but what one person uses cannot be used by anyone else ('rival'); so it is rational for each person to consume as large a share of the resource as he or she can, without heed to the consequences of everyone else acting in the same way. In the case of fisheries, this means that each fisherman will fish as intensively as possible, because prudent fishing by one fisherman to protect the stock will almost certainly only lead to larger catches by other fishermen. This results in overfishing: that is, fishing at a higher level than is sustainable biologically, referred to as the maximum sustainable yield (MSY). It leads to depletion and possible destruction of the very fish stocks on which fishermen's livelihoods depend. Economic theory suggests that the best solution to the tragedy of the commons is to make it possible to exclude people from consuming the resource by assigning property rights, but in the case of sea fisheries this is not an easy matter. For a start, there has to be an assignment of property rights over the seas, and then there has to be some way of assigning property rights (or at least 'harvesting rights')[1] over

---

1   Harvesting rights are the right to take so much of the resource over a certain period and are not normally assigned in perpetuity.

the fish swimming in these seas. Another problem arises from the fact that fish stocks can migrate over national jurisdictions, so fisheries' management requires international cooperation and a mutual recognition between nations of fishing rights awarded.

These issues would have to be faced by the UK government, or the devolved administrations, if the management of our maritime fisheries were in national hands. Since the earliest days of UK membership of the EEC/EU, however, property rights over the fish in the seas around the UK have been ceded to the Community, and almost all aspects of fisheries are managed through the European Common Fisheries Policy (CFP). For more than 30 years, aspects of the CFP have been supposed to conserve fish in EU waters; nevertheless, by 2008 the European Commission itself estimated that, of the stocks of fish for which information was available, 80 per cent were being fished above MSY, compared with a global average of 25 per cent. Worse still, 30 per cent of these EU stocks being fished beyond MSY were now outside safe biological limits, meaning that stocks might be unable to recover (COM 2008). Alongside this, the contribution of the fishing industry (fishing, fish processing and aquaculture) to EU GDP had fallen from 1 per cent in the early 1970s to less than half a percent in 2009, and the number of people engaged in the industry throughout the EU had fallen from 1.2 million in 1970 to about 400,000 in 2009 (El-Agraa 2011).[2]

This European-wide pattern of industry decline is reflected in the UK. While landings into UK ports of the free-swimming pelagic fish (such as herring and mackerel) have fluctuated considerably since 1970 and showed an overall decrease of just 19 per cent to 2013, those for the more valuable seabed demersal fish (such as cod, plaice and haddock) have been in almost continuous decline, plummeting by 81 per cent from 778,600 tonnes

---

2   This decline is even sharper than it might seem, since the 1970 figures apply to the EU15 (the countries that made up the EU before the 2004/7 enlargement), whereas the 2009 figures apply to the EU27.

to 149,000 tonnes over the same period.[3] The size of the fleet has also fallen, both in response to the economic pressures resulting from falling catches and also because of EU and UK government encouragement to decommission vessels. Numbers of vessels fell from 8,667 in 1996 to 6,399 in 2013, with a resulting reduction in terms of capacity from 274,532 gross tonnage (GT) to 200,697 GT. The number of regular and part-time fishermen has shrunk too – from 19,044 in 1996 to 12,152 in 2013, and by nearly a half since 1970 (Marine Management Organisation 2014: Tables 3.7, 2.1 and 2.6).[4] UK fish consumption is falling, but, in spite of this, the industry is unable to satisfy demand. In 2013, the UK was a net importer of 286,000 tonnes of fish, with a value of £1.3 billion, equal to roughly one-third of total UK consumer expenditure on fish (ibid.: Tables 4.5 and 4.1).

From these figures, it seems that the CFP has served the UK fishing industry very badly. This chapter looks at the history of the CFP to try to understand why this should be. This is quite complex, but it falls fairly clearly into six time periods.

## 1957–69: the conception and early development of the CFP

Common European policies on fishing have their origins in the 1957 Treaty of Rome, which stated that there should be a common agricultural policy (the CAP) and, almost accidentally, defined agriculture to include the products of fisheries.[5] Initially, however, little attention was given to fisheries management.

---

3   These figures include landings into UK ports by non-UK-owned vessels and exclude landings by UK-owned vessels into non-UK ports. For more details, see Marine Management Organisation (2014).

4   Whilst the number of part-time fishermen continues to fall, there has, however, been a small increase in the number of regular fishermen since 2011.

5   For full details of the legal basis for the EEC/EU competence over fisheries and fish products, and how this has been amended by treaty changes over the years, see Churchill and Owen (2010).

But the development from 1962 onwards of a common market in fish (which entailed the removal of EEC internal barriers to trade and the implementation of a common external tariff) had implications for the six individual member states. In particular, France and Italy, who both had fairly inefficient fishing sectors previously protected by high import tariffs, were faced with steeply rising fish imports. These threatened domestic producers' profitability and, as a result, their governments began to agitate for a CFP that would include a structural fund to provide aid to enable the modernisation of their fishing fleets. Not much was done, however, until 1970, when the application to join the EEC of the UK and three other nations (Norway, Denmark and Ireland) with either big fishing industries or significant coastlines[6] led to a scramble to establish an *acquis communautaire* (body of Community law) in the area of fishing, which the new accession nations would have to accept if they were to join.

## 1970–82: the establishment of common Community waters

On 30 June 1970, on the eve of the formal accession negotiations, the EEC Council of Ministers hurriedly agreed two Regulations, which formed the basis of the first fully-fledged CFP. Council Regulation 2142/70 established the common organisation of fisheries markets, encouraging fishermen to band together to form Producers' Organisations (POs) that would centralise market supply in major centres and oversee quality and marketing. It also set up a market intervention system with the aim of establishing price floors for fish, similar to the price-support system of the CAP. The other Regulation (2141/70) met demands for structural aid for the industry by providing access to the European Agricultural

---

6  Ireland has a long coastline and thus had potential legal claims to sovereignty over a large area of sea, but at that time it had a relatively small fishing industry.

Guidance and Guarantee Fund (EAGGF) for funds to modernise fishing fleets. Most significantly, however, it established the principle of *equal access* to fishing grounds, thereby giving boats registered in one member state the same access to the maritime fishing grounds of any other member state as boats registered in that state. It meant that the EEC member states would no longer have control over their own fishing grounds. Rather, fishing waters would be a common Community resource, open to exploitation by all member states. This posed obvious dangers of increased overfishing, particularly as the initial proposals contained no conservation measures for fish stocks.[7] Largely because of fears about the potential cost of this to their fishing industry, the Norwegians decided in a referendum in 1972 (and again in 1994) not to join the Community after all.[8]

At the time Regulation 2141/70 was adopted, national sovereignty over fishing waters in Europe was largely governed by the 1964 European Fisheries Convention, which had given coastal states sovereignty over waters twelve nautical miles (nm) out to sea from their 'baselines'.[9] These 12 miles were divided into a 0–6 nm zone in which the coastal state had exclusive fishing rights, and a less exclusive 6–12 nm zone in which those foreign states that had 'habitually fished' in this zone between 1953 and 1962 could also fish in the same areas, roughly at the same rate as they had previously. Outside these zones lay the high seas over which no nation had exclusive fishing rights. Initially, then, the EEC equal access principle legally applied only to the 12-mile zones, and, because of huge resistance from the accession

---

7 At the last minute, a bland supplementary preamble was added to Regulation 2142/70, simply stating that 'implementation of the common organization must also take account of the fact that it is in the Community interest to preserve fishing grounds as far as possible'.

8 It was also one of the main reasons why Greenland, having gained autonomy from Denmark, withdrew from the EEC in 1985.

9 The low-water mark on the shore, or, in the case of bays, a straight line drawn across the bay.

nations and particularly their concerns about conservation of stocks, it was eventually agreed that this right should be partially derogated (put off) for a transitional ten-year period until 1983, when it would be reviewed again. During this period, equal access would not be allowed in the 0–6 nm zone, or in those parts of the 12 nm zone where it was deemed that coastal communities were especially dependent upon fishing.[10] In the 1983 reforms of the CFP, this derogation was extended to the full 12-mile zone, as a means of protecting coastal communities. Ironically, because of the recognition that there was better fish conservation in these waters, this derogation was renewed again in 2003 and, most recently, in the 2013 CFP reform.[11] Because of this, the UK still largely retains exclusive national fishing rights in 'inshore' waters, but this does not exclude these waters from other aspects of CFP regulation;[12] nor does it mean that these waters are legally safe from the equal access principle, which will be reviewed again in 2022.

The principle of equal access is, however, of great significance beyond the UK's inshore waters. By the 1970s, some coastal nations had extended their property rights over marine resources up to 200 nm from their baseline,[13] and, although this was not fully legalised until the 1982 UN Convention on the Law of the Sea, it was already clear by the mid-1970s that such 200 mile exclusive economic zones (EEZs) would almost certainly be upheld in international law. Iceland established a 200 nm EEZ in 1975, followed by the US, Canada and Norway in 1977. This had profound

---

10  Negotiations on that principle eventually excluded about one-third of the British coastline from equal access, although the historic rights of other member states to fish in these areas remained as before.

11  See Regulation (EU) Number 1830/2013, Preamble (19).

12  For instance, since conservation measures are an exclusive EU competence, member states must get agreement for any conservation measures they make in their inland waters.

13  Or, where the coastlines of two nations are closer than 400 nm, to the median point between them.

consequences for Northern European fisheries, especially the UK distant-water fleets, based in Scotland and North East England, which had traditionally fished in these waters, and which, from then on, would only be able to do so by negotiation and at reduced levels.[14] So, this trend towards 200 nm EEZs meant a significant diversion of fishing effort, not only by Community fishing fleets but also by similarly affected third-party states, into the northern waters around the EEC.

In 1976, responding to this perceived double threat on fish stocks, the EEC agreed that member states with coastlines bordering the North Sea and the North Atlantic should themselves simultaneously adopt 200 nm fishing zones on 1 January 1977. This was done by national legislation in each member state: in the case of the UK, by the Fishing Limits Act 1976.[15] Because of the equal access provision, however, this essentially extended EEC property rights over a vast area of sea.[16] Since by that time it was becoming obvious that many European fish stocks were overfished, two crucial questions immediately presented themselves: firstly, how to limit catches so that stocks might be conserved, and, secondly, how to allocate these limited fishing opportunities between the member states. A related important third issue was how to shrink the capacity of the Community fishing fleet (both in terms of tonnage and engine power), which was now recognised as being too large in relation to the fishing opportunities – a problem that had actually been made worse by the provision of European structural funds to modernise the fleet.

---

14  The negotiating text drafted at the conclusion of the third session of the UN Conference on the Law of the Sea (UNCLOS) in 1975 laid down that a coastal state would only be obliged to grant other states access to exploit the proportion of the available fish catch it was unable or unwilling to catch itself.

15  In fact, the UK would have created a 200-mile fishing zone unilaterally if need be: see Hansard, 20 October,1976, Col. 1459.

16  Fishing limits were also later extended in the West Atlantic, the Skagerrak and Kattegat and the Baltic, but not in the Mediterranean.

## 1983–92: the development of a fisheries management system

Given how much was at stake, it is perhaps not surprising that it took more than six years of squabbling between the nine member states to come to any agreement as to what should be done. Eventually, however, the EEC worked its way to a more comprehensive CFP, adopted in 1983, which defined the objectives of the new system as being to 'ensure the protection of fishing grounds, the conservation of the biological resources of the sea and their balanced exploitation on a lasting basis and in appropriate economic and social conditions' (Council 1983a). The main means for attempting to do this would be via the setting of an annual Total Allowable Catch (TAC) for each of the main commercial fish stocks.[17] This was to be formulated initially by the Commission in the light of available scientific advice,[18] and agreed by the Council of (fishery) Ministers. These TACs would then be divided into *national* quotas for each fish stock. The Regulation also gave the EEC the legal powers to introduce other 'technical' conservation measures, which included such things as closing areas of the sea to fishing at certain times of the year to protect spawning and immature fish; restrictions on the use of fishing gear, such as the type of nets used; and the minimum size of fish that could be landed.

To ensure all this was implemented, the CFP introduced control measures to police the system: these required all EEC skippers of boats over 10 metres to maintain standardised logbooks in which to record details of their catch; all member states to establish an inspectorate to check on fish landings; and the

---

17  That is, fish species in certain defined areas of the sea – thus, sole in different areas of the North Sea, for example, are regarded as different fish stocks from those off the West Coast of Scotland.

18  The basic Regulation also provided for the establishment of a Scientific and Technical Committee for Fisheries, now the Scientific, Technical and Economic Committee for Fisheries (STECF), in order to provide this information.

setting up of a small multinational team of fisheries inspectors (originally thirteen, now 25) within the Commission to run spot checks on the national procedures.

Clearly, so far as the UK was concerned, the most important aspect of the policy was how the division of TACs into national quotas would be made.[19] The 1983 'basic Regulation' 170/83 stated that this should be on the principle of 'relative stability', which meant that the proportional share of the catch of each fish stock taken by any EEC member state should stay roughly the same (Council 1983a). After intense negotiations, it was decided this would be based on the average of past catches in the reference period 1973–8, with some adjustment under the so-called Hague Preferences to give preferential treatment to regions particularly dependent upon fishing (some northern parts of the UK, Greenland and Ireland) and reflect the loss of catches by distant-water fleets as a result of the introduction of the 200-mile fishing zones by Norway and Iceland. Because of this, the relative stability principle has had a huge part to play in determining the fortunes of national fishing industries. In the case of the UK, in spite of our having contributed around 62 per cent of the waters of the 'common community pond', because so much British fishing during the reference period had been in distant waters, it ended up with a quota of just 37 per cent of the Community total by weight, and, because it was skewed heavily towards lower value fish, only 13 per cent in cash terms (Booker and North 2005).[20]

In spite of these measures, however, it was clear by the beginning of the 1990s that the CFP was failing in its management of

---

19 The very important related issue of how to divide a nation's quota amongst national fishermen was left for each member state to decide, and, over the years, quite different methods have emerged. For the present UK method, see the appendix to this chapter.

20 Similarly, Ireland, with an underdeveloped fishing industry in the 1970s, ended up with a quota amounting to a mere 4.4 per cent of the total. See Booker and North (2005: 251).

fish stocks. Four main problems can be identified, all largely the product of the tragedy of the commons playing itself out in new ways. In spite of reforms, these problems have been a feature of the CFP ever since. The first was the fact that effective implementation depended on fishermen's compliance with technical conservation measures, their keeping of accurate details of fish catches and landings[21] and determined monitoring and policing of the system by member states, including halting the catch of particular fish stocks once national quota limits had been reached. Since it was in the economic interest of both fishermen and member states not to comply, many did not, particularly as at that time virtually no penalties were imposed on member states breaching their quota allocation or failing to comply with technical conservation measures.

A second problem was that the TACs were set at too high a level. There were two reasons for this. First, in advising on TACs, the Commission lacked accurate data on fish catches (and therefore fish stocks), and it also had inadequate scientific advice. Second, in the Council meetings, fishery ministers regularly pushed TACs to levels above those advised by the Commission in order to avoid their own national quotas from being cut. In effect, it was the fisheries ministers who were contributing to the problem of the Commons, rather than the fishermen themselves.

The third major problem was the fact that TAC limits attempt to control fish *landings*, not the number of fish *caught*, including those discarded (usually dead) back into the sea. This practice of discarding arises for many reasons, including juvenile fish being caught under the specified legal landing size; legal but smallish fish being discarded in favour of higher-value larger fish, a practice known as 'high-grading'; and, in mixed fisheries, species of fish being caught as a 'by-catch' to the main target fish and being considered uneconomic to land, or there being no available quota for them.

---

21 Including in non-EEC ports, and offloading at sea into other vessels.

The fourth problem was that, in spite of an awareness that the size of the Community fishing fleet needed to correspond to fishing opportunities, the structural arm of the CFP was still providing funds for 'economically appropriate expansion' and modernisation of the fishing industry. This provided for subsidies from the EAGGF of 35–50 per cent of the costs of such investment (Council 1983b). From 1987 onwards, targets in the form of multiannual guidance programmes (MAGPs) were introduced to reduce fleet tonnage and engine power (Council 1986, 1990). However, as with the TACs, the Council set these at levels above those advised by the Commission. The result of this was that, over the period 1983 to 1991, fishing capacity actually *increased*, providing a strong economic incentive to continue to fish above quota.

All these problems were exacerbated by the entry of Portugal and, more especially, Spain into the EEC in 1986. At that time, Spanish fishermen had a fleet approximately three-quarters of the size by tonnage of the total of all the other EEC members. However, they added little to Community fish stocks, as their destructive fishing methods had virtually exhausted their own waters. To avoid Spain's complete disruption of the CFP, complex transitional arrangements were put in place, under which only a limited number of Spanish vessels would be allowed access to Community fishing grounds, and then not before 1 January 1995. It was planned that full integration would only take place in 2003. In return for this delay, Spain was given substantial aid from the EAGGF. This was supposedly to reduce the size of the fleet, but much of it was actually used to modernise boats and, hence, increase their fishing capacity. Spain also circumvented the interim ban from wider Community waters by 'quota-hopping': that is, setting up fishing businesses in other EEC countries, particularly the UK, and so qualifying for a share of those countries' quotas – a legal practice under the 'right of establishment' Community rules, even though the boats might be manned by

Spanish fishermen and the fish caught landed in Spain.[22] In any case, faced with a Spanish threat to veto the 1995 EU enlargement (when Sweden, Finland and Austria joined), from 1996 the Spanish fleet was allowed equal access to EU waters, so putting further pressure on fish stocks.

## 1993–2002: the introduction of vessel licensing and effort controls

In 1993, reforms of the CFP were introduced. These included multiannual plans for fisheries management, in the hope that these would avoid dramatic variations in TACs, and so allow the industry to plan ahead better; mandatory licensing of all Community fishing vessels; and regulation of fishing 'effort'[23] instead of, or in addition to, the TAC limits. None of this did much to improve fish conservation or the economic health of the fisheries sector. As the Commission's Green Paper (COM 2001) noted, there had been limited progress in adopting multiannual approaches. Effort management had proved unsuccessful, largely because it too was subject to bargaining by the fisheries ministers within the Council,[24] who continued to systematically fix both TACs and MAGPs above levels proposed by the Commission. In addition, there remained considerable variations between member states in the enforcement of the system and the imposition of penalties for infringement.

---

22  In spite of the requirement introduced in 1999 that British registered fishing vessels over 10 metres in length and landing over 2 tonnes of quota stocks annually must demonstrate an economic link with fishing communities in the UK, numerous vessels fishing against UK quota are part- or wholly owned by non-UK citizens.

23  That is, the product of the capacity of a fishing vessel and its activity, normally expressed in terms of days allowed at sea.

24  One of the constant criticisms made by the industry about effort management is that it has introduced yet more complex regulatory micromanagement into the system. And, because of the numerous derogations negotiated in Council, it has so far proved to be a very ineffective conservation measure.

Excess fleet capacity was a significant problem, particularly as structural aid, provided since 1994 under the Financial Instrument for Fisheries Guidance (FIFG), continued to enable fleet modernisation; this, because of 'technological creep' through improved fishing gear, was increasing the ability to harvest fish more than just fleet tonnage and engine power might suggest. Because of all this, many fish stocks, particularly demersal species such as cod, hake and whiting, were on average 90 per cent lower in the late 1990s than they had been in the early 1970s. They were now outside safe biological limits. At the same time, much of the fisheries sector was characterised by poor profitability and steadily declining employment, with jobs in fish catching, for instance, declining by 22 per cent overall in the period 1990–98 (COM 2002).

## 2003–13: reform of the CFP

As the 2002 Green Paper shows, the staff at the Commission seem to have long recognised the problems in the workings of the CFP (many of which continued to stem from the competing interests between EU member states, and the inability of some member states to take the need for conservation measures seriously). But they have been fairly helpless to do anything about them. The Commission held extensive consultations with stakeholders in the industry over the period 1998–2002; in response to their deep dissatisfaction with the system, the Council adopted yet another new basic CFP Regulation, which came into force at the beginning of 2003 (Council 2002). The main aspects of this were the following.

- The adoption of multiannual management or *recovery* plans for selected fish stocks (the latter, involving stocks deemed to be outside safe biological limits, might involve the closing of sea zones to fishing for periods of time).

- The replacement of MAGPs with an 'entry/exit' regime, whereby any new fishing capacity created with or without the use of EU public money should be matched with the withdrawal of at least the same amount of capacity.
- The introduction of tighter measures of control and enforcement. This included the installation of satellite-based monitoring systems on board all larger fishing vessels;[25] that fish could only be sold from a fishing vessel to registered buyers or at registered auctions (to help stamp out demand for 'black' or illegal non-quota fish); and tougher sanctions against infringements of the CFP, to be applied both by member states against fishermen, and by the EU Commission against member states. It also allowed for a greater degree of cooperation between member states on enforcement matters, which led to the creation of a Community Fisheries and Control Agency (CFCA), operational since 2007.
- The establishment of a Community Fleet Register (CFR), which means the Commission now holds regularly updated details on all commercial fishing boats, each of which is assigned a unique CFR number, so aiding control and enforcement and the entry/exit regime.
- The establishment of Regional Advisory Councils (RACs) to feed stakeholder advice to the Commission. These would cover distinct fishing zones and be made up primarily of representatives of the fisheries sector, but they would also include other interested parties, such as environmental groups.

By 2008, six RACs had been set up. They were generally considered a success, enabling much greater input from those with

---

25 The requirement applied to vessels longer than 18 metres as from January 2004, and to vessels longer than 15 metres as from January 2005 (Council 2002: Article 22).

detailed knowledge of local fishing conditions into the distant Brussels-based policymaking process. Other aspects of reform, however, failed. As far as the policy of multiannual management of fisheries was concerned, by 2008 only four recovery plans and four management plans had been adopted, and annual TACs (by this time set for around 130 commercial fish stocks) continued to be the main instrument of fisheries management. These were still being set on average about 48 per cent higher than MSY (COM 2008: 331). An added problem was that, even when scientific evidence pointed to the need for big reductions, existing EU rules meant TACs could not be reduced (or increased when stocks were recovering) by more than 15 per cent per annum. Crucially, too, member states had lacked the political will to speed up a reduction in fishing capacity: this continued to fall at roughly the same annual rate of between 2 and 3 per cent that it had over the previous decade. Even this small reduction was broadly offset by technological progress in fishing efficiency – some estimates put fishing overcapacity throughout the EU in 2008 at 40–50 per cent (House of Lords 2008: 23, 28).

This problem of overcapacity was made much worse by the continued misuse of the EU Structural Fund, supposedly mainly intended to aid vessel decommissioning or alternative employment for fishing communities. Of the €3.2 billion provided by the FIFG between 2000 and 2006, approximately €1.5 billion went to Spain (three and a half times the total sum given to the UK, Germany and Poland combined). Spain used 60 per cent of this for vessel construction and modernisation, thereby further increasing the size and power of the Spanish fleet (Poseidon Aquatic Resource Management 2010).[26] Finally, a damning report by

---

26 The FIFG was replaced in 2007 by the European Fisheries Fund, which provided financial assistance to the European fisheries sector of €4.3 billion over the period 2007–13, €1.12 billion of which went to Spain, compared with €134 million to the UK (COM 2014). The EFF has now been replaced by the European Maritime and Fisheries Fund (EMFF), which is planned to provide €5.7 billion over the period

the European Court of Auditors in 2007 found that the system of control, inspection and sanctions remained inadequate: catch data was neither complete nor reliable, the inspection system remained poor and few infringements were followed up with penalties sufficient to act as a deterrent. The report found the failure of the system was greatest in Spain, where, for example, quota monitoring ignored the catches by vessels under 10 metres in length, even though such vessels accounted for 67 per cent of the fleet. As the European Union Committee of the UK's House of Lords concluded in its extensive 2008 report:

> on most indicators the 2002 reform of the Common Fisheries Policy has failed: overcapacity in the fishing fleets of the Member States, poor compliance, uneven enforcement, and a stiflingly prescriptive legislative process all persist, while fish stocks remain depleted (House of Lords 2008: 6).

In more recent years, however, there have been small signs of improvement in conservation. By 2009, about 41 per cent of pelagic fish and 29 per cent of demersal fish were being managed under long-term management plans, and these enabled annual TACs to be varied by up to 30 per cent. The TACs were also being set slightly closer to the scientific advice, though they were still well above MSY. New monitoring and control procedures had been put in place, including better data collection and wider implementation of electronic logbooks, enabling real-time catch recordings (Council 2009). By 2010, it appeared that some fish stocks in the North East Atlantic were recovering, and by 2012 the percentage of stocks overfished in these waters had fallen from 94 per cent in 2005 to 47 per cent. It is notable, however, that 75 per cent of the stock in the Mediterranean remains overfished (COM 2013).

---

2014–20, over one-fifth of which will go to Spain, compared with 4.6 per cent to the UK. For details, see http://ec.europa.eu/fisheries/cfp/emff/index_en.htm (accessed 14 September 2015).

In 2009, the Commission published yet another Green Paper (COM 2009) inviting further debate on the ways the CFP might be much more radically reformed.[27] One of the most notable aspects of this was the Commission's recognition of the very poor economic health of the EU fisheries sector (in several member states, the cost of fishing to the public budget in terms of national and EU aid actually exceeded the total value of the fish caught) and, in an attempt to improve this, its desire to see fishing opportunities set at levels that could restore stocks to MSY (COM 2009: 7).[28] The other urgent and related[29] matter was to reduce discards. There are hugely varying estimates of how bad discarding under the CFP has been, but a paper produced by the Commission in 2007 estimated that, for the period 2003–5, discard rates were running at 20–60 per cent of the catch weight for typical fisheries exploiting demersal fish. Between 1990 and 2000, in the North Sea alone, it was estimated that around 500,000–880,000 tonnes of fish were discarded annually (COM 2007).[30] Another estimate by NUFTA[31] and Greenpeace (2008) suggested that around 1.3 million tonnes of fish were being discarded annually in the North East Atlantic. The Commission itself was keen to see an

---

27  For a detailed UK parliamentary discussion of the proposed reforms, see House of Commons (2010–12).

28  The other reason for this policy was that, at the 2002 World Summit on Sustainable Development, the EU had pledged to set fishing opportunities within MSY by 2015.

29  If stocks are fished beyond MSY, there are more likely to be fewer large mature fish, so more discards through 'high-grading' may take place.

30  The EU's STECF has systematically been collecting data under the data collection Regulation 1543/2000 (now the more stringent Regulation 199/2008) since 2002; the 2003–5 discard rate is based on these figures. However, they did not then have data for all sea areas; earlier figures are from the UN's Food and Agriculture Organisation (FAO).

31  NUFTA, the 'New Under Ten Fishermen's Association', is a UK campaigning organisation representing commercial fishermen with boats less than 10 metres in length and/or not belonging to the large fish Producer Organisations, which are referred to as 'the Sector'. Most of the UK's pelagic and demersal fish are caught by the Sector; about half the shellfish are caught by the 'under 10s'.

end to discards, and by 2011 there was mounting public pressure, particularly in the UK, for an immediate end to the practice.[32] This demand was eventually supported by Maria Damanaki, the EU Commissioner for Maritime Affairs and Fish, but it was opposed in the June 2012 Council meeting by a number of fisheries ministers, including the French and Spanish.

## 2014 onwards: last chance for the CFP?

Eventually, a compromise on discards was reached and enshrined in the December 2013 CFP new basic Regulation (COM and Parliament 1380/2013). This came into force at the beginning of 2014. The key aspects of these new proposals are the following.

- From 2015 onwards, starting with pelagic fish, a ban on discards is being gradually introduced on a fishery-by-fishery basis. This is referred to as the 'landing obligation' and means that, by 2019, all fish subject to quota will have to be landed and will count against quota; small fish below 'minimum conservation size' will not be allowed to be sold for human consumption. TACs may be raised slightly to take account of the fact that fish will no longer be discarded, and, because of possible greater demands on quota, the ability of member states to 'bank and borrow' against subsequent years' quotas is to be increased from 5 per cent to 10 per cent.[33]
- A legal commitment that exploitation rates within MSY should be achieved by 2015 where possible, and by 2020 at the latest, for all fish stocks.

---

32 Spearheaded by the celebrity chef Hugh Fearnley-Whittingstall and his 'Fish-Fight' campaign, which is estimated to have attracted 700,000 supporters.

33 There will be money available from the EMFF, the new fisheries structural fund set up in 2014, to facilitate the discard ban by, for example, enabling vessels to install new gear to reduce by-catches, and enabling Fish Producer Organisations (FPOs) to fund marketing campaigns to promote the consumption of lesser-known fish.

- A renewed commitment to the management of fish stocks under multiannual plans, which will be based on MSY targets and include conservation measures where necessary.
- A proposed new form of regional government, whereby member states with a direct interest in a fishery shall, in consultation with the RACs (renamed Advisory Councils), make joint recommendations to the Commission. The role of the Advisory Councils will also be strengthened, and four new ones will be established.
- Member states will be required to produce and publish an annual report on the capacity of their fleet, including whether there is any structural overcapacity. If there is, they will be required to produce an action plan with a clear timetable setting out how this will be addressed.

These changes to the CFP are significant, but the fact that the implementation dates for both the ban on discards and the requirement to fish within MSY have been delayed because of protests from some fisheries ministers could have serious consequences. The World Wide Fund for Nature (WWF) has argued, for instance, that the delay until 2020 in fully implementing fishing at MSY may be too late to save some fish stocks (WWF 2013).

Other problems remain: for instance, the regionalisation proposal is not truly one of subsidiarity, delegating decision-making powers down to the member states and relevant stakeholders, but maintains, and might even increase, the involvement of the Brussels bureaucracy (see House of Commons 2010–12: 9–13). In addition, since obligations under the Lisbon Treaty, which came into force in 2013, mean that CFP legislation now has to be agreed by both the Council of the EU *and* the European Parliament, legislative procedures surrounding the CFP may be even more cumbersome than, and as prone to competing national self-interest as, they have been to date. Indeed, it is not clear how the central problem of the CFP, the infighting to secure the highest possible

TAC for individual member states, has been overcome. So, there is no assurance that this latest reform, welcome though it is, will serve what remains of the UK fishing industry any better than the previous CFP has over the last 40 years.

It is difficult to avoid the conclusion that the UK would have done better to retain national control over its fisheries as, for example, Norway, Greenland and Iceland have done. Withdrawal from the CFP is almost certainly not an option whilst the UK remains a member of the EU. But if it were to choose to leave, then the UK could immediately rescind the EU's equal access principle over fishing waters and take control of the complete UK 200 nm zone, at the same time regaining complete sovereignty over inshore waters. With property rights firmly vested with the UK's own national government, fisheries management could then be carried out according to the long-term interest of UK nationals, taking on board the lessons learnt from the CFP and fisheries management systems in other parts of the world. The UK government already has in place its own detailed system for allocating national quotas (at present set by the EU) amongst competing UK fishermen. It also has a system of policing these harvesting rights[34] and for quite rigorously regulating the capacity of the industry (see the appendix to this chapter). In the short term, this system could easily be continued, the only crucial difference being that overall national quotas for each fish stock in UK waters would now be determined solely by the UK itself, based on best national and international scientific advice, rather than through bargaining by the fisheries ministers within Council of the EU meetings. It would also be national (rather than essentially European Commission) policy to determine the best conservation measures. In addition, it would be up to the UK government to decide on what terms (if at all) it wished to

---

34 Although inshore fishermen in Devon admit policing needs to be tighter and more patrol vessels are needed (author's discussions).

continue to allow fishing businesses owned by non-UK nationals to have access to UK harvesting rights. At present, for instance, 23 per cent of the English fishing quota is allocated to one giant Dutch-owned fishing vessel, the *Cornelis Vrolijk*, which lands its entire catch in the Netherlands (Greenpeace 2014).

Management of fisheries could be conducted at the most appropriate ecological unit for the fish stock concerned: probably sea basins (such as the North Sea, the Irish Sea, the Celtic Sea and the English Channel) for most demersal species, and larger areas for migratory pelagic fish, with the UK entering into bilateral arrangements over fish management and conservation with the EU or other nation states as appropriate, as Iceland, Greenland and Norway do at present.[35] Over the longer term, the UK might follow the examples of New Zealand and Iceland and experiment with ways of making the quota allocated to individual fishing vessels more fully tradable than it is at present (Gissurarson 2000; OECD 2011).[36] Both of these nations seem to have been far more successful in managing their fisheries than has the EU.

## Appendix: the UK system for apportioning national fishing quotas

The UK divides the national quota it is allocated for each fish stock subject to TAC between *groups* of licensed fishing vessels largely on the basis of fixed quota allocation (FQA) units. These are abstract units of measurement based on vessels' historic share of national landings of this fish stock, usually the period

---

35 Norway, for instance, shares 90 per cent of its fisheries' harvest stocks with other nations, so national TACs are set in cooperation with Russia, Iceland, the Faroe Islands, Greenland and the EU.

36 In fact, as the method of allocating a national quota between fishermen is a national rather than an EU competence, there is nothing to stop the UK at present from making quota more fully tradeable between its fishermen. Individual EU member states have experimented with a variety of 'rights-based' quota management schemes (COM 2007).

1994–6. Essentially, they are a right to harvest fish. For vessels over 10 metres long, these FQAs are assigned to individual vessels' licences; for those under 10 metres, they are held as a block by the four fisheries administrations (see below). *The FQA units are not fixed allocations of quota to the vessel in question: they are used as a mechanism for allocating the quota.*

The UK government first divides the quota for each fish stock between the four devolved fisheries administrations (FAs): DEFRA/ The Marine Management Organisation (England), Marine Scotland, The Welsh Government, and the Department of Agriculture and Rural Development (Northern Ireland). This is largely on the basis of the share of the UK FQA units held by the vessels registered with each of the FAs. Each FA has discretion as to how it allocates its share of the quota, but for England it is roughly as follows.

1. The total quota is apportioned between three groups:
   (a) 'The Sector' (vessels that are members of one of the 23 UK Producer Organisations).
   (b) The non-Sector pool (vessels over 10 metres that are not members of, or assigned to, a PO).
   (c) The 10-metres-and-under pool (the 'inshore fleet', vessels under 10 metres that are not members of a PO).
   For groups (a) and (b), this apportionment is on the basis of the FQA units assigned to vessels in the group; for group (c), it is based on the relative proportion of landings by this group in the period 2008–12. About 95 per cent of the UK's fishing quota is held by the Sector. Because of concern about the need to sustain the 78 per cent of the UK fishing vessels that make up the inshore fleet, are vital for local communities and which also practice the most sustainable fishing, there is now an 'underpinning' arrangement to top up the quota allocation of the 10-metres-and-under fleet to a guaranteed minimum level. Many consider this to be inadequate

and think that the underpinning arrangements need to be amended so as to provide more of the quota to smaller vessels.

2. The management of quota within these three groups is as follows:

    (a) POs are responsible for managing their own quota allocations and making sure they are not exceeded. Some set monthly catch limits; others issue annual vessel or company quotas.

    (b) Quota allocations for the non-Sector pool and the 10-metres-and-under fleet are managed by the fisheries administrations. Each vessel's licence sets out the stocks that the vessel is not permitted to fish. For the non-POs, it also sets out monthly catch limits for the stocks the vessel is able to fish and land, which may be varied during the year as the national quota limit is reached. Apart from fish stock under particular pressure, where monthly catch limits may also be set, individual vessels in the under-10-metre fleet are generally allowed to fish without restriction until the overall quota allocation for the group has been taken in full, but this may be varied within the year.

Very limited markets operate within this system.

1. Since, in order to control the size of the UK fleet, no new fishing licences are currently created, in order to licence a vessel for the first time, an old licence (referred to as a 'licence entitlement') sufficient to cover the size and power of the boat, and the type of fishing required, has to be bought from previous licence holders removing their vessels from the fishing fleet.

2. The FQA units attached to old licences may be traded separately.

3. Subject to various rules, some annual quota swapping, or 'quota leasing', can take place. The UK as a whole can swap its quota with another EU member state. The FAs can also swap their quotas between themselves and with other EU member states, as well as negotiate quota swaps for all three groups between themselves, with the other two groups or with another EU member state.

## References

Booker, C. and North, R. (2005) *The Great Deception*. London: Continuum.

Churchill, R. and Owen, D. (2010) *The EEC Common Fisheries Policy*. Oxford University Press.

COM (1991) Report from the Commission to the Council and European Parliament on the Common Fisheries Policy. SEC (91) 2288, European Commission.

COM (2001) Green paper on the future of the Common Fisheries Policy. COM/2001/0135, European Commission.

COM (2002) Communication from the Commission on the reform of the Common Fisheries Policy. COM/2002/0181, European Commission.

COM (2007) An analysis of existing Rights-Based Management instruments in Member States. FISH/2007/03, European Commission.

COM (2008) Reflections on further reform of the Common Fisheries Policy. Working Document, European Commission.

COM (2009) Reform of the Common Fisheries Policy. Green Paper COM(2009) 163, European Commission.

COM (2013) Communication from the Commission concerning a consultation on fishing opportunities for the year 2014. COM(2013) 319, European Commission.

COM (2014) Seventh Annual Report of the Implementation of the European Fisheries Fund. COM(2014) 738, European Commission.

COM and Parliament (2013) Regulation (EU) 1380/2013.

Council (1983a) Council Regulation (EEC) 170/83.

Council (1983b) Council Regulation (EEC) 2908/83.

Council (1986) Council Regulation (EEC) 4028/86.

Council (1990) Council Regulation (EEC) 3944/90.

Council (1992) Regulation (EEC) 3760/92.

Council (2002) Regulation (EC) 2371/2002.

Council (2009) Regulation (EC) 1224/2009.

Council and Parliament (2014) Regulation (EU) 1380/2013 of 11 December 2013.

El-Agraa, A. (2011) *The European Union.* Cambridge University Press.

European Court of Auditors (2007) Special Report No. 7/2007.

Gissurarson, H. (2000) *Overfishing: The Icelandic Solution.* London: Institute of Economic Affairs.

Greenpeace (2014) Our net gain. Blog Post, *Greenpeace.* http://www.greenpeace.org.uk/blog/oceans/our-net-gain-20141118 (accessed 14 September 2015).

Hardin, G. (1968) The tragedy of the commons. *Science* 162: 1243–8.

House of Commons (2010–12) Environment, Food and Rural Affairs Committee. EU proposals for reform of the Common Fisheries Policy, Volumes 1–3.

House of Lords (2008) The progress of the Common Fisheries Policy. HL Paper 146-1.

MMO (2014) UK Sea Fisheries Annual Statistics Report 2013. Marine Management Organisation.

OECD (2011) Fisheries Policy Reform: National experiences. Report, Organisation for Economic Co-operation and Development.

Poseidon Aquatic Resource Management (2010) FIFG 2000–2006 Shadow Evaluation. Final Report for Pew Environment Group.

Wise, M. (1984) *The Common Fisheries Policy of the European Community.* London: Methuen.

WWF (2013) Recovery of European fish stocks and the Reform of the Common Fisheries Policy. Analysis, World Wildlife Fund.

# 11 STUCK IN BRUSSELS: SHOULD TRANSPORT POLICY BE DETERMINED AT EU LEVEL?

Kristian Niemietz and Richard Wellings

## Introduction

EU policy has a substantial impact on the transport sectors of member states. While transport policy debates are typically framed at national level, in reality the choices available to policymakers are tightly constrained by decisions made within EU institutions. Strategic objectives are increasingly determined by the European Commission's Directorate-General for Mobility and Transport,[1] the Directorate-General for Regional and Urban Policy and other Commission bodies, before being approved or rejected by the European Parliament and the Council of Europe.

The exact process is more complex, with the Commission consulting with interested parties and representatives of member states before adopting a particular policy. The Parliament and Council may also suggest changes to legislation. Moreover, EU transport policy intersects with various international agreements involving non-EU parties, for example, the 'Open Skies' arrangement with the US, and free-trade treaties more generally. Member states also have a degree of flexibility in their implementation of EU requirements. Policy processes within the EU therefore appear to exhibit a significant degree of pluralism, together

---

1 For an introduction, see http://ec.europa.eu/transport/about-us/index_en.htm (accessed 7 September 2015).

with checks and balances. However, as Vaubel (2009, and Chapter 3 of this volume) has pointed out, it is clear that the European institutions have a vested interest in the greater centralisation of powers because this enhances their power and prestige. This tendency is evident in transport, as in other sectors. Indeed, the policy process in general is heavily politicised and clearly very far removed from a classical liberal approach, under which resource allocation and other decisions would typically be made by non-state actors engaging in voluntary exchange within a framework of general rules.

This chapter summarises the key policies imposed across the Union and examines their economic impact. The final section considers the extent to which transport policy should be determined by supranational bodies rather than smaller administrative units.

## The aims of EU transport policy

The main objectives of EU transport policy can be placed into two broad categories.[2] The first aim is to increase economic and social cohesion by improving transport links in order to reduce barriers to trade and address the locational disadvantages of relatively poor and peripheral regions. A further aspect of the cohesion strategy is the harmonisation of regulation, with the stated aim of making it easier for firms to operate and compete in different member states. An implicit objective of such policies may be to cement the Union by artificially deepening social and economic links between member states beyond the level that would arise in a market setting, thereby enhancing the power of EU institutions, breeding mutual dependency and raising the potential costs of exit.

---

2   A third important area would be safety, although such regulation also forms part of the harmonisation agenda.

The second broad objective is to reduce the impact of the transport sector on the environment. The EU has made a commitment to reduce by 2020 overall greenhouse gas emissions by 20 per cent compared with 1990 levels (EC 2014). Looking further ahead, the European Commission proposes that the EU sets a target of reducing emissions to 40 per cent below 1990 levels by 2030, with 80–95 per cent under consideration for 2050 (ibid.). Given that the transport sector is currently responsible for approximately one-fifth of the bloc's greenhouse gas emissions, the impact of such targets is likely to be substantial. Furthermore, environmental concerns are not limited to climate change. Restrictions are gradually being tightened on the emissions of a range of pollutants that negatively affect urban air quality.

## Key policy initiatives

The ambitious objectives of EU policy translate into concrete policies that are already having far-reaching effects on the transport sectors of member states. While it is not possible to list every measure, the key implications are listed below.

### Developing trans-European networks

The EU will continue to spend large sums funding infrastructure such as new high-speed railways, motorways and airports in Southern and Central Europe. Smaller amounts have also been spent on schemes in depressed old industrial areas in Northern Europe. Transport has been allocated around €26 billion under the Connecting Europe Facility (CEF), the financing instrument to be used in the EU's 2014–20 budget period to invest in transport, energy and ICT infrastructures (EC 2013a: 16). This is a relatively small amount compared with spending on transport infrastructure by member states, although the skewed geography of the projects means it is highly significant for certain regions.

### Harmonising regulation and industry structures

Transport industries will be integrated further at EU scale through regulatory mechanisms such as open access rules. For example, owners of rail infrastructure will be forced to allow different operators to use their tracks, and full vertical integration will be prohibited. Rules will be standardised across the whole bloc, with EU institutions taking a much larger role in the development of new regulation. Similar steps have been taken in the aviation and shipping industries.

### Modal shift from road to public transport

EU policymakers propose to meet environmental targets by encouraging a major modal shift from road to other modes of transport. By 2050, the aim is for more than 50 per cent of all medium-distance passenger and freight transport to go by rail and waterborne transport. To help achieve this, the length of the EU's existing high-speed rail network should be trebled by 2030 (EC 2014: 19). Within cities, the plan is to halve the use of petrol and diesel cars by 2030 and ban them completely by 2050. Vehicle emissions regulations will continue to be tightened, while legislation will encourage greater use of low-carbon fuels.

## Economic impact

Some of the EU transport policies outlined above have clearly imposed very heavy costs on both taxpayers and consumers, and this burden is likely to increase over time as radical environmental targets are pursued.[3] The benefits are perhaps harder to quantify, but they may include efficiency savings from harmonisation and cross-EU competition, together with enhanced infrastructure in

---

3   For examples, and some cost estimates, see Gaskell and Persson (2010).

peripheral regions and improvements in environmental goods such as air quality. Any empirical analysis of the impact of EU policy is hampered by the absence of relevant counterfactuals: it is not possible to determine which policies alternative institutions would have adopted. Nevertheless, economic analysis does enable broad conclusions to be made about the success or failure of EU policy, both in terms of its own objectives and its wider economic effects.

## New infrastructure

The development of new infrastructure in the bloc appears to have been a particularly stark policy failure. This profoundly politicised process, which has prioritised 'cohesion' over maximising economic returns, has meant significant resources have been diverted to poor value schemes, where the costs have almost certainly outweighed the benefits.[4] Even where returns have been positive – and projects have encouraged growth by lowering the costs of trade – in many instances, the opportunity costs have still been substantial, i.e. the funds may well have delivered much greater returns if invested elsewhere.

A series of 'white elephants' have been constructed, such as heavily loss-making high-speed railways and barely used airports in peripheral regions. Typically, member-state governments have contributed a large share of the funding for EU-backed schemes, imposing significant costs on taxpayers in some of the bloc's poorest areas. In the context of high government debt, the deadweight losses from the tax burden are likely to be particularly high (see Feldstein 1995). Indeed, wasteful spending on loss-making infrastructure – which, in turn, requires ongoing state subsidies – has arguably made a

---

4   For detailed analyses of schemes, see, for example, Nicolaides (2014), Kriström (2012) and De Rus and Inglada (1997).

significant contribution to the current fiscal crisis in countries such as Greece and Italy.

By contrast, private sector entrepreneurs would invest where they expected to maximise their profits. Similarly, a public sector infrastructure programme that maximised value for money for taxpayers would engender a very different pattern of investment to current EU policy.

Cooperation in transport infrastructure projects already exceeds the EU's boundaries, with non-EU members participating in individual projects selectively. As far as cross-border infrastructure projects are concerned, what the ideal relationship between the UK and the EU should be is very much a secondary question.

Indeed, the 'core network corridors' (EC 2013b) being developed are pan-European rather than pan-EU. EEA member Norway is a participant in the creation of the 'Scandinavian–Mediterranean Corridor', while EFTA member Switzerland is a participant in the creation of the 'Rhine-Alpine Corridor'. The UK forms part of the 'North Sea-Mediterranean Corridor', which stretches from Ireland to Southern France. We cannot assess here how economically sensible the UK's participation is, but this question is not directly related to the questions over the UK's exact future relationship with the EU. On its own, a 'Brexit' would probably have no impact in this regard, simply because 'international cooperation' is not the same as 'EU integration'.

## Market structures

The economic impact of EU regulation has also been mixed, partly depending on the sector to which it has been applied. For example, in the case of rail, EU open access rules have effectively prohibited genuine private ownership of the infrastructure by removing the right to exclude. And while some member states have gone further than the requirements of the directive in imposing particular structures on the rail industry, the EU approach has encouraged fragmentation of the sector, undermining traditions of vertical integration that had emerged through a market discovery process during the nineteenth century. One consequence has been an increase in transaction costs in the industry, due to the need for complex contractual arrangements between separate firms. This has translated into higher taxpayer subsidies in the UK (Wellings 2014). Ideally, the degree of vertical integration would be determined by market processes, such as mergers and demergers, that reflected the costs and benefits of different organisational structures.

EU aviation policy, with similar objectives to the interventions in the rail market, has arguably been far more successful in terms of delivering economic benefits. This perhaps partly reflects the nature of aviation markets, with the EU approach more in tune with 'natural' market structures than is the case on the railways. The sector was also historically highly protectionist, with both airports and airlines typically under state ownership and the latter often heavily subsidised by member-state governments and viewed as 'national champions'. EU rules on state aid have helped reduce, though not eliminate, these market distortions. Indeed, the single market appears to have enhanced competition and improved efficiency, with, for example, low-cost airlines free to operate across the bloc. To what extent this would have happened without EU intervention is an open question.

One of the ironies of EU integration is that while the EU has taken on a host of responsibilities that would be better borne at the national, regional or local level, it has been slow in areas where the efficiency gains from international cooperation have been obvious. Air traffic control is one such area. European airspace is still fragmented along national borders, which is wholly inappropriate for air travel. Thus, while US air space is governed by one single air traffic management organisation, governance of the European air space is shared among 38 different ones

(Langner and Schwenke 2011). Fragmentation raises costs in various ways, the most obvious one being the cost of air traffic management itself – the average American flight controller handles twice as many flights as the average European flight controller. It also leads to unnecessarily long flight paths.

The total cost of fragmentation is not precisely known, but the comparison of domestic with otherwise similar international flights, or of European cross-border flights with American cross-state-border flights gives an indication. According to one estimate, fragmentation costs are in the area of €3.4 billion per year. The EU has recently sped up the process of moving to a single European airspace. A first step is the creation of nine so-called functional airspace blocks (FABs), which are airspaces jointly managed by between two and nine countries. FAB boundaries are meant to be closer approximations of traffic routes than national boundaries.

This is an area where there is a strong rationale for international cooperation. However, while EU policy appears to be delivering economic benefits, it is not clear that the EU is a necessary institution for such agreements. Non-EU members such as Norway and Iceland form part of the Northern FAB, for example, together with Denmark, Sweden, Finland and Estonia. Switzerland is part of the central European FAB, together with France, Germany and the Benelux countries, while Bosnia-Herzegovina is part of an Eastern European FAB. It is quite conceivable that the Single European Sky will expand further in the future, ceasing to be a truly 'European' arrangement. So again, on its own, a 'Brexit' would be unlikely to make much difference in this policy area. As in the case of cross-border road infrastructure projects, 'international cooperation' and 'EU integration' are two very different subjects.

While beyond the scope of the current political debate, it is in principle well worth exploring to what extent governments need to be involved in air traffic control at all. In the US context, the chairman of the House Transportation and Infrastructure

Committee (Congressman Bill Shuster) has recently proposed a privatisation of air traffic control.[5] If such a solution were adopted in Europe, it is very unlikely that it would be organised along national boundaries, or indeed EU boundaries.

## Environmental policies

The long-term costs of the environmental component of EU transport policy probably far outweigh the burdens imposed by the funding of new infrastructure and intervention on industry structures. Many of these costs are hidden, however, and are not readily appreciated by taxpayers and consumers, who may face higher prices but fail to comprehend their connection to EU policy. Key additional costs include increased public transport subsidies resulting from modal shift, more expensive vehicles as a result of environmental standards, and higher fuel costs because of biofuels requirements and the Emissions Trading Scheme (ETS).

There are numerous economic objections to the imposition of environmental targets, including methodological problems in calculating the 'social cost' of carbon, but the discussion of these is beyond the scope of this chapter (see, for example, Niemietz 2012: 132–39; Whyte 2013). However, if the objective of reducing $CO_2$ emissions is taken as given, then tools that replicate market mechanisms – such as a carbon tax or a cap-and-trade system – are more cost-effective than a piecemeal approach. The government decides on the volume of emission reductions but leaves it up to firms and households to work out the least painful way of implementing them. What that 'least painful way' is varies from firm to firm, and from household to household, depending on

---

5 *Wall Street Journal* (2015) Rep. Bill Shuster releases 'principles' for bill to privatize U.S. air-traffic control, 15 June. http://www.wsj.com/articles/rep-bill-shuster-releas es-principles-for-bill-to-privatize-u-s-air-traffic-control-1434398386 (accessed 7 September 2015).

individual preferences and circumstances. In addition, the optimal mix of carbon abatement strategies cannot be known in advance; it has to be found out through trial-and-error processes. Market-oriented systems allow for experimentation, and they ensure that the knowledge thus created diffuses more quickly than under alternative systems.

With this in mind, the European Emissions Trading System (ETS) is a workable, if far from perfect, solution.[6] Once an overall carbon cap is specified, there is no case for doing anything else on this front. However, the EU is pursuing a multi-pronged approach to carbon abatement, particularly in transport, and the different components of its strategy blatantly contradict each other. The whole point of the ETS is to allow each individual household and firm to work out their own carbon abatement plan, rather than impose any one plan on the whole population. Yet the EU's approach can be described as setting an overall target first, and then still dictating detailed plans for particular sectors, including transport.

In 2009, the EU introduced mandatory emission standards for new vehicles. Until 2015, the average $CO_2$ emission level of new passenger cars was to be cut from about 160 g/km to 130 g, with separate targets for other vehicle types (ICCT 2014). Average emission levels of new cars were already showing a downward trend at the time, but they fell by no more than 1 per cent per annum, so the EU targets required substantial additional investment in carbon abatement. In 2013–14, the EU set more stringent follow-up targets for 2020, with the most important one being a 95 g/km target for passenger cars. The problem with this policy is not necessarily that the targets are too stringent, but that the approach is extremely prescriptive and inflexible. It is not limited to setting overall targets for the industry as a whole: rather, each individual vehicles manufacturer has its own individual set of targets. Those

---

6    Emissions are discussed further in Chapter 14 of this book.

manufacturer-specific targets are set according to the composition of their car fleet, with manufacturers of heavier vehicles being
allowed a higher level of emissions. This is why Daimler and BMW,
which produce relatively large and heavy cars, were given target
levels of 140 and 139 g/km for 2015 (101 and 100 g/km for 2020),
while Toyota and Fiat, which produce relatively small and light
cars, were given targets of 128 and 123 g/km (92 and 89 g/km for
2020). The policy is already producing the inefficiencies that one
would expect. Unsurprisingly, some manufacturers found it much
easier to meet their targets[7] than others: in 2012, Peugeot-Citroën,
Toyota and BMW had already overfulfilled their targets, while
others had yet to get there (ibid.).

Compare this to a hypothetical policy of a 'sub-ETS' applied
only to the car industry. Such a policy would have been illogical
– why should a unit of carbon emitted by a car be treated any differently from a unit of carbon emitted by an airplane or a factory?
– but less illogical than the policy actually in place. Under this
hypothetical 'cars-only ETS', the most likely outcome would have
been that the overachievers would have cut their emissions even
more, and sold the permits thereby freed up to those carmakers
who faced the greatest difficulties in reducing emissions. The
total volume of emission reductions would have been the same,
but it would have been implemented by those manufacturers
who had the means to achieve those reductions at the lowest cost.

Note also that the targets refer to the average emissions, not
to the total emissions, of a carmakers' fleet. In a cars-only ETS,
one possible response would have been to simply produce fewer
cars, rather than to change their engineering drastically. Especially for an upmarket producer, focused more on margins than
volume, this might well have been the preferable alternative. But
it is an alternative that the EU approach does not recognise. A

---

7   The Volkswagen scandal has unearthed evidence that some manufacturers have
    systematically misled regulators and the public about the real emissions perfor-
    mance of the vehicles they produce.

manufacturer who reduces his or her production volume will still have to achieve the same reduction in average emissions on the remaining car fleet, while, conversely, a manufacturer who increases his or her production volume will not have to keep total emissions constant through sharper cuts in average emissions.

There are various other distortions in the EU carbon standards. The term 'average emissions' is somewhat misleading, because it is not the actual emissions that will be compared against the target level. It is a hypothetical value, which is calculated using a politically determined formula that gives special weights to features the EU wants to encourage. For example, if a company produces two cars emitting 45 g of $CO_2$ per km and one car emitting 90 g, its 'average emissions' in this sense will not be 60 g/km, but 52 g/km, since the EU awards so-called super-credits to cars that emit less than 50 g of $CO_2$ per km. This introduces additional distortions, as reducing emissions from 50 g/km to 49 g/km counts for more than reducing emissions from, e.g. 60 g/km to 59 g/km. Manufacturers can also obtain credits for using so-called eco-innovations, i.e. politically favoured technologies.

In short, the whole approach is dirigisme taken to the extremes. And a similar criticism also applies to the Fuel Quality Directive (2009/30/EC), the Renewables Directive (2009/28/EC) and the Biofuels Directive (European Parliament and Council 2009a; 2009b; 2003). These directives define targets for a reduction of the greenhouse gas intensity of fuels, and for the inclusion of bio- and other renewable fuels in the fuel portfolio. By contrast, a relatively cost-effective ETS-only approach to carbon abatement could be summarised as 'a unit of carbon is a unit of carbon is a unit of carbon'.

## Centralisation versus competition and discovery

The shortcomings of EU transport policy outlined above raise serious questions about current institutional structures, and whether alternative arrangements could improve economic outcomes. Indeed, economic theory suggests that the present approach will result in the misallocation of resources due to knowledge problems, perverse incentive structures, politicisation and the disproportionate influence of special interests over the decision-making process.[8]

A key aspect of this centralised approach to transport policy is the imposition of one-size-fits-all regulations on the whole of the Union. Businesses may derive benefits from uniform rules because the same products and services can be traded across a vast region. For example, bespoke production lines catering to the regulatory requirements of different countries are unnecessary, bringing economies of scale. The costs associated with monitoring compliance may also be reduced. Having said this, in many cases such economies will be limited because, say, variations in language and cultural tastes mean goods and services must be tailored to specific markets in any case. And, clearly, potential economies of scale will vary by sector, depending on production methods, etc.

Unfortunately, a one-size-fits-all approach cannot take into account local time- and place-specific circumstances, leading to large inefficiencies. Take the example of vehicle standards. The benefits of air pollutant controls on vehicles may be concentrated in large cities where pollution levels are said to have a negative impact on health. Yet drivers in rural areas, where any benefits are negligible, will face substantial costs meeting standards imposed across the entire EU. In such circumstances, a dispersed approach to regulation is more appropriate, with local institutions making decisions based on the costs and benefits in their location. Ideally, these local institutions would include 'proprietary communities' based on voluntary agreements, which would

---

8    On knowledge problems, see, for example, Hayek (1945); on incentive structures and special interests, see Olson (1965).

have strong incentives to reflect the subjective preferences of their customers, unlike local governments (Beito et al. 2004).

Dispersed, bottom-up regulation has a number of additional advantages compared with the centralised, top-down regulation imposed at a supranational level. In particular, it creates competition between competing jurisdictions, which has several benefits. If regulations (or indeed taxes) are especially burdensome in one location, then businesses and consumers may have the opportunity to move elsewhere to reduce costs. Indeed, the possibility of exit is of immense importance in the preservation of economic and other freedoms more generally (see, for example, Scott 2009), and it may also act as a constraint on predatory politicians. In the context of jurisdictional competition, governments imposing heavy regulatory and tax burdens risk a vicious circle of business exit, falling growth and lower revenues.

Competing regulatory jurisdictions also enable a discovery process to take place. Different administrations may adopt different rules and structures, which leaves scope for some innovation and experimentation. Successful models may then be copied in other locations, and failed models abandoned. Through this process of evolution and emulation, the economic efficiency of institutions is likely to increase over time. Indeed, it has been hypothesised that Europe's former economic pre-eminence partly resulted from the dynamic effects of its division into numerous competing units (Raico 1992; Diamond 1997).

## Regulatory scale as market discovery process

It can be seen that one-size-fits-all policies suffocate competition and undermine the discovery process that may bring economic benefits via a process of evolution and emulation. The exit option is also significantly undermined. At the same time, such centralisation produces losses when policies do not take account of time- and place-specific conditions. Yet, clearly, for some economic activities there may be substantial efficiency gains from standardisation across a large geographical area.

This raises the question of how the optimal geographical scale of regulation and other policies should be determined. In other words, there are both economies and diseconomies of scale. If the economies of scale outweigh the diseconomies of scale, there will be efficiency gains from increasing the scale of regulation, or vice versa. Yet, given that such trade-offs are dynamic, varying over time and space and by economic sector (see above), it seems highly improbable that the EU would form the optimal unit. Similar limitations also apply to member states, although their boundaries at least sometimes reflect linguistic and cultural divisions – or, indeed, natural boundaries such as the English Channel[9] – that may be relevant to the trade-off in some sectors.

The main point, however, is that politicians and central planners face insurmountable problems if they attempt to determine the optimal geographical scale at which regulation and other policies should be decided and imposed. This reflects the problems outlined above, such as knowledge limitations and poor incentive structures. Fortunately, there is an approach to regulation that is far more effective at adapting to highly varied, ever-changing trade-offs, and utilising dispersed, subjective knowledge specific to particular times and places.

In contrast to a top-down, highly centralised and politicised process, rules systems can be developed by market institutions themselves. Indeed, there are numerous historical examples of successful private regulation, such as the evolution of 'merchant law' (*lex mercatoria*) – a system of courts and regulation for traders across medieval Europe (Benson 1990). Similarly, major financial markets, including the London Stock Exchange, operated under private regulation for most of their history, with intrusive statutory

---

9   In some instances, the transaction costs associated with such natural boundaries (e.g. high shipping costs) may make certain exchanges uneconomic.

controls a relatively recent phenomenon (Arthur and Booth 2010). Such arrangements can address alleged market failures, such as information asymmetries and externalities, while competition between different rules systems facilitates a discovery process that encourages efficiency gains. One element of this market process is discovering the optimal *scale* of regulation, from local to transnational. Under this model, firms and individuals are free to exit one rules system and join another (or none at all), which means that there are strong incentives for private institutions to evolve rules that reflect the preferences of market participants.

Operating outside established rules systems would typically have significant costs, such as making it more difficult to gain the trust of potential customers. Major European car manufacturers could, for example, join a private regulatory body that assured certain vehicle safety standards. Smaller firms, perhaps new market entrants, might decide not to participate in such a framework (or indeed set up a competing standards body with less stringent requirements). They would seek a competitive advantage by selling vehicles more cheaply by not implementing stringent safety rules, but they would also risk deterring those customers who sought the reassurance of an established regulatory body. Ultimately, the decision would rest with consumers, with such market segmentation potentially delivering significant welfare gains for drivers who valued lower prices (and alternative spending options) over high safety levels.

There are, however, some practical problems with moving towards systems of private regulation. In certain sectors, markets are non-existent or heavily distorted because of government ownership or the nature of 'public goods'.

Prime examples of the former include road networks and state control over land use. Private regulation of roads would deal with issues such as the potential externalities from unsafe vehicles (Knipping and Wellings 2012). Similarly, private rules for both roads and land use could address local externalities such as noise and urban air pollution (see Beito et al. 2004). For example, vehicles not meeting certain quality standards could be excluded from a private neighbourhood. Yet, government controls effectively prohibit these and similar solutions based on private property and voluntary agreements. Indeed, the imposition of EU measures – often in addition to pre-existing state intervention – may further crowd out private regulatory options.

Policies of deregulation and privatisation at various administrative levels would facilitate the development of non-government systems of rules. However, in the absence of such an approach, a workable second-best option might be a light-touch approach to regulation that genuinely devolved limited powers to small political units, such as local authorities. This would at least facilitate some degree of competition and tailoring of rules to place specific conditions, though unfortunately local governments are still subject to the problems associated with special interest influence and politicisation.

Another set of problems relates to externalities potentially affecting large geographical areas, such as sulphur dioxide (acid rain) and $CO_2$ emissions (global warming). Given the pathologies of government regulation, including insurmountable economic calculation problems, there is clearly a high risk that the costs of intervention will outweigh the benefits. Nevertheless, there may be a theoretical case for transnational regulation of certain activities in an environment where voluntary, market-based alternatives are suppressed. It is, however, difficult to identify externalities for which EU regulation represents the most appropriate geographical scale. In the case of global warming, for example, effective measures might have to incorporate major emitters such as China, India and the US, to avoid 'carbon leakage'.[10]

---

10  Carbon leakage is the phenomenon whereby mitigation measures in one region lead to an increase in emissions in another region that does not impose similar measures, for example through energy intensive industries relocating from the EU to China.

## Conclusion

The EU is playing an increasingly important role in transport policy across the region. The economic impact has been mixed, with very heavy costs imposed on businesses and consumers but also some benefits from the removal of pre-existing interventions by member states. While it is extremely difficult to estimate these costs and benefits, it is clear that in economic terms EU policy has been very far from optimal. This reflects calculation and incentive problems inherent to centralised planning and one-size-fits-all policymaking, and it suggests the EU is typically not an appropriate institution for the development and implementation of transport policy.

There are, therefore, strong arguments for allowing regulations and investment decisions, together with institutional scale, to be determined by market processes rather than political and bureaucratic mechanisms. A radical programme of deregulation would help facilitate this. Where remaining state intervention makes this difficult, there should be a bias towards political decentralisation to make better use of local knowledge, reflect local preferences and facilitate competition between jurisdictions. Transnational agreements may bring significant economic benefits in some areas, but the optimal scales of regulatory institutions vary markedly from sector to sector. In this context, there is a strong case for moving away from an EU-centric approach and towards a patchwork of voluntary cooperation between private rulemaking bodies, infrastructure entrepreneurs and the institutions of local governance.

This would not, of course, preclude transregional and transnational cooperation, but it would be in a more decentralised setting, with such cooperation clustering around specific areas, and its relative merits assessed on a case-by-case basis. 'Ever-closer union' would not be an aim in itself, and there would be no set of institutions with an open-ended remit and a vested interest in their own growth.

Indeed, in the areas where there is a case for large-scale international cooperation, it is very unlikely that the EU itself is the right scale. In those areas, such cooperation is already established or emerging, and it already exceeds the boundaries of the EU. When it comes to emissions trading, air traffic control or cross-border transport projects, the distinction between the EU, the EEA and the EFTA is relatively unimportant. Some of these schemes even extend to countries that are not part of any of these arrangements. In this sense, transport is a policy area that already illustrates the distinction between project-based cooperation, which is a matter of cost–benefit analysis, and political integration, which is a matter of political preferences.

## References

Beito, D. T., Gordon, P. and Tabarrok, A. (eds) (2004) *The Voluntary City: Choice, Community and Civil Society.* Oakland, CA: The Independent Institute.

Benson, B. L. (2011) *The Enterprise of Law: Justice without the State.* San Francisco: Pacific Research Institute.

De Rus, G. and Inglada, V. (1997) Cost-benefit analysis of the high-speed train in Spain. *Annals of Regional Science* 31: 175–88.

Diamond, J. (1997) *Guns, Germs, and Steel: A Short History of Everybody for the Last 13,000 Years.* New York: Vintage.

EC (2013a) Transport: connecting Europe's citizens and businesses. Report, European Commission Directorate-General for Communication, Brussels.

EC (2013b) The core network corridors. Trans-European Transport Network, European Commission, Brussels. http://www.tentdays2013 .eu/Doc/b1_2013_brochure_lowres.pdf

EC (2014) Climate action. http://ec.europa.eu/clima/policies/strategi es/2020/index_en.htm

Feldstein, M. (1995) Tax avoidance and the deadweight loss of the income tax. Working Paper 5055, National Bureau of Economic Research, Cambridge, MA.

Gaskell, S. and Persson, M. (2010) Still out of control: measuring eleven years of EU regulation. Report, Open Europe, London.

Graham, D. (2007) Agglomeration, productivity and transport investment. *Journal of Transport Economics and Policy* 41(3): 317–43.

Hayek, F. A. (1945) The use of knowledge in society. *American Economic Review* 35(4): 519–30.

ICCT (2014) EU $CO_2$ emission standards for passenger cars and light-commercial vehicles. Policy Update, International Council on Clean Transportation.

Knipping, O. and Wellings, R. (2012) *Which Road Ahead: Government or Market?* London: Institute of Economic Affairs.

Kriström, B. (2012) Economic evaluation of the high speed rail. Report to the Expert Group for Environmental Studies 2012: 1, Finansdepartementet, Stockholm.

Langner, B. and Schwenke, M. (2011) Der einheitliche europäische Luftraum: Single European Sky. Stand und Ausblick. CEP Studie, Centrum für Europäische Politik, Freiburg.

Nicolaides, P. A. (2014) Is the EU funding white elephants in transport? *European Structural and Investment Funds Journal* 1: 31–7.

Olson, M. (1965) *The Logic of Collective Action: Public Goods and the Theory of Groups*. Cambridge, MA: Harvard University Press.

Raico, R. (1992) The rise, fall, and renaissance of classical liberalism. *Freedom Daily*, 23 August.

Scott, J. C. (2009) *The Art of Not Being Governed: An Anarchist History of Upland Southeast Asia*. New Haven, CT: Yale University Press.

Vaubel, R. (2009) *The European Institutions as an Interest Group*. London: Institute of Economic Affairs.

Wellings, R. (2014) The privatisation of the UK railway industry: an experiment in railway structure. *Economic Affairs* 34(2): 255–66.

Whyte, J. (2013) *Quack Policy: Abusing Science in the Cause of Paternalism*. London: Institute of Economic Affairs.

# 12  BANK REGULATION: STARTING OVER

David Mayes and Geoffrey Wood

The recent financial crisis led to substantial demands on tax-payers around the world to provide funds to prevent financial institutions from collapse. An understandable response has been to say that the regulations in place before that crisis were inadequate, and that they must be tightened so as to prevent these problems arising again. While understandable, framing the issue in this way has led to too narrow a question and to an answer that is both damaging and inadequate. In this chapter, we first set out why we think this to be the case, and then outline what we think should be done instead.

In our view, the general interest is to have a financial system that intermediates efficiently and helps absorb the shocks to the real economy. That is, one in which individual failures may worry but do not seriously threaten other members of the system, and in which those who bear losses are, at least in general, those who knowingly chose to risk doing so. This is important everywhere, but particularly in the UK, where not just the financial sector as a whole but the banking sector in particular is very large, both in absolute terms and relative to the economy.

We therefore pay particular attention to what has been done in the EU with regard to banking regulation, as this inevitably affects the UK. But our first step is to set out the principles by which regulations are to be judged; only then can EU actions sensibly be considered.

The next section summarises the kind of banks we are talking about, and why they matter. We then turn to the causes, in an accounting sense, of bank failures. We deal first with liquidity shortage, and then turn to failure through loss of capital. How these can be ameliorated where appropriate and contained when necessary, and how risks can be properly assigned, are then set out.

A time when the country is contemplating a new start in its relationship with the EU is a good time to think about starting again with regulating the banking sector. Is there a need for international cooperation in banking regulation, supervision and law? Do we need the set of international supervisors and bailout authorities that are promised, or do we just need coordination so as to avoid conflicts? We also touch briefly on whether the answers we provide would be different for banks in countries that are in the euro zone.

## Banks and bank failures

The type of banks we are dealing with are fractional reserve banks – banks such as Barclays or the Royal Bank of Scotland. They take deposits and make loans. It seems almost otiose to point out we are dealing with this kind of bank except that, in the wake of the crisis, there have been proposals to return to 'cloakroom banking', as espoused, for example, by Henry Simons (1936). These are banks that take deposits and keep them. They are like the places one leaves one's coat at the theatre, which do not lend out the coats deposited with them, but return them to their owners when required. Cloakroom banks would differ in their operations from theatre cloakrooms only in that they would not promise to return exactly the same notes as had been deposited by the customers, but notes to the same value. Such systems raise very interesting questions, but discussion of these would not take us towards anything bearing on current proposals. Fractional reserve banks need liquidity, and they need capital. Both needs arise from the same cause, their lending out some of the money they receive. They hold back some of the money deposited so as to meet the day-to-day demands of their customers for cash. And they need capital, their own funds, so that if some of the loans they made are not repaid, or are not repaid in full, they can still pay their depositors – for if they cannot, they have to close down.

Problems arise if they on some occasion do not have enough liquidity, or do not have enough capital.

Before going on, a further distinction is necessary – between an individual bank and the system as a whole, or in substantial part. We are of course concerned, if an individual manufacturing or retailing firm fails, to ensure that it brings down as few other firms as possible. This is why there are laws relating to bankruptcy. These laws, among other things, ensure that creditors are paid out in an orderly prescribed sequence, so that creditors can have at least some idea of what they will eventually receive, and can plan accordingly, fairly early in the insolvency process. But even in particularly hard cases, when many workers lose their jobs or many poor people lose money, the usual response is to try to mitigate the failure's consequences rather than to stop it happening. Why, then, in the recent crisis was there a rush to prevent *banks* failing? There are at least two reasons. First, the failure of one bank, even a small one, can trigger a panic run for cash from other banks, and, as they find themselves with insufficient to pay their depositors, they fail in turn. Eventually, a large part of the system may fail. Second, the bank that seems likely to fail may itself be a large part of the system. Such failures lead to destruction of bank deposits, nowadays a large part of the money stock, and thus produce the kind of sharp monetary squeeze that causes recession. They also destroy the channels of transmission of credit from lenders to borrowers, so that, as the economy starts to recover from the money stock contraction, the pace of recovery is inevitably sluggish.

Concern then is with the system, not, in principle, with any one institution. In this paper, we address first how to prevent an individual failure spreading to the system and, second, what to do if one bank is, or soon will be, a substantial part of the system. The first part of that question was addressed in the nineteenth century, and it was addressed not in the abstract but in the face of failures triggered by loss of liquidity.

Before turning back to the nineteenth century and its possible lessons, we of course acknowledge that banking has changed since then. Banks have become much bigger relative to their economies, and in many cases relative to the banking systems in which they operate.[1] They carry out a much wider range of activities than they did then. Banks have become more international: while in the nineteenth century they carried out many activities overseas, not many banks provided a full range of banking services in every country in which they operated. There was neither bank regulation nor bank supervision: in Britain, banks were regulated by exactly the same laws as governed other firms (this remained the case until 1979), and the only supervision was by banks monitoring their counterparties and the Bank of England seeing what was going on in markets. Few banks now are unlimited liability partnerships. That last may seem a modest point compared with the others, but when we consider how the lessons of the nineteenth century may need to be modified for the twenty-first, it turns out to be of considerable importance.

## Liquidity and the lender of last resort

In 1793, war was declared between France and Britain:

> That dreadful calamity is usually preceded by some indication which enables the commercial and monied men to make

---

1   See Capie and Rodrik-Bali (1982) for discussion of aspects of this process in the UK.

preparation. On this occasion the short notice rendered the least degree of general preparation impossible. The foreign market was either shut, or rendered more difficult of access to the merchant. Of course he would not purchase from the manufacturers; ... the manufacturers in their distress applied to the Bankers in the country for relief; but as the want of money became general, and that want increased gradually by a general alarm, the country Banks required the payment of old debts. ... In this predicament the country at large could have no other resource but London; and after having exhausted the bankers, that resource finally terminated in the Bank of England. In such cases the Bank are not an intermediary body, or power; there is no resource on their refusal, for they are the *dernier resort*.

This is how Francis Baring, writing in 1797 of the dramatic events of 1793, introduced the notion of the Bank of England as the 'last resort' of the banking system. The concept was soon afterwards developed very substantially by Henry Thornton (1802). Further refinements were introduced by Walter Bagehot, most notably in *Lombard Street* (1873), but also in his writings in *The Economist* and elsewhere. Throughout the nineteenth century, the Bank of England's practice in the task gradually evolved.

A sudden lack of liquidity can, as Francis Baring set out, readily bring down a large part, or even all, of a banking system. What to do to prevent this being an almost inevitable consequence of such an event was fully explained, in the context of a Britain then on the Gold Standard, by Bagehot in 1848:

It is a great defect of a purely metallic circulation that the quantity of it cannot be readily suited to any sudden demand; it takes time to get new supplies of gold and silver, and, in the meantime, a temporary rise in the value of bullion takes place. Now as paper money can be supplied in unlimited quantities, however sudden the demand may be, it does not appear to us that there is any objection on principle of sudden issues of paper money to meet sudden and large extensions of demand. It gives to a purely metallic circulation that greater constancy of purchasing power possessed by articles whose quantity can be quickly suited to demand. It will be evident from what we have said before that this power of issuing notes is one excessively liable to abuse because, as before shown, it may depreciate the currency; and on that account such a power ought only to be lodged in the hands of government ... It should only be used in rare and exceptional circumstances. But when the fact of a *sudden* demand is proved, we see no objection, but decided advantage, in introducing this new element into a metallic circulation.

Or, in other words, the central bank should sharply increase the supply of money to match the sudden demand for it.

That summarises nineteenth-century theory on the subject. Because the central bank was the monopoly note issuer, it was the ultimate source of cash. If it did not, by acting as lender of last resort, supply that cash in a panic, the panic would continue, get worse and a widespread banking collapse would ensue, bringing along with it a sharp monetary contraction.

Practice of that preventative developed rapidly. Sterling returned to its pre-war gold parity in 1821. The first subsequent occasion for emergency assistance from the Bank of England was in 1825. There had been a substantial external drain of gold, and there was a shortage of currency. A panic developed, and there were runs on banks. The types of bills the Bank would normally discount soon ran out and the panic continued. If a wave of bank failures was to be prevented, the banks would have had to borrow on the security of other types of assets. On 14 December, the Bank of England suddenly deviated from its normal practice; it made advances on government securities offered to it by the banks instead of limiting itself to discounting commercial bills.

The next step was taken in 1866, with the Overend and Gurney crisis.

Overend, Gurney, and Company originated with two eighteenth-century firms, the Gurney Bank (of Norwich) and the London firm of Richardson, Overend and Company. By the 1850s, the combined firm was very large; its annual turnover of bills of exchange was in value equal to about half the national debt, and its balance sheet was ten times the size of the next largest bank.[2] It was floated during the stock market boom of 1865. By early 1866, the boom had ended. A good number of firms were failing. Bank rate had been raised from 3 per cent in July 1865 to 7 per cent in January 1866. After February, bank rate started to ease, but, on 11 May, Gurney's was declared insolvent.

To quote the *Bankers' Magazine* for June 1866, 'a terror and anxiety took possession of men's minds for the remainder of that and the whole following day'. The Bank of England for a brief time made matters worse by hesitating to lend even on government debt. The Bank Charter Act (which, among other things, restricted the note issue to the extent of the gold reserve plus a small fiduciary issue) was then suspended, and the panic gradually subsided.

The failure in 1878 of the City of Glasgow Bank was much less dramatic. It had started respectably, was managed fraudulently and failed. There was fear that the Bank Charter Act would have to be suspended again, but no major problems appeared: 'There was no run, or any semblance of a run; there was no local discredit.' Other Scottish banks took up all the notes of the bank; Gregory (1929) conjectures that they acted in that way to preserve confidence in their own note issues.

In summary, in nineteenth-century Britain, ample provision, on security, of cash from the central bank to the banking system

---

2    It was, however, substantially smaller, relative to available estimates of British national income for that time, than Britain's large banks now are relative to national income.

ensured that one bank's running out of cash did not lead to panics causing other banks to fail as well. The system was protected in the face of occasional liquidity-driven failure. Note that individual banks were allowed to fail if they ran out of even the crisis-lowered quality of collateral that the Bank of England would accept; see the example of Overend and Gurney.

Central banks today have generally accepted their lender-of-last-resort responsibility. Indeed, central banks started doing so, following the Bank of England's lead (the Banca d'Italia explicitly stated that they were following that lead) from the late nineteenth century. The responsibility goes by a number of names: in Britain, for example, it is now being subsumed under the heading of maintaining financial stability, but it is accepted everywhere. This is not to say that practice is always perfect. For those who wish to read of difficulties in this task, there is an abundant literature on the failure in 2007 of Northern Rock. But if practice is needed to produce perfection, deviations from perfection are welcome. (The euro area, with its system of central banks, has somewhat novel arrangements, but these seem entirely workable.)

Lender of last resort, then, can deal with liquidity crises, and it has been tested, and shown to work, intermittently since the nineteenth century. It has worked every time it was used; and on the occasions it was not used (the US in 1930 and onwards, for example), individual failure spread across the system.

## Loss of capital in the nineteenth century

Loss of liquidity was the subject of theorising from which policy conclusions were derived. In general, following the nineteenth-century laissez-faire view, banks that ran out of capital were allowed to fail. They were the authors of their own misfortune, through either imprudence or being excessively burdened by ill fortune.

But there was a most instructive exception in 1890 – the (first) Baring crisis. Barings was a large bank of great reputation; in 1877, when Treasury bills were introduced, Bagehot praised them as being 'as good as Barings'. It nevertheless became involved in a financial crisis in Argentina. The Argentinian government found difficulty in paying the interest on its debt in April 1890; then, the national Bank suspended interest payments on *its* debt. This precipitated a run on the Argentinian banking system, and there was revolution on 26 July. Barings had lent heavily to Argentina. On 8 November, it revealed the resulting difficulties to the Bank of England. The Bank (and the government) were horrified, fearing a run on London should Barings default. A hurried inspection of Barings suggested that the situation could be saved, but that £10 million was needed to finance current and imminent obligations. A consortium was organised, initially with £17 million of capital. By 15 November, the news had leaked, and there was some switching of bills of exchange into cash. But there was no major panic and no run on London or on sterling. The impact on financial markets was small. Barings was liquidated, and refloated as a limited company with additional capital and new management.

Observe, however, that there are major differences between this bailout and those that took place at the start of the twenty-first century. The management of Barings lost their jobs, and most of their capital in the bank. Fresh capital was provided not by the taxpayer but by other banks in the British banking system, who had identified a common interest in preserving the reputation of that system. These other banks had the capital to lend. Unlike Barings, they had not lost money in Argentina, nor indeed life-threatening amounts elsewhere. It might appear, then, that this example of a capital injection is of little assistance in guiding us in present-day banking. But that is not the case, for these very significant differences help us see much more desirable reforms than those currently being considered.

## Banking in the twenty-first century

The nineteenth-century approaches to liquidity and capital crises that we have described did, broadly speaking, achieve what we consider to be in the general interest: a financial system that intermediates efficiently and helps absorb the shocks to the real economy; in which individual failures may worry but do not seriously threaten other members of the system; and in which those who bear losses are, at least in general, those who knowingly took on the risk of doing so.

In what ways do these earlier approaches need to be modified so as to achieve the same result in the twenty-first century? We first summarise the relevant changes to the banking system that we touched on earlier, and then consider what needs to be done to achieve our desired outcome.

Banks have become much bigger relative to their economies. They carry out a much wider range of activities than they did then, both domestically and overseas. Banks have become international: in the nineteenth century, they carried out many activities abroad, but not many banks provided a full range of banking services in every country in which they operated. Furthermore, there was neither bank regulation nor formal bank supervision in Britain. This last seems to us to have implications for current proposals, which involve international cooperation in banking regulation, supervision and law, along with international supervisors and bailout authorities. Perhaps we actually just need coordination so as to avoid conflicts.

As is clear from our earlier remarks, in our view the key to the successful operation of the banking sector is to be able to cope with failures in a way that does not destabilise the financial and economic system. That ability needs not merely to exist but to be viewed as credible by those running banks, those who own them, those who lend to them and, of course, to depositors and borrowers. Above all, it must appear credible to governments, as they are the ones who step in and use taxpayers' funds if they fear for the stability of the financial system.

It has long been clear that ordinary bankruptcy does not offer the ability to cope with failures of any but small banks. It brings transactions to a halt, depositors cannot get access to their funds (even after accounting for any losses) for a substantial period of time, and the problems will be transmitted immediately to counterparties who may, in turn, fail. Because the outcome is uncertain, there will be a general loss of confidence. However, it took the global financial crisis for most authorities to realise this. The aspects of the new legislation in the US (Dodd–Frank Act), the EU (Bank Recovery and Resolution Directive) and elsewhere that have introduced a *lex specialis* to enable a resolution of bank failures virtually overnight are therefore welcome. Such schemes apply the same principles as bankruptcy law, including the maintenance of a hierarchy of creditors, but compress the whole process of establishing claims, valuing the assets and realising that value through sale and liquidation, into a few hours rather than many years (without requiring a fire sale of assets at the prevailing distressed prices).

However, that on its own does not appear sufficient to ensure a purely private sector solution to the problem. The first reason is simply that liquidity beyond what could be achieved through lender of last resort is likely to be needed to effect the immediate resolution. In the US, this is achieved through the Federal Deposit Insurance Corporation's (FDIC's) assets, and in future with the help of the Orderly Liquidation Authority (OLA) enabling temporary funding from the taxpayer. The EU hopes it has achieved the same result by setting up resolution funds in each member state, but these funds are small in comparison with those of the US, even after appropriate adjustment for size of economies. Second, it has usually been necessary in recent crises for the authorities to issue some sort of guarantee against further loss in order to restore confidence in the system and get new lending restarted in order to enable the recovery of the real economy. The need for this action implies that the credible ability to handle the resolution of each individual bank may not be sufficient for confidence in the system. That is an example of systemic risk. There is more to financial stability than the case-by-case treatment of individual members of the financial system.

## Size and structure

In the early literature on bank failure (that is to say, literature from the mid-twentieth century on, since in the nineteenth century individual bank failure was a source of concern only insofar as it threatened the banking system), it was thought that it was simply the size and complexity of the largest banks that made it impossible for their problems to be resolved without a taxpayer bailout. This belief still seems to be held. The response of the authorities since the financial crisis has, however, been less than transparent in this regard. Banks are being required to put together confidential recovery and resolution plans that spell out how they can be resolved immediately in the face of any plausible failure. Initial experience in the US, at any rate, has not been promising where the first draft from every such large bank has been rejected by the Federal Reserve and the FDIC as implausible.

There is a second side to this concern, in that not all activities undertaken by banks, and particularly by more diversified financial groups, need be subject to immediate resolution. They can be handled by ordinary insolvency. The question, therefore, is whether it is sensible to separate out these activities from the essential banking functions, or at least to protect the banking functions from problems in the rest of a group's activity. Doing so would help to simplify the group's structure for the immediate resolution, which has to be possible for part of the group. Here, there has been little agreement internationally about what should be done, and the proposed legislation in the EU is currently stalled. But, in any case, it is clear that with more institutions performing bank-like functions, and more thus being vital to the continuing operation of the financial system, the *lex specialis* approach will have to be extended somewhat.

One problem in implementing these principles is simply that splitting up the large financial groups would be expensive for them, and with strong lobbying power they have been able to avoid change. Perhaps this issue will be resolved through the resolution plans, but it is beginning to look as if the largest institutions are still not resolvable in a useful sense (expeditiously and without threatening contagion) in a crisis. This would not only fail to remove the risk of the taxpayer being called upon but would distort competition in the rest of the industry.

## Incentives

When reviewing incentives, attention has focussed on incentives *within* the institution. These are important, of course, but as the example of both Barings and the City of Glasgow Bank's failures showed, incentives within the *industry* are also important. In both cases, there was seen to be a collective interest: in the Barings case in the reputation of London as a financial centre, and in the Glasgow case in the reputation of the notes of every individual bank in the area. This collective interest is not only useful in the case of outright failure. It can also be useful in helping to prevent failure, if not of a troubled institution then certainly the failure of institutions in the same system. For if one firm were seen as at risk through either folly or deliberate excessive risk taking of one sort or another, then other firms would reduce or eliminate their exposures to it. An example of this being useful is provided by the experience in London of the now-defunct Bank of Credit and Commerce International (BCCI). Because the London discount houses (specialist interbank market makers) could not get sufficient information on the BCCI, and did not like what little they could get, they collectively did not deal with it. Thus, when the BCCI was suddenly closed, there were, to the pleasure and surprise of the Bank of England, no adverse knock-on effects within the banking system.

Questions do arise, however, as to whether, in a setting where so many banks are international and engaged in extensive cross-border business, such a common interest would be felt; and, of course, it is of little relevance if the whole, or greater part, of a banking system is in danger.

## Cross-border

We have deliberately avoided discussing the problems of banks whose activities run across borders in order to keep the analysis simple; but if organising a resolution in a single jurisdiction is proving too difficult, as it currently seems, it will be much harder where separate proceedings have to be started for resolution in each jurisdiction, even if they are to be linked. Cooperation is essential, yet cannot normally be compelled, as these are arrangements between sovereigns.

While effective cooperation may well be the optimal solution (although so far there is only assertion to support this), we have to ask what should be done if it cannot be achieved. The UK and the US have come to the conclusion that the likely workable solution is that the home country solves the problem for the banking group as a whole. In the US, this is particularly straightforward, as the usual structure of such a group is through a holding company with the component banks as affiliates (generally wholly owned). As long as the creditors of the holding company can be written down far enough, then just one authority can implement a resolution of the entire group, largely irrespective of the concerns of the others, as the activities in their jurisdiction will be saved. While there is some fear that some groups may run out of creditors to bear the losses, such an approach is usually likely to succeed.

The obvious alternative is to insist on splitting up the group along jurisdictional lines for each vital activity – and to ensure that each divided part is resolvable, which entails both that it is adequately capitalised and that it has the capability of independent operation after resolution. This is what New Zealand has insisted on with its 'Open Bank Resolution'. All main retail operations must be locally incorporated, separately capitalised and capable of operating on their own overnight. Achieving such separability implies substantial preparation, not just in terms of organisation but in computer systems so that the resolution can be performed in the few hours available.

However, the EU is in danger of being in a halfway house, where cooperation among jurisdictions is required but these arrangements are not regarded as being fully credible. Wherever such credibility does not exist, the foundation for an adequate regulatory regime is not present. And such credibility cannot be achieved without better disclosure, which itself would do much of the job by encouraging good behaviour by institutions. In any event, we discuss the special case of the EU in a little more detail just before concluding.

## Capital

The principal regulatory response internationally has been to demand that banks hold more capital against risks – particularly equity capital, followed by other securities that can be 'bailed in'. Indeed, the whole resolution scheme in the EU is predicated on there being enough capital. While having enough risk-weighted capital is the requirement for registration, the requirement for resolvability is a *total capital* requirement (composed of both external and internal elements). Thus, to an extent, the risk-weighted and leverage ratios at the heart of the Basel system are becoming non-binding. Indeed, this idea was taken up in the Financial Stability Board recommendations presented to the Group of Twenty (G20) in Brisbane in November 2014. Each bank, particularly those judged as systemically important, has to be able to have adequate total loss-absorbing capacity (TLAC) so that it can withstand the plausible range of failures without having to call on secured creditors or the taxpayer. This is simply an extension of the previous bankruptcy arrangements, where the shareholders bear the first loss, followed by the subordinated debtholders, other junior creditors and then senior unsecured creditors.

Prior to the new insolvency laws mentioned above, a firm would enter into a disorderly failure once shareholder capital was exhausted. Now, because these other creditors can be 'bailed in' and required to bear the losses, there is no need for the firm to stop trading. All short-term liabilities, those involving derivative markets and those involving other financial institutions, will be kept whole, so that the failure of the one institution does not feed on to the failure of others – providing confidence is maintained and depositors do not run.

Thus, in many respects, the requirements to hold greater risk-weighted assets under Basel III have been overtaken by the requirement to hold adequate 'bailinable' capacity (TLAC). But the overtaking is not complete, for bailing-in might in turn threaten the solvency of other institutions; bailinable debt is not suitable for all to hold. This is why it is particularly important that it be made clear that, although capital requirements do have a role in absorbing shocks and, hence, reducing the risk of failure, their primary role is not to prevent failure, but to allow orderly resolution after failure.

## Depositors

The system has become complicated in recent years by the increasing importance of depositor protection. Deposits are unsecured loans to banks, yet they are made in the main by people who are not well informed, who are unable to monitor the bank's performance and, moreover, who are likely to be seriously affected by failure, as the bank deposit is their main financial asset. Before the financial crisis, the common international position was that the deposits of 'ordinary people' ought to be fully protected. This implied limited coverage, usually to some level between one and two times GDP per head – not that this was ever the explicit explanation of the chosen limit. Since the crisis, protection levels have become much higher and now fully cover almost all depositors, going far beyond what the ordinary person needs. This restricts the amount of funds available for bailing in.

Since derivatives, covered securities, short-term financing and other preferred creditors are excluded from being bailed in, the pressure on the remaining securities could become substantial, especially if, unlike in New Zealand, depositors are part of the preferred group. Depositor preference is now becoming the norm, with (in the EU) the deposit insurer/guarantor becoming super-preferred, should it have to pay out on behalf of the depositors despite the preference.

Ironically, this solves by the back door the problem of the increased moral hazard from having high deposit insurance coverage levels for large banks. With preference, depositors are unlikely to be caught up in insolvency. Except to the extent that their funds have to provide liquidity support until the bank is fully resolved, such insurance will not be called on, and it is the senior unsecured creditors, most of whom are capable of monitoring the performance and risk-taking of the bank, who are the group that is exposed to the risk of bank failure at the margin. Deposit insurance will then in practice only remain for the smaller banks, which can be closed without the need to keep their primary banking operations running. (However, it is our expectation that bailing-in will be applied even to relatively small banks, as it may often be easier to keep them running than organise rapid sales to other providers.)

## The EU response

The EU has responded to the lessons of the financial crisis largely by implementing what it calls 'banking union'. This comprises enhanced capital and supervisory regulation,[3] with the creation of a Single Supervisory Mechanism (SSM) run by the European Central Bank (ECB),[4] a Bank Recovery and Regulation Directive requiring all member states to have the tools for speedy resolutions, where losses are assigned to shareholders and creditors in the manner we describe.[5] In addition, a new Single Resolution Board (SRB) has been appointed to oversee such resolutions, with funds contributed by levies on the banks to facilitate this.[6]

3  Directive 2013/36/EU of the European Parliament and of the Council of 26 June 2013 on access to the activity of credit institutions and the prudential supervision of credit institutions and investment firms, amending Directive 2002/87/EC and repealing Directives 2006/48/EC and 2006/49/EC, available at http://eur-lex.eur opa.eu/legal-content/EN/TXT/PDF/?uri=CELEX:32013L0036&from=EN (accessed 2 September 2015), and Regulation (EU) No. 575/2013 of the European Parliament and of the Council of 26 June 2013 on prudential requirements for credit institutions and investment firms and amending Regulation (EU) No. 648/2012, available at http://eur-lex.europa.eu/legal-content/EN/TXT/PDF/?uri=CELEX:32013R0575& from=EN (accessed 2 September 2015). See also Castaneda et al. (2015).

4  Regulation (EU) No. 1022/2013 of the European Parliament and of the Council of 22 October 2013 amending Regulation (EU) No. 1093/2010 establishing a European Supervisory Authority (European Banking Authority) as regards the conferral of specific tasks on the ECB pursuant to Council Regulation (EU) No. 024/2013, available at http://eur-lex.europa.eu/LexUriServ/LexUriServ.do?uri=OJ:L:2013:287 :0005:0014:EN:PDF (accessed 2 September 2015).

5  Directive 2014/59/EU of the European Parliament and of the Council of 15 May 2014 establishing a framework for the recovery and resolution of credit institutions and investment firms and amending Council Directive 82/891/EEC; Directives 2001/24/ EC, 2002/47/EC, 2004/25/EC, 2005/56/EC, 2007/36/EC, 2011/35/EU, 2012/30/EU and 2013/36/EU; and Regulations (EU) No. 1093/2010 and (EU) No. 648/2012, of the European Parliament and of the Council, available at http://eur-lex.europa.eu/legal -content/EN/TXT/PDF/?uri=CELEX:32014L0059&from=EN (accessed 2 September 2015).

6  Regulation (EU) No. 806/2014 of the European Parliament and of the Council estab- lishing uniform rules and a uniform procedure for the resolution of credit institutions and certain investment firms in the framework of a Single Resolution Mechanism and a Single Resolution Fund, and amending Regulation (EU) No. 1093/2010, available at

The EU also made a proposal in January 2014 for the restructuring of banking groups, but this is stalled at the time of writing.[7] Facilities for the lender of last resort function already exist and have been extensively used.

In the context of the difficulty of getting agreement from 28 countries, this is a major achievement, but it is convoluted: a consequence of having to get round the difficulty. Whether it will work in practice and restore confidence that orderly failures can be achieved remains to be seen. What the EU has done is not a move towards the kind of desirable regulatory framework that we developed earlier in the paper. Our view, therefore, is that when the crisis is eventually over, and the problems with banks are no longer entwined with the sovereign debt problems of the most affected countries, the EU should start again.

The new structure needs three main things.

- *A resolution entity that can handle resolutions of any bank, however complex and cross-border, in a manner that does not threaten financial stability.* The present SRB only applies to the euro area and other states that choose to join. This conflation of a monetary area with international banking is mistaken and based on the need to avoid renegotiating the EU treaties, not on the logic of the problem. Any system that does not include the UK, the member of the EU that has

http://eur-lex.europa.eu/legal-content/EN/TXT/PDF/?uri=CELEX:32014R0806& from=EN (accessed 2 September 2015), and Council Implementing Regulation (EU) 2015/81 of 19 December 2014 specifying uniform conditions of application of Regulation (EU) No. 806/2014 of the European Parliament and of the Council with regard to ex ante contributions to the Single Resolution Fund, available at http://eur -lex.europa.eu/legal-content/EN/TXT/PDF/?uri=CELEX:32015R0081&from=EN (accessed 2 September 2015).

7    European Commission (2014). Proposal for a Regulation of the European Parliament and of the Council on structural measures improving the resilience of EU credit institutions, available at http://eur-lex.europa.eu/legal-content/EN/TXT/? uri=CELEX:52014PC0043 (accessed 30 October 2014).

some of the most significant banks and the most important financial market, is seriously flawed.

- *Access to adequate funds to effect resolutions and convey the confidence that further problems can be handled.* This can only be handled with access to temporary financing from the state, along the lines of the OLA in the US – which state does, of course, raise difficulties in the case of the EU.
- *A single legal framework where the activities of these large institutions can be handled in one jurisdiction.* The single point of entry approach, where the home country can handle the entire problem, would work, but the only alternative is to require banks to register as European companies governed by a single European regulatory regime.

There are four other aspects to be sorted out.

- *A genuine single supervisory mechanism that covers the whole of the EU is required.* How centralised this should be is a matter of opinion, but it should not be part of the ECB, as this creates a convoluted decision-making structure, as not all parties are represented on the Governing Council of the ECB. More importantly, it creates a conflict of interest between the role as lender of last resort and that of supervisor. When the opportunity arises, the EU should create an independent institution, perhaps based on the European Banking Authority (EBA), and unrelated to the euro area.
- *The issue of the appropriate constraints on banking group structure and banking activities needs to be addressed head-on.* It should not, as at present, be left to the hope that the supervisory and regulatory authorities will be able to come up with a scheme for each bank that will make them resolvable.

- *The EU has ducked the issue of a common deposit guarantee scheme. This needs to be brought back onto the agenda.* Insurance companies are quite capable of running several different schemes, so a single entity does not need to imply a single approach to guarantees. Of course, we could simply follow the US example and have the deposit insurer as the resolution authority.

- *Lastly, the EU is caught in the same trap as all of the other main countries in perpetuating a system of capital buffers based on risk weighting.* Failures occur through errors in risk management and crisis through common errors across much of the banking system. The opportunity exists with the leverage ratio, the emphasis on equity and the concept of TLAC to make the whole of this system much simpler and more robust.

Taken together, these measures would provide a simple, coherent structure, where each party has a clear role, and banks are resolvable and, hence, have a clear incentive to run themselves more prudently – and, even if that fails, to seek a private sector solution before the resolution authority steps in. But whether such changes to the existing plans are possible in the EU is far from clear. They require the EU to 'start again'. That has not often happened; but the present context of British negotiations over future EU status is just such an opportunity. The EU has the opportunity to do the job properly rather than restrict itself to the present arrangements, which were largely determined by political constraints.

## Concluding remarks

In our view, the effective regulation of banks to provide a stable and efficient banking system in which the public can have confidence, and where there is little fear of a call on the taxpayer except in the short run, entails quite a simple system with four main ingredients – all of which have been highlighted in the global financial crisis.

1. All banks need to be readily resolvable overnight in such a manner that functions felt vital to the stability of the financial system can be kept operating without a break. This must not only be practicable at the time but must appear credible to all those involved with the banks (owners, managers, depositors, counterparties, regulators, government and taxpayers) all the time.

2. Such resolvability requires that all banks must hold adequate loss-absorbing capacity in the sense that all losses can be assigned to shareholders and then unsecured creditors in increasing order of seniority, without including those parts of the financial sector that would merely increase the chance of further institutions failing.

3. Such resolvability also requires that banks should be simple enough to ensure that such a rapid resolution is possible. While there is a plausible argument that this can be achieved if resolutions are applied with a single point of entry at the group level, or by having a bank divided upon national lines, the success of intermediate arrangements is yet to be plausibly demonstrated.

4. Lastly, it is essential that the failure of one institution, especially a large one, should not result in instability in the rest of the system through a lack of liquidity and confidence. We therefore see an enhanced role for the lender of last resort function developed in the nineteenth century, where the central bank advances unlimited credit against adequate collateral to institutions that are believed solvent. Enhanced, because we see that extra funds will be required, both to execute these resolutions

in the short run with the required rapidity, and to provide the confidence that, should other banks get into difficulty, they can also be handled in the same manner. Only the state can do that by being able to draw on the 'unlimited' funding that could be provided by the taxpayer. Here, there is clearly a problem for those countries that are already so severely indebted that the idea of raising further funding is implausible.

What cannot be done for any banking system that is to remain efficient is removing the risk of future failures and crises. But the simple framework we suggest, building on what is already being created following the financial crisis, would tend to reduce the risk of such failures, because there is a stronger incentive for bank owners and management to run their institutions more prudently, with reinforcing pressure from those who fear they might be bailed in in the event of failure. This would not take us fully back to incentives of the strength implied by the partnership model, but it would move us in that direction.

There would also be a clear incentive affecting regulators to produce lower-cost failures, in the sense of losses to shareholders and creditors, through rapid action and avoidance of the costs of bankruptcy.

However, the failure of any large institution will always represent a shock to the economy as a whole. Being able to bail in rather than bail out a bank will not mean that somehow losses can be absorbed costlessly. The term loss-absorbing capacity can give the impression that somehow it could mop up the problem like a sponge, wring it out down the drain and rebound to normal afterwards. The real impact will depend on where the losses fall. If they can be absorbed by hedge funds and pension funds, then this will limit the short-run impact on the general population. But if they were to lead to the failure of pension funds, this would simply transfer the problem from one part of the financial economy to another and require that matching special provisions were in place to resolve pension funds in a manner that minimised the impact on the real economy and the taxpayer.

But simplicity and clarity will do much. If incentives are clear, they are usually responded to.

## References

Bagehot, W. (1848) The currency problem. *Prospective Review*, 297–337.

Bagehot, W. (1873) *Lombard Street*. London: Henry King.

Capie, F. and Rodrik-Bali, G. (1982). Concentration in British banking 1870–1920. *Business History* 6: 107–25.

Castaneda, J., Mayes, D. G. and Wood, G. (eds) (2015) *Banking Union in Europe*. London: Routledge Taylor and Francis.

Gregory, T. E. (1929) *Select Statistics, Documents and Reports Relating to British Banking 1832–1928*. Oxford University Press.

Simons, H. (1936) Rules versus authorities in monetary policy. *Journal of Political Economy* 44(1): 1–30.

Thornton, H. (1802) *An Enquiry in to the Effects of the Paper Credit of Great Britain*. Reprinted 1978 (with introduction by F. A. Hayek). Fairfield, NJ: Augustus Kelly.

# 13 YOUNG, SINGLE, BUT *NOT* FREE – THE EU MARKET FOR FINANCIAL SERVICES[1]

Philip Booth

## Introduction

The EU has been increasing its role in financial regulation over the last four decades. At first, the main focus was on promoting trade within the union in a way compatible with the four freedoms: the free movement of goods, services, capital and people. As part of this agenda, the EU prohibited member states from introducing certain forms of regulation that inhibited free trade in services and the free movement of capital. Attempts to promote consistency of regulation tended to involve a process known as 'mutual recognition'. In other words, member states were broadly free to develop their own regulatory frameworks within which financial institutions operated; companies from one member state could then operate freely in other member states whilst being regulated by their home state. In discussing how regulation at the EU level has become detached from the original founding principles of the EU, this chapter will focus on the regulation of insurance services, though there will also be some discussion of other non-bank financial services. Banking is covered in Chapter 12.

Insurance often gets dwarfed in popular press discussion by debates over the banking sector. However, the insurance sector in the UK is the largest in the EU and makes up 7 per cent of the

---

1  Parts of this chapter borrow heavily from Booth and Morrison (2012).

total world market, employs 320,000 people and is responsible for the investment of £1.8 trillion.[2] A narrowly defined measure of non-bank financial services is only slightly smaller in terms of contribution to national income than the contribution of the banking sector defined widely; in turn, insurance is the largest sector within non-bank financial services.[3]

Elements of this mutual recognition approach remain with regard to trade in insurance services. The principle of EU law is still that insurance companies domiciled in one EU country can conduct business elsewhere in the EU under supervision of the home state. However, the European financial regulator now has an overarching authority. Furthermore – and much more importantly – more powers have accrued to the central authorities within the EU, and, as a result, regulation is in the process of becoming harmonised.

From 2011, supervision of financial services began on a pan-EU basis. The EU financial regulatory authority is made up of three supervisory bodies: the European Banking Authority (EBA), the European Securities and Markets Authority (ESMA) and the European Insurance and Occupational Pensions Authority (EIOPA). The desire of these organisations to centralise regulation is clear. For example, the EBA states: 'Whilst the national supervisory authorities remain in charge of supervising individual financial institutions, the objective of the European supervisory authorities is to improve the functioning of the internal market by ensuring appropriate, efficient and harmonised European regulation and supervision.' ESMA notes that it aims to create a unified rule book. In the field of insurance, the Solvency II agenda is unifying regulation at the EU level. In effect,

---

2  See https://www.abi.org.uk/~/media/Files/Documents/Publications/Public/ Migrated/Facts%20and%20figures%20data/UK%20Insurance%20Key%20 Facts%202012.ashx (accessed 31 July 2014).

3  See Burgess (2011). The measure of banking output includes anything that is produced by banks, even if the services are not banking services as such.

national regulators are becoming subsidiaries of the EU regulatory bodies.

It is argued in this chapter that unifying regulation is not necessary to promote free trade in insurance and other non-bank financial services. Although unified regulation might reduce the transactions costs of trade between countries, it does not necessarily promote a better business environment in general, as a higher level of regulation may reduce overall economic activity in financial services. It is concluded that it would be perfectly reasonable for groups of states to develop unified approaches to regulation outside the remit of the EU if they believed that doing so would reduce costs and bring other benefits. However, the role of the EU, enforced through the ECJ, should simply be to ensure that national regulations do not impede or significantly distort trade: the EU should not create a level playing field or harmonise regulation.

## The regulation of insurance companies pre-1970

The justifications for insurance company regulation are different from those for banking regulation. Systemic risk is a much less important consideration in insurance.[4] Instead, issues such as dealing with information asymmetries and enforcing opaque contracts are much more important (see Booth and Morrison 2007). Furthermore, though there are protection schemes for customers of insurance companies – akin to deposit insurance schemes – they do not have the same importance as deposit insurance schemes in banking. The winding-up of failed insurance companies is normally much easier than the resolution of banks, and, especially in the case of life insurance, there is less time pressure when winding-up an insurance company.

---

4   The UK's insurance regulator, the Prudential Regulation Authority, states: 'Nevertheless it is clear that insurers are not systemic in the same way as banks.' See Debbage (2013).

Insurance markets in the UK were regulated between 1870 and Britain's entry into the then common market by a set of principles that were established in the 1870 Life Assurance Companies Act (see Booth 2007). Although it was amended and consolidated on various occasions, its basic principles remained clear for 100 years. A deposit was required for new entrants into the insurance market; all companies had to publish actuarial reports and publish the basis upon which those reports were calculated (though no specific basis was required); and a special mechanism was adopted for winding up failed insurance companies. These principles, whilst remaining in place for over a century, gradually evolved to give greater powers to the regulator (generally the Board of Trade) to intervene in the affairs of the company if an insurance company was close to insolvency. The 1870 Act was certainly very successful in the sense that it was not intrusive – except in one respect[5] – and led to a long period of very stable insurance markets, especially in the life insurance sector.

## The EU, the single market and free trade

Entry into the common market meant that UK insurance regulation had to be compatible with EEC regulation. In the early days of British membership, EEC regulation had two main aims. The first was to ensure that insurance regulation in member states was lightly coordinated. The second was to allow insurance companies in one member state to transact businesses in other member states.

In these early stages, there were various European requirements that had to be fulfilled, but the principle was one of 'mutual recognition', though that term was not always used explicitly. In

---

5   The deposit requirement may well have prevented new entry by small companies.

essence, there were some basic EU[6] regulatory principles that had to be enshrined in the laws of member states, but, beyond that, an insurance company domiciled in one country (say, the UK) could do business in another EU country (say, Belgium) through a branch whilst being regulated from the UK.

The basic EU regulatory principles included an explicit margin of solvency and some other regulations that were adopted by the UK in the Insurance Companies Regulations 1981.[7] These EU regulations did not add substantially to the regulatory burden in the UK, although it could be argued that their arcane, opaque and obsolete nature helped reinforce the mismanagement of Equitable Life, which was closed to new business because of its solvency position in 2000. Certainly, the adoption of EU regulation by the UK accelerated the erosion of what had been known as the 'freedom with publicity' approach to insurance regulation, which was enshrined in the 1870 Act.

Nevertheless, this system of mutual recognition allowed – indeed encouraged – regulatory competition. If insurance companies were over-regulated in Denmark, for example, it was possible for a UK company to establish a branch in Denmark, regulated by the UK Board of Trade, and sell into the Danish market. Of course, if customers preferred the more stringent regulation of the Danish insurance companies, they could still buy policies issued by Danish companies.[8]

There were certainly very wide differences between regulatory regimes in the EU at that time. The differences in regulation are summarised by the following quotation:

---

6   Henceforth, 'EU' will be used to describe what is now called the European Union – it having gone through various name changes since Britain joined.

7   These related to the valuation of assets and liabilities.

8   Consumer protection issues were not covered by EU competences, so UK companies operating branches still had to obtain product approval in some of the more dirigiste regimes.

[In the] U.K., Ireland and to some extent the Netherlands a liberal system of supervision of insurance operates ... At the other extreme is West Germany and the Scandinavian countries. The guiding principle there is one of tight supervision on conservative bases as the best means of protecting consumers (Ferguson et al. 1989: 455).

The later Third Life Directive, which had to be implemented by 1994, arguably strengthened the principle of regulatory competition, whilst, in general, promoting deregulation by prohibiting some forms of insurance regulation. For example, under this directive, a member state was not allowed to require foreign firms selling business to obtain approval for policy terms or impose restrictive conditions on the investment of assets (especially in relation to government bonds). These were prohibitions on regulation that were designed to promote trade and should not be seen as intrusive regulations.[9] It could certainly be argued that the Third Life Directive (and the associated directive in relation to non-life insurance) was a step towards a free-trade environment in which an insurer domiciled in one country could operate without hindrance in another EU country; it also encouraged deregulation in certain member states.

## The beginning of the end of mutual recognition and deregulation

The European Commission regarded the situation that existed under the Third Life Directive as unsatisfactory because it inhibited, in its view, the development of the single market. In the Commission's words:

---

9    See, for example, http://europa.eu/rapid/press-release_P-91-8_en.htm (accessed 4 September 2015).

The rationale for EU insurance legislation is to facilitate the development of a Single Market in insurance services, whilst at the same time securing an adequate level of consumer protection ... Many Member States have concluded that the current EU minimum requirements are not sufficient and have implemented their own reforms, thus leading to a situation where there is a patchwork of regulatory requirements across the EU. This hampers the functioning of the Single Market.[10]

It can certainly be argued that the Third Life Directive has not been a success in terms of encouraging the writing of cross-border insurance business. Figures are not available for the life insurance industry, but in 2010 the non-life insurance industry wrote only £731 million of cross-border business through branches rather than separately regulated subsidiaries:[11] this compared with over £22 billion of premium income written by Lloyds of London alone in 2010[12] and £13 billion of premium income written by a single insurance company (Aviva) through separately regulated non-UK subsidiaries in 2013. The value added by the EU cross-border insurance business under the Single European Passport is clearly tiny. However, there is a vast amount of trade in insurance services both within the EU and outside, but without using the single passport system

There are three logical responses to this situation. First, we could regard the mutual recognition and single passport approach as a 'bit-part player' that is complementary to the freedom of all EU insurance companies to establish subsidiaries in all other EU countries and be regulated by the country in which

---

10  See http://ec.europa.eu/internal_market/insurance/docs/solvency/solvency2/ faq_en.pdf (accessed 4 September 2015).

11  Figure from Association of British Insurers Data Bulletin, 2011.

12  http://www.lloyds.com/~/media/files/lloyds/investor%20relations/2010/annual %20results/files/ar2010.pdf (accessed 4 September 2015).

the business is written. In other words, the EU could have just carried on with the existing system established under the Third Life Directive. Second, we could move in the direction chosen by the EU towards uniform regulation in all EU countries. Third, we could allow all countries to adopt their own independent regulatory frameworks. If the third approach were taken, trade in insurance services would only be possible through subsidiaries established in other member countries, but there would be no reason why pairs of countries or groups of countries should not choose to unify their regulation. This might be particularly beneficial for smaller countries and countries that share similar legal frameworks, and it will be considered below.[13] It certainly should not be thought, however, that free trade requires harmonisation of regulation, as is also discussed below.

## From common market to single market, harmonisation and centralisation

The EU has been able to centralise financial regulation at the European level with few political obstacles. From January 2011, three European Supervisory Authorities became responsible for supervising financial services across the EU. For the insurance sector, the relevant supervisor is the EIOPA. It is very clear that it is the role of the EIOPA to draft a single set of regulations, and the role of national regulatory authorities is merely to supervise firms and ensure that they apply the EU-wide rule book.

---

13  In meetings I had with the Polish and Bulgarian ministries of finance in the early 1990s, it was interesting to note that the English translations of both the 1990 Polish Insurance Law and the proposed Bulgarian Law (which, I believe, was never passed) were identical (with the same translation errors in both). Indeed, the proposed Bulgarian Law was probably translated into Bulgarian from the English translation of the Polish Law. Translation difficulties aside, this is a perfectly reasonable way for countries to move forward – adopting common regulatory frameworks if they so wish outside the structures of the EU.

One example of the way in which regulation is being central-ised is the new system of insurance capital regulation known as Solvency II. This regulatory framework involves an extraordi-narily complex system of calculating capital requirements that requires insurance companies to hold capital sufficient to ensure that they have, according to the models used, a probability of in-solvency of less than one-in-200 over a one-year period. In taking this approach, those framing the regulation repeat exactly the same mistakes as the framers of the Basel approach to banking regulation (see De Soto (2009), and see below). The approach – which is largely incomprehensible except to the expert – requires exceptionally complicated rule books to deal with all types of business in 27 different countries. Other pillars of Solvency II require that insurance businesses are governed in a way that promotes effective risk management and enhances transparency and disclosure.

Whilst I do not approve of the new approach to insurance regu-lation and believe it will do little to promote free trade, it is worth noting that, in the absence of the centralisation of EU insurance regulation, the UK regulator would probably have developed a similar regulatory framework to that being adopted in the EU. In-deed, the UK has had substantial influence on the development of Solvency II. But the main purpose of this chapter is not to discuss the efficacy or otherwise of particular aspects of the EU regula-tory system; it is to question the whole approach of centralising regulation at the EU level rather than allowing member states to determine their own approaches. The new labyrinthine regulatory system is merely an example of the effect of centralisation.

## Single market or free market?

As already noted, there is tension between the concepts of a free market and a single market. The two are not necessarily the same, though they were assumed to be by the Conservative government that ratified the Single European Act in 1986.[14] We are moving to a situation where the same regulations will apply across the financial sector and throughout the EU, but, at the same time, financial services companies will be heavily circumscribed everywhere within the EU. In other words, the market will be single but not free. Insurance is one notable example of this. Freedom to trade would be circumscribed – both within and between countries – by the restrictive regulatory framework that contrasts greatly with the tradition of 'freedom with publicity' and decentralised systems of regulation that existed in the UK until at least 1970. The whole philosophy of the UK insurance regulatory framework had been to allow insurance companies the freedom to do as they wished, as long as they explained what they were doing.

As noted above, an alternative to unifying regulation would be to allow each country within the EU to regulate insurance companies as they wished. At the same time, following the principle of free movement of services, any company from any country could be allowed to establish a subsidiary in another member country. A subsidiary of a UK company established in, for example, Spain would be regulated by, in that case, the Spanish regulator. That subsidiary could still buy services provided by the UK subsidiary, but the regulation of the business sold in Spain would be by the Spanish government.

---

14 See, for example, Mrs Thatcher speaking in 1988: 'Action to get rid of the barriers. Action to make it possible for insurance companies to do business throughout the Community. Action to let people practice their trades and professions freely throughout the Community. Action to remove the customs barriers and formalities so that goods can circulate freely and without time-consuming delays. Action to make sure that any company could sell its goods and services without let or hindrance. Action to secure free movement of capital throughout the Community. All this is what Europe is now committed to do. In 1985 the Community's Heads, Government gave a pledge to complete the single market by 1992. To make sure that it was not just a pious hope, they made that pledge part of the Treaty, as the Single European Act.' http://www.margaretthatcher.org/document/107219 (accessed 4 September 2015).

There would be no single market under this regime. There would be increased transactions costs from trade, and it is possible that freedom to trade could be circumscribed within countries that chose onerous regulatory regimes. However, this approach should not lead to discrimination between companies from different countries, and so freedom to trade between countries would be promoted, as long as subsidiaries were established to conduct business. British companies establishing in Spain would be treated the same way as Spanish companies. Free trade would certainly still be possible, and trade could not be prohibited by member governments under EU law. For example, the French government could not prohibit a UK company from selling insurance services in France as long as the UK company set up a French subsidiary. The economic activity could still be undertaken in the UK through the mechanism of the French subsidiary buying services from the UK head office: this happens in reverse with the offshoring of call centres by many UK insurance companies today. The benefits of trade and comparative advantage would be retained, but there would be no single market. Any vexatious regulation that inhibited trade (for example, requiring insurance companies domiciled in Spain to invest all assets in Spanish bonds and Spanish listed companies, or requiring insurance companies domiciled in Spain to only use Spanish-speaking workers to provide policy-administration services) would not be permitted and should be overruled by the ECJ in enforcing the basic freedoms within the EU, using appropriate legislation to do so.

## The costs and benefits of uniform EU regulation

The mechanisms put in place under the Single European Act have led directly to the centralisation of regulation. In the development of Solvency II, it appears that no attempt was made to promote regulatory competition using mutual recognition. Indeed, HM

Treasury (2008: 7) suggests that only two options were seriously considered by the European Commission in assessing the costs and benefits of Solvency II – one was to wait for an international solvency regime, and the other was the development of an EU solvency system. It appears that approaches that did not involve centralisation were not even considered – the only question was whether centralisation should be at the EU or at the world level. However, the problems of over-regulation that arise when regulation is centralised at the EU level could have been anticipated: indeed, they were explained in Migue (1993).

If the central authority of a federation of states or regions is given the power to regulate, then interest groups can influence the use of that power for their own benefit and to undermine the comparative advantage of other member states – thus introducing trade distortions in a subtle way. We saw after the financial crisis, for example, the attempts by EU member states to impose a financial transactions tax. If that had been enacted, this would have fallen disproportionately on the UK, with perhaps 50 per cent of all revenues coming from the UK. As it happens, the imposition of such a tax was impossible because of the unanimity requirement on matters of taxation. Matters to do with insurance regulation can, however, be determined by qualified majority voting and, given the processes that were set in place in the Financial Services Action Plan (see Bank of England 2003), this means that the EU bureaucracy or a collection of states can effectively determine insurance regulation across the EU to the detriment of certain countries that have a comparative advantage in insurance services, or to the detriment of consumers. The same applies to other areas of financial regulation (see below).

Vaubel (2007) shows how the institutions within the EU, post-the Lisbon Treaty and enlargement, are especially susceptible to rent seeking and the tactic of 'raising rivals' costs'. After 2017, legislation can be passed by a qualified majority representing only 65 per cent of the population of the EU (or 55 per cent of the member states). Migue (1993), recognising these problems, describes harmonisation of regulation as a 'menace' to true federalism, an impediment to freedom to trade and an impediment to ensuring that the appropriate regulatory environment is developed for each member state.

In addition to these problems, the adoption of uniform systems of regulation can make financial systems more prone to systemic risk. If the regulatory system fails, or if it distorts financial activity in the way that the Basel Accord encouraged securitisation in the banking system, for example, international regulation can increase the likelihood of the whole system failing (see, for example, the chapter by Alexander in Booth (2009)). In this context, it is interesting that HM Treasury (2008) states explicitly: 'Solvency II is based on a three-pillar approach used in the Basel II banking accord.' This document was published at the height of the banking crisis, without any apparent recognition of the failure of regulation in that crisis. Swarup (2012) shows how the design of insurance regulation under Solvency II is likely to encourage, perversely, insurance companies to invest in risky sovereign bonds. These incentives apply to all insurance companies in all EU countries, as they face the same regulatory requirements. If there should be a sovereign bond crisis, all EU insurers could be affected in the same way, given that the regulations will encourage herding.

Furthermore, a uniform approach to regulation, which rejects the concept of regulatory competition, also prevents us benefiting from a trial-and-error process, in which regulators in different countries can learn from the successes and mistakes of others. There is a real possibility that regulation will become fossilised at the EU level and will not be adaptable to the different situations pertaining in different EU countries in relation to, for example, different legal systems.

Of course, there are possible benefits from the harmonisation of insurance regulation. The UK Treasury undertook a regulatory impact assessment of regulatory harmonisation under the EU's

Solvency II process that was published in 2008 (HM Treasury 2008), though this was hardly rigorous. This assessment concluded that there would be ongoing net benefits of £96.6 million a year in the UK from Solvency II, and that potential benefits might include the following:

- increased security for consumers;
- fewer distortions to trade;
- more transparency for investors, and therefore reduced cost of capital;
- the ability to use different strategies for risk mitigation without discrimination;
- more efficient use of capital resulting from the ability to exploit efficiencies for groups operating across the EU.

The Treasury assessment also pointed out that UK firms would benefit from the fact that the Financial Services Authority imposes both the current EU capital requirements (pre-Solvency II) as well as an approximation to the forthcoming capital requirements under Solvency II. However, that is just an indication of how over-regulated UK insurers are currently, and not a justification for uniform regulation or any particular level of regulation.

In the analysis, however, no consideration was given to the possibility that a much more liberal regime would still provide incentives for insurance companies to be transparent to providers of capital and manage their businesses in such a way that policyholders were protected – this was the basis of the 'freedom with publicity' approach that was so successful in the UK from 1870 to 1970. It was assumed in HM Treasury (2008) that information asymmetries necessitated insurance regulation for consumer protection, and that benefits would flow from that. However, during the century from 1870 to 1970, there were only two failures of insurance companies – neither of which harmed non-profit policyholders – despite there being no explicit capital requirements for much of that period.[15] Furthermore, there was no discussion in the document of the problems of removing regulatory competition, the problems of using a 'one-size-fits-all' regime, or of the potential for the fossilisation of the regulatory regime as a result of it being determined at the central EU level.[16] There was also no discussion of the potential costs of the new EU regulatory regime imposing capital requirements that were too high in respect of certain types of activity, or of the costs of favouring particular asset classes such as sovereign bonds.

## Other areas of EU financial regulation

The EU has been in the process of trying to unify all aspects of non-bank financial regulation for many decades. This process does not just apply to insurance business; it also applies to hedge funds, private equity, pension funds, rules to which quoted companies must adhere, and so on.

Since 2005, companies issuing equity have been required to produce information in line with the Prospectus Directive (amended in 2010). The Directive requires that all companies with new issues of shares traded on a regulated market have to meet EU-wide harmonised requirements in terms of the information that they provide. This then provides a 'passport', which will allow shares to be traded on any regulated EU market, thus promoting a single market.

This approach is predicated upon two errors. The first is the assumption that the government or a government financial regulator needs to determine the information that is put before

---

15  See Booth (2007). It is a moot point exactly when capital requirements were brought in.

16  Although I do not approve of the changes to the regulatory regime that followed the Equitable Life crisis, the Financial Services Authority was able to react quickly. It is inconceivable that the central EU bureaucracy would react to events in a specific country within a decade, if at all.

the market before an offer for sale of shares. Such things can be determined by the stock exchange, and exchanges can compete according to the effectiveness of the requirements they impose on companies. A well-managed exchange with appropriate requirements for companies and a high degree of confidence amongst investors will be attractive to investors and lower the cost of capital.[17] Indeed, companies themselves have an incentive to provide the right sort of information to the market in order to lower their cost of capital. The second is that, even if the regulation of company information is determined by the government, different requirements imposed by different governments do not intrinsically inhibit trade. Some governments may choose to have no information requirements at all except those imposed by exchanges; some governments may accept the prospectuses authorised by other EU member states; and some governments may have their own requirements. The only reason for the EU to be involved would be if governments imposed requirements on companies domiciled in one member country that were, in effect, protectionist, or if they prohibited companies domiciled in another member country from seeking a listing or quotation on an exchange in their country.

There are several other Directives relating to 'market abuse', company transparency, the operation of markets (MiFID) and the compulsory application of accounting standards. More recently, the Alternative Investment Fund Managers Directive has been implemented. This applies regulations to previously unregulated sectors such as private equity funds and hedge funds. The regulations apply both to funds established in the EU (even if managed outside the EU) and funds marketed in the EU (even if managed and/or established outside the EU).

---

17  See Arthur and Booth (2010) for a discussion of this issue and Stringham (2015) for a comprehensive and original review of the literature.

The extension of EU competencies in these areas is not necessary for the free movement of capital or services, though it could be argued that it reduces the transactions costs of trade and reduces the costs of regulated entities complying with many different regimes. Arguably, regulation in these areas is not required at all – as the UK historical experience suggests. Furthermore, there can be no 'correct' approach to regulation, and, therefore, a multiplicity of approaches may provide opportunities for experimentation and learning from different approaches. Given that EU regulation in these areas is not necessary to achieve the key objectives of the Union, and that the desirability of any regulation at all can be disputed, it would seem sensible to take a different approach and allow cooperation between EU countries that wished to unify their regulation: cooperation that could be extended outside the EU if desired. This approach will be expanded upon in the conclusion.

## Conclusion

In all sectors of financial services, there has been increased centralisation of regulation at the EU level, together with an increase in the general level of regulation. We should be very clear what this entails. The EU has, in effect, tried to reduce the transactions costs of trade by unifying regulation. However, if this process leads to higher levels of regulation or inappropriate regulation, the costs of doing business, whether between or within countries, will be increased. As the EU develops its role in the financial sector further, there is no effective check on centralisation and increasing levels of regulation. A unanimity requirement for new regulation is probably necessary to achieve such a check.

If countries wish to obtain the additional advantages of unifying regulatory systems in order to lower transactions costs, they can do that through intergovernmental agreements. This is likely to be simplest amongst countries that have similar legal traditions, and it need not only involve EU countries. For example, there is no reason why the UK, Ireland, Canada, South Africa, Australia and New Zealand could not unify their insurance regulatory systems. Alternatively, they can agree to recognise each other's regulatory systems following the principle of mutual recognition.

If Britain were to leave the EU, it could be argued that its financial services industry would lose the protection of the EU institutions when it came to promoting free trade with the other member countries: other countries could impose regulation that raised the cost of UK firms doing business. However, against that, the UK would be free to develop its own regulatory system and negotiate agreements with other countries. The likely worst-case scenario is that UK companies undertaking business in the EU would have to establish subsidiaries abiding by EU regulation.

In summary, if the UK is to remain in the EU, the UK should demand reform along the following lines in order to promote an approach based on competitive federalism.

- All EU countries should be permitted to develop their own systems of insurance and securities market regulation.
- Any country that developed a system of regulation that distorted or impeded trade should be referred to the ECJ.
- Any pair or group of countries could freely choose to adopt the same systems of regulation, or mutually recognise each other's systems so that a company domiciled in one of the countries party to the agreement could operate in another country through a branch under the regulation of the country of domicile. These arrangements could also be made by EU countries with non-EU countries.
- The EU *could* have its own central system of regulation, into which member states could opt, and individual companies

could opt if they wished. This would reduce business costs for larger entities operating in a number of EU countries.[18]

- An insurance company or other financial entity from any member state should be able to operate in another member state by establishing a subsidiary in that member state regulated by the receiving state. The subsidiary could, of course, buy services from other subsidiaries within the group. As such, for example, a UK insurance group could set up a subsidiary in Slovakia, the capital and sales practices of which would be regulated by the Slovakian government. However, the Slovakian company could be entirely serviced by the UK subsidiaries. Both the free movement of capital and of services would be achieved through this mechanism.

Under this scheme, harmonisation, insofar as it is desirable at all, can occur through agreement between member states without being imposed from the centre.

This approach would enable free trade to be promoted without unifying regulation. Transactions costs would be higher, but these could be ameliorated by bilateral or multilateral agreements between member states and by the trading of services between subsidiaries under a holding company. Furthermore, multilateral agreements could be extended to non-EU countries. This approach would promote regulatory systems that responded to competitive pressure and allow best practice to be copied

The same principles apply to securities markets and corporate governance and reporting regulation. Different countries having different rules regarding the contents of prospectuses, accounting standards and so on does not, in principle, inhibit trade. Indeed, until 1986, such matters were not generally determined by government in the UK. Insofar as rules relating to such matters

---

18  This is not unlike the US system, where states have the responsibility for regulation but nearly all states adopt the same model.

are used for protectionist purposes by individual countries, they should be prohibited by the ECJ. The harmonisation of regulation at the EU level is neither necessary nor desirable.

It is highly unlikely that the EU will evolve in a liberal direction that will allow the approach suggested above to be adopted. The UK can remain in the EU with, it would appear, ever-more-centralised and costly systems of regulation. Alternatively, the UK could leave the EU, liberalise its financial regulation and cooperate with other countries that wish to promote free trade in financial services. The ideal, though, would be to return to a regulatory regime that was designed to promote the four freedoms within the EU and free trade outside. Unfortunately, that is not on offer.

As noted, it should not be assumed that a return to the liberal regulatory regimes on which a successful, respected and prudent financial services industry was built in the UK is immediately on the political agenda domestically, even if the UK were to withdraw from the EU. When it comes to financial regulation, the UK has moved a long way since the early 1980s, when it could point to a century-long liberal tradition, certainly with regard to non-banking financial services regulation (see Booth 2014). Indeed, in some areas, it is the British government that has been pushing for more regulation at the EU level.

## References

Arthur, T. and Booth, P. (2010) *Does Britain Need a Financial Regulator?* Hobart Papers 169. London: Institute of Economic Affairs.

Bank of England (2003) The EU financial services action plan: a guide. *Bank of England Quarterly Bulletin* 43(3): 352–65.

Booth, P. M. (2007) 'Freedom with Publicity' – the actuarial profession and insurance regulation from 1844–1945. *Annals of Actuarial Science* 2(1): 115–46.

Booth, P. M. (ed.) (2009) *Verdict on the Crash*. Hobart Papers 37. London: Institute of Economic Affairs.

Booth, P. M. (2014) Stock exchanges as lighthouses. *Man and the Economy* 1(2): 171–87.

Booth, P. M. and Morrison, A. D. (2007) Regulatory competition and life insurance solvency regulation in the European Union and the United States. *North American Actuarial Journal* 11(4): 23–41.

Booth, P. M. and Morrison, A. D. (2012) Promoting a free market by ending the single market – reforming EU financial regulation. *Economic Affairs* 32(3): 24–31.

Burgess, S. (2011), Measuring financial sector output and its contribution to GDP. *Bank of England Quarterly Bulletin* 51(3): 234–46.

Debbage, S. (2013) The rationale for the prudential regulation and supervision of insurers. *Bank of England Quarterly Bulletin* 53(3): 216–22.

De Soto, J. (2009) The fatal error of Solvency II. *Economic Affairs* 29(2): 74–7.

Ferguson, D. G. R., Croucher, P. E., Franklin, N. A. M., Henty, J. M., Parmee, D. C., Saunders, A. and Shaw, G. J. M. (1989) A single European market for actuaries. *Journal of the Institute of Actuaries* 116(III): 453–507.

HM Treasury (2008) Solvency II: a partial impact assessment. http://web archive.nationalarchives.gov.uk/20130129110402/http://www.hm-tr easury.gov.uk/d/solvencyii_finalia_090608.pdf (accessed 4 September 2015).

Migue, J. L. (1993) *Federalism and Free Trade*. Hobart Papers 122. London: Institute of Economic Affairs.

Slaughter and May (2004) *The New EU Prospectus Directive*. Slaughter and May: London, UK.

Stringham, E. P. (2015) *Private Governance: Creating Order in Economic and Social Life*. Oxford University Press.

Swarup, A. (2012) A well-intentioned folly: the macroeconomic implications of Solvency II. *Economic Affairs* 32(3): 17–23.

Vaubel, R. (2007) *The European Institutions as an Interest Group: The Dynamics of Ever-Closer Union*. Hobart Papers 167. London: Institute of Economic Affairs.

# 14 BETTER ENERGY AND CLIMATE POLICY

Matthew Sinclair

EU climate policy is too heavy on grandiose targets and draconian regulations. It is too light on more modest measures, which might be a more effective European contribution to addressing what is a global problem.

Of course, British politicians have not been passive victims of the development of EU climate policy. There have been some exceptions recently, but the general pattern is still that the British government has been among the most enthusiastic advocates for more ambitious targets, and more draconian climate regulations.

That does not mean that the EU does not bear a significant measure of blame for the dysfunctional state of UK climate policy. The effect of EU-level policymaking in this area is not primarily in the regulations that were put in place; it is the fact that they are still in place.

Since the direction of EU climate policy was set, there have been a number of crucial developments: the diplomatic process that was supposed to lead to a binding global climate agreement at the Copenhagen Summit in 2009 has failed; despite a notional success at the more recent Paris conference, the major emitters have still not committed to binding emissions targets comparable with those embraced by the EU; it has become clear that the requirements of some of the EU's policies are very onerous, particularly the renewable energy targets, which the government is keen to avoid renewing; the recession has meant that there are a whole range of other pressures on family living standards; and the burden of climate policy has compounded the challenge of necessary fiscal adjustments.

All those developments should have been the spur for a new and more appropriate set of climate policies. Former Canadian Prime Minister Stephen Harper and former Australian Prime Minister Tony Abbott announced their opposition to carbon taxes and emissions trading in June 2014, with Harper saying that action to mitigate climate 'must not destroy jobs and growth in our countries' (Kennedy 2014). Unfortunately, in Europe the changes have been superficial. The same dysfunctional structure of climate policy is still in place.

The new and difficult problem of decarbonising modern, industrial economies – one group of academics has described it as a 'wicked' problem for the complexity of the systems policymakers are trying to control (Prins et al. 2010) – was never well suited to the EU. Politicians saw the supranational scale of the EU as an advantage, but that scale has actually meant too little flexibility to try new ideas, see which work best and quickly reform or scrap those measures that are proving ineffective. British ministers too often simply take EU targets as a given. They look no further than the next steps along a proscribed road to meeting those targets, rather than lifting their eyes to the horizon and considering a better direction altogether.

Climate policy is therefore quite different from policy areas such as the Common Fisheries Policy (Rotherham 2009, and Chapter 10 of this book) or the regulation of financial services (Europe Economics 2014, and this volume's Chapter 13). The principal problem is not that our interests differ, or that we have a different conception of how the regulations should function. In most other member states, the present direction of EU climate policy creates similar problems to those it is creating for the UK, although the scale of the problems created does vary.

If the UK leaves the EU, there will be a natural opportunity to think again about the direction climate policy has taken thus far. If the UK remains a member state, climate policy will remain a crucial test of whether a bloc of 500 million people and nearly thirty member states is too large and unwieldy to fulfil its own ambitions – an ocean tanker in a world that rewards agility.

I will try to do three things in this chapter: explain the depth of the challenge facing a society wanting to emit less $CO_2$, and persuade you that you should probably care less about whether computer models of the climate are reliable, and more about whether the policy being pursued is effective and affordable; set out why the EU's climate policies are failing, and why they are unlikely to be fixed with modest reforms; and, finally, I will propose an alternative course of action, which I think would be more realistic, more effective and less of a burden on families and businesses. I hope we can consider an alternative, in or outside the EU.

## The problem

Wrigley (1988) described how energy, generated by burning fossil fuels, was crucial to the Industrial Revolution. An enormous supply of energy was available, and using more energy did not mean more pressure on agricultural land and therefore the food supply. He cited Émile Levasseur – a nineteenth-century French economist – who wrote that steam engines were providing the equivalent of 'deux esclaves et demi par habitant de la France' (two and a half 'slaves' for every inhabitant of France). Update his calculations to reflect final energy consumption, and each inhabitant of Britain enjoyed the services of 97 mechanical slaves in 2009 (Sinclair 2011: 34).

We should therefore not be surprised that since the Industrial Revolution economic growth has been associated with increasing fossil fuel consumption. Equally, we should understand why attempts to restrict the use of fossil fuels and use more expensive sources of energy could have enormous implications for our future standard of living. There are consequences to giving up the services of those mechanical slaves or paying them more.

If climate policy is to be a realistic political prospect, it cannot be premised on voters accepting substantially lower incomes now, in return for somewhat lower temperatures at some point in the future. Pielke (2010) called that the 'iron law' of climate policy.

There have been concerns for some time that fossil fuels might not be a sustainable basis for continuing economic growth. The first objection was that the supply of fossil fuels was limited, and, over time, they would become steadily scarcer and more expensive. The Bureau of Mines in the US warned in 1914 that US oil reserves would be exhausted by 1924. The Department of the Interior warned in 1939 that the world's petroleum reserves would last thirteen years. Those predictions and others since (Will 2010) have steadily been proven wrong, as new reserves have often been discovered or become profitable to extract more quickly than existing reserves have been depleted.

The most recent and most striking example of this is the enormous development of shale gas and other unconventional resources in the US. The US produced five million barrels of crude oil a day in 2008; it produced around seven and a half million barrels a day in 2013, a 50 per cent increase in five years (US Energy Information Administration 2014a). It produced around twenty trillion cubic feet of natural gas in 2008; it produced more than twenty-four trillion cubic feet in 2013 (US Energy Information Administration 2014b). Other new resources are being developed. The Japanese government has been investigating the potential to access enormous reserves of methane hydrates, which are found near coastlines on the ocean floor (Mann 2013).

The second and more credible objection to the continued and increasing use of fossil fuels to power a growing industrial economy is that resulting greenhouse gases will contribute to dangerous changes in the global climate. The Kaya identity – named for the Japanese economist Yoichi Kaya – describes how economic growth will tend to increase greenhouse gas emissions, though the process will be moderated if the emissions intensity of GDP is falling (Prins et al. 2010):

Emissions = Population × GDP per capita × Energy intensity of GDP × Emissions intensity of energy

We can expect that so long as fossil fuels constitute the most reliable, available and affordable source of energy for most purposes, this basic relationship will hold. The emissions intensity of GDP does tend to fall over time, but the world economy tends to grow fast enough that global greenhouse gas emissions continue to rise.

The Royal Society (2014) reports the current conventional scientific understanding of the implications of rising greenhouse gas emissions:

Greenhouse gases such as carbon dioxide ($CO_2$) absorb heat (infrared radiation) emitted from Earth's surface. Increases in the atmospheric concentrations of these gases cause Earth to warm by trapping more of this heat. Human activities – especially the burning of fossil fuels since the start of the Industrial Revolution – have increased atmospheric $CO_2$ concentrations by about 40%, with more than half the increase occurring since 1970.

[...]

If emissions continue on their present trajectory, without either technological or regulatory abatement, then warming of 2.6 to 4.8 °C (4.7 to 8.6 °F) in addition to that which has already occurred would be expected by the end of the 21st century.

As the Royal Society (2014: 5) notes, the greenhouse effect itself has been well established in experimental science. However, there is considerable uncertainty over the scale of the complex positive and negative feedback expected to amplify or mute that initial effect. Uncertainty over that feedback (without which expected climate change would be considerably more modest) results in the substantial range for expected warming. It is also the basis of most criticisms from sceptics of the current, conventional science.

Increases in global temperature are expected to create a range of harms. Those harms are best expressed in terms of the social cost of carbon, the expected harms now and in the future of emitting a tonne of $CO_2$-equivalent greenhouse gas.[1] Nordhaus (2011) estimates the social cost of carbon to be \$12 per tonne of $CO_2$ (in 2005 prices). His results are comparable with the wider literature, and there does not seem to be a trend upwards or downwards in estimates of the social cost of carbon over time (Tol 2011). However, the social cost of carbon itself is expected to steadily rise over time.[2]

Those with relevant expertise will continue to debate the science of climate change, but it is unrealistic and unhelpful for policymakers to insist on a greater degree of certainty than researchers investigating a complex system such as the global climate can reasonably be expected to provide. Time, energy and talent have been wasted debating the validity of climate models, which could have been better used in scrutinising the policies purporting to reduce emissions.

---

1  $CO_2$ is the most important greenhouse gas overall and the most pressing challenge for policymakers, but other greenhouse gases are significant and often make a greater contribution to the greenhouse effect for each tonne emitted. For example, methane is expected to contribute 21 times as much as $CO_2$ to global warming for each tonne emitted over a 100-year time horizon.

2  There is also the more remote possibility of a catastrophic outcome (Weitzman 2009), and much higher social costs, but many attempts to distinguish climate change from other potential catastrophes are based on 'armchair climate science' (Manzi 2008).

Once you start to scrutinise those policies, it becomes clear that, whatever understanding you have of the science of climate change, it does not change the conclusion. European climate policy is failing on its own terms.

## The EU response

Climate policies adopted across the developed world have been remarkably similar. Prins and Rayner (2007) argue that the Kyoto Protocol was created by 'quick borrowing from past practice with other treaty regimes dealing with ozone, sulphur emissions and nuclear bombs' and fails because it relies too heavily on an unrealistic attempt to create 'a global market by government fiat, which has never been done successfully for any commodity'.

There are four principal elements to EU climate policy:

1. targets for emissions reduction;
2. the Emissions Trading System (EU ETS);
3. renewable energy subsidies;
4. green taxes.

There is also a range of requirements for greater energy efficiency (for example, in regulations setting requirements for average fuel efficiency for motor vehicles).

While the EU stands out in terms of the degree to which it has adopted ambitious targets and policies aimed at reducing greenhouse gas emissions, it does not stand out in terms of reductions in emissions intensity. To the extent that the EU has reduced emissions relative to – for example – the US, it has done so because its economy has grown more slowly (see Figure 5). At the same time, there is no discernible change in the trend for emissions intensity in the late 1990s and early 2000s with the introduction of the principal climate change policies. European climate policy does not appear to have been effective in terms of reducing emissions intensity thus far.

Figure 5    **Emissions intensity, Europe versus the US**

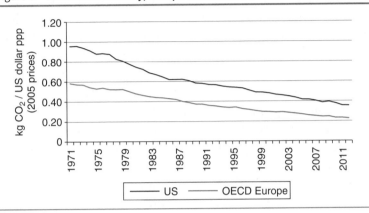

I will not set out all the detailed problems that have beset the current policies.[3] I will instead focus on why they have not just failed so far but can be expected to continue to fail, even if reforms address some of the more minor issues in the future.

## Targets for emissions reduction

There are now three important sets of targets for emissions reductions. The EU as a whole is to reduce emissions by 80 per cent below 1990 levels by 2050; 40 per cent below 1990 levels by 2030; and 20 per cent below 1990 levels by 2020.

Without remarkable progress in reducing emissions intensity, those targets have the potential to require dramatic reductions in living standards. The Kaya identity makes it easy to understand why that is the case. If an economy were to grow at a little over 2 per cent a year from 1990–2020 and reduce its emissions

---

3   See Sinclair (2011) for a more comprehensive and detailed analysis of the various policies enacted in various member states and elsewhere.

intensity at a similar rate, as developed European economies have over the same period (2.2 per cent from 1990 to 2000; 2.1 per cent from 2001 to 2011), then the result is obvious: it would take a reduction in national income of 20 per cent from the expected level to cut emissions by 20 per cent. If the EU is not able to do better, then the targets will require a reduction in national income to 40 per cent below expected levels by 2030.

Pielke (2009) studied the UK's targets under the Climate Change Act using the same method and concluded that the rates of decarbonisation needed (4–5 per cent a year, on average, over decades) would be unrealistic compared with the record up to that point. Very little has changed since, except that a recession has reduced GDP below the level expected and therefore made the short-term targets easier to meet.

Despite all that sacrifice, meeting the targets would not necessarily make any significant difference to the expected global temperature. Crucially, those targets are for reductions in producer emissions (emissions produced in member states of the EU), not consumer emissions (emissions produced supplying demand in the member states of the EU). Helm (2009) describes the problem this creates:

> This international dimension raises perhaps the most important aspect of the 20 per cent overall target: it is based on production of carbon within the EU, and not on consumption. Thus the EU can achieve its targets if it switches carbon production that would have taken place within the EU to overseas, and then imports back the goods and services which would have caused the emissions internally. And, to the extent that energy-intensive industrial production is shifting globally from developed to developing countries (which it is), the 20 per cent target can be achieved without reducing carbon concentrations globally by the implied amount. Indeed, if the production techniques in developing countries are less carbon-efficient

than in developing countries, and if we add the emissions from shipping, aviation, and other transport, it could even increase emissions.

Research for the British government has found that this is not just a theoretical issue. While UK producer emissions (emissions in the UK, whether the relevant activity is serving domestic or export consumers) fell by 20 per cent between 1990 and 2009, consumer emissions (emissions serving UK consumers, whether they occur within the UK or abroad) rose by 13 per cent (Scott and Barrett 2013).

The targets only make any sense in the context of a global agreement. The process by which such an agreement was supposed to come about collapsed at the Copenhagen summit in 2009. Thanks to *Der Spiegel*, we even have a recording of the moment at which EU leaders failed to secure the support of the major emitters they would need to make such a global agreement meaningful, with Nicolas Sarkozy accusing the Chinese government of hypocrisy (Rapp et al. 2010). An accord was eventually reached without European leaders in the room.

Many of the developed economies that were supposed to be bound by the Kyoto Protocol have subsequently repudiated it or rejected the use of specific climate targets. The US Senate made clear that they would not ratify the Protocol. Japan reduced its emissions target for 2020 in 2013, to 3.8 per cent below 2005 levels (3.1 per cent above 1990 levels). Canada withdrew from the Protocol in 2011. In Australia, legislation to establish a carbon tax first appeared set to be passed with bipartisan support. That bipartisan support then collapsed (taking the career of Malcolm Turnbull, then leader of the centre-right Liberal Party, with it). The central carbon tax was eventually passed, but despite a campaign pledge not to introduce it, and in the face of opposition from a Liberal Party then elected to form a new government, who pledged to repeal the regulation.

Targets for cuts in producer emissions without international coordination are not meaningful. They can enormously distort policy, which is constantly judged in terms of whether it meets the targets, rather than whether a policy is effective and represents good value. Even when and if each set of targets is met, it can be a hollow victory if emissions are rising elsewhere.

## Emissions trading

Under the EU ETS, relevant organisations[4] are required to hold an emissions allowance for each tonne of $CO_2$ they produce. Those allowances are either allocated or auctioned and can then be traded, generating a market price and therefore creating a cost (buying an allowance) or opportunity cost (not selling an existing allowance). That creates a neat incentive for firms to cut emissions in the least expensive way possible in theory, without requiring politicians to set a price.

There have been a number of problems with the implementation of the EU ETS: fraud, which, at one point, accounted for 90 per cent of trades on some markets (Europol 2009); significant windfall profits, even in competitive markets, as firms were given allowances for free, but the need to hold those allowances increased the marginal cost of production and therefore prices (Sinclair 2011); and member states allocating too many allowances to their firms, leading to an early collapse in the price and a transfer from UK firms of around £1.5 billion over the first three years, as the British government was more parsimonious (Open Europe 2006). The carbon floor price further increases the burden on British industry, without cutting overall emissions at all (Sinclair 2011).

However, it is also important to understand that the problems the ETS has faced are not simply a result of flaws in its

---

4    Over 11,000 power stations and industrial plants in 31 countries are covered, plus airlines. See http://ec.europa.eu/clima/policies/ets/index_en.htm (accessed 14 September 2015).

implementation. Reforms have addressed some of those initial challenges, but they cannot address its more fundamental weaknesses.

The most pressing problem facing the EU ETS is the sheer instability of the carbon price. It has repeatedly collapsed (Sinclair 2009): first when it became clear that many countries had over-allocated emissions allowances to domestic industries, and then again when the recession led to a reduction in demand. That instability has two crucial effects: it undermines the effectiveness of the carbon price in encouraging investments to reduce emissions, as those investments are subject to greater risk; and it exacerbates the burden on industry as firms struggle to plan with an uncertain component in their costs.

That instability in the price was thought to be a result of the various problems in the implementation of the EU ETS. Actually, the problem is that, unlike in other industries, where the impact of an increase in demand on prices is mitigated by an increase in supply, in the emissions market supply is fixed. That means any change in demand is entirely reflected in the price.[5]

That might not matter if demand were predictable, and the supply of allowances could therefore be planned to ensure a reasonable price. Unfortunately, demand is inherently unpredictable: governments cannot predict recessions; all kinds of policies can be enacted by the EU or individual member states; new technologies can disrupt the market. The carbon price will always be unstable. It could spike in the future, causing enormous economic harm, as easily as it has collapsed up to now. Instability in the price will always undermine the efficacy of emissions trading.

---

5  It is easier to understand this problem if you think about other markets in which supply is fixed, such as the housing market. When more people want to live in a city where construction is easier, more houses are built. In places such as London, where supply cannot keep pace, prices increase sharply. Krugman (2005) characterised housing markets that saw a boom in prices before the financial crisis as making up the 'Zoned Zone', and those where more housing could be constructed, and a boom therefore never get started, as the 'Flatland'.

## Renewable energy subsidies

Twenty per cent of final energy consumption in the EU as a whole must come from renewable sources by 2020. The targets for individual member states vary, and the UK target is the most ambitious.

Onshore wind has generally cost about twice as much as conventional energy,[6] offshore wind has cost about three times as much, and solar has cost even more. That would not necessarily be a lasting problem if we were willing to be patient. Over time, those technologies might become more affordable. However, the rate of improvement is often overstated: a key official target for a reduction in the cost of offshore wind appears likely to be missed (Sinclair 2013); progress in reducing the cost of solar power is real but overstated, as proponents of the technology mix up lasting technological progress with the temporary effects of Chinese industrial policy.

However, we are trying to push prohibitively expensive technologies into action now, using the lure of extravagant subsidies to secure private investment. Over £200 billion of investment is needed in the UK energy sector by 2030 in addition to the around £150 billion that would be needed to maintain supply without the decarbonisation targets (Atherton and Redgwell 2013). The implications are obvious: profits have to rise so investors can make a return on that enormous investment, and prices then have to rise to pay for those profits.

There does not seem to have been any plan for how the public would be persuaded to accept that outcome as legitimate. It is quite easy for campaigners with an axe to grind to portray that combination of rising prices and rising profits as evidence that energy firms are profiteering at the expense of consumers.

---

6   There is a debate over the aesthetic qualities of onshore wind. My sense is that both sides are right: onshore wind turbines are not ugly in themselves, but they make many views less beautiful. New York is a beautiful city, but that does not mean there would be nothing lost if we covered the Lake District in skyscrapers.

On one level, that story is accurate: firms are going to make larger profits at the expense of higher prices for their customers. But those higher prices and profits are necessary for climate policy to be effective. They are a feature, not a bug, of the measures put in place by exactly the same politicians now lambasting those companies for supposed profiteering.

Investing enormous amounts of money in deploying uneconomic renewable energy is therefore expensive and not politically sustainable. There have already been retrospective subsidy cuts in Spain and an effective windfall tax in Germany, in the form of the tax on nuclear assets (Atherton 2010: 10), and those political risks mean even higher returns are needed.

The normal criticism of government interventions designed to subsidise specific technologies is that they are trying to pick winners. Here, governments are instead almost deliberately picking losers. The most expensive sources of energy receive the most generous subsidies. They are doing this because the targets are sufficiently ambitious that every opportunity to increase the use of renewable energy has to be taken, even if – as in the case of renewable heat – the costs are clearly greater than the benefits (Renewable Energy Forum 2010).

Politicians should be working to support the development of economic alternatives to fossil fuels for the future. Instead, they are focused on targets to deploy inadequate alternatives now. The tail is wagging the dog. The short-term costs are enormous at a time when there are many other priorities for investment, and many other pressures on the living standards of European families.

## Green taxes

Many economists regard green taxes as the ideal climate policy. Mankiw (2006), for example, has advocated higher taxes on motor fuels and termed the 'elite group of pundits and policy wonks'

287

who support higher Pigovian taxes[7] the 'Pigou Club'. Worstall (2010) called for a broader, neutral carbon tax and the repeal of other climate policy. They argued that a carbon tax could correct for externalities, and people would then only consume fossil fuels if the benefit to them was worth more than the costs to others. Further regulation would not be needed. All that is much easier said than done.

First, you need to establish the correct social cost of carbon, the right level at which to set a carbon tax. There is an enormous range in academic and official estimates of the social costs of climate change, and they can vary enormously depending on your assumptions, such as for the long-run discount rate (Tol 2011).

Then you need to take into account all the other positive and negative externalities. Motoring taxes at European levels cannot be justified by the social cost of carbon alone (Dunn 2009). Proponents of higher taxes therefore add other externalities, from the costs created by accidents via traffic noise to congestion on the roads (normally the largest component). They rarely include the many positive externalities associated with driving, such as reduced congestion on public transport.

All kinds of inequities emerge. Why do we not apply an emissions tax to agriculture, to account for the methane produced by ruminating cows?[8] Why are motorists subject to taxes to account for the noise they create but factories, for example, are not? Why are motorists subject to taxes to account for the particulate emissions their cars create, when those particulate emissions are already regulated in other ways?

You can view these double standards as a lamentable result of the political process, and not an indictment of the policy in itself.

---

7   A 'Pigovian Tax' is intended to correct market prices for 'negative externalities' – costs imposed by economic activity that are not fully paid for by those benefiting from the activity. The first economist to advocate such taxes was Arthur Cecil Pigou (1877–1959).

8   Instead, we subsidise farms handsomely.

The reality is that the Pigovian principle of intervening to align private incentives with the social good can justify such a wide range of taxes and subsidies, and is so analytically complex, that it just becomes a rationale for politicians to impose whatever taxes they like. Or, as Manzi (2009) put it:

> In order to achieve the 'fairness and social optimality' that we started with when discussing the [global warming] effects of carbon, we are logically led to demanding that the government measure the social value of almost every economically significant action, and then set up incentives to manage the population so as to achieve social goals. Because this is an impossible analytical task, in practice this means the purely political management of society based on relative power. What is this but unadulterated socialism in a green dress?

Green taxes also start to confuse the point of the tax system. Is it a means to raise revenue, or an instrument of social control?

Many policymakers like to imagine a neat transfer from reliance on taxes on labour income, for example, to taxes on greenhouse gas emissions. The Chancellor of the Exchequer – George Osborne (2006) – entitled a speech in opposition: 'Pay as you burn, not pay as you earn'. Unless these taxes are expected to be entirely ineffective in changing behaviour, there will be a shortfall in funding as emissions intensity falls. Greater instability will be introduced into the tax system.

Vehicle Excise Duty was reformed to make the rate more dependent on vehicle emissions, and revenue has steadily declined as cars have become more efficient. Politicians are now considering expensive new reforms to make up the difference (Odell and Pickard 2012).

Of the three main policies that are in place now, green taxes look the best on an economist's blackboard. There are better alternatives that reflect a more realistic role for government. The tax system is best left with one simple, but more than challenging enough, objective: creating the least economic distortion possible while raising the revenue needed to finance government services.

## An alternative

It is important to note that all the policies discussed in the last section really require global government. The EU has been seen as a second-best alternative – emissions might be less likely to leak outside its wider borders – and as a more effective interlocutor with global institutions, with greater negotiating weight than any member state negotiating alone.

In both respects, it is failing. The International Energy Agency (2013) currently expects that, due to high energy costs, resulting from climate policy and a failure to match US development of domestic hydrocarbon reserves, Europe will lose 10 per cent of the global export market in emissions intensive industry by 2035. Chemicals firm BASF recently announced it is shifting investment to the US (Gummer 2014), and where investment goes today the balance of economic activity will go tomorrow. And, as mentioned earlier, European leaders were not even in the room when the Copenhagen Accord was finally negotiated (Rapp et al. 2010).

The crucial reason why climate policy has gone so wrong is that policymakers have been answering the wrong question. They have been answering the question: 'If there were a global government that wanted to restrict emissions, what would it ask European member states to do?'

They are waiting in vain for a final global deal. Politicians in the major emitting economies will not bind themselves to restrict emissions if it entails substantial increases in energy costs for families and businesses in their country. Even modest increases in energy costs have led to riots (Pielke 2010) and revolutions in developing countries; when push has come to shove, developed countries outside Europe have not put compliance with the Kyoto Protocol before their economic health.

I think a much more meaningful question is this: 'What can European member states, which make a limited contribution to global emissions, but which possess considerable financial and technical resources, do to improve our chances in the face of potential climate change?'

What would you do, if you had £1 million, £10 million or £100 million and were asked to do something about climate change?

I do not think you would achieve very much spending the money subsidising an offshore wind turbine. I think you would be much better advised to either take sensible precautions to ensure that your crops, your home, your transport infrastructure and your rivers and coastline were not disrupted more than they needed to be if the climate warmed, or fund the development of new alternatives to fossil fuels by supporting new research.

Defenders of the current approach might argue that governments have funded measures to adapt to climate change, and they have funded R&D. The Technology Strategy Board has helped to fund a new Longitude Prize, and several of the options they are considering relate to climate change. Those efforts have largely been a distraction at the margins of climate change policy. Funding for adaptation has often been shorthand for attempts to bribe developing countries to participate in international climate change deals.

There is a role for supranational institutions in the kind of climate policy that I will sketch out here. They could have a non-trivial role as fora in which countries can share best practice and perhaps agree on a sensible division of labour. However there is no need for the kind of grand, utopian global deals upon which current climate policy was always premised. The best climate policy does not really need the EU. Whether or not better climate policy is possible inside the EU depends on whether the institutions can show a new flexibility in this area.

## Resilience

No country is safe in the face of natural disasters, but the consequences tend to be far more severe in poorer countries with dysfunctional institutions. People are poorer and therefore closer to the edge, more likely to be malnourished or in ill-health already. Institutions are weaker and therefore will be slower in recognising problems and less able to provide support to those affected. As most countries have become more prosperous and more democratic since the 1920s, 'mortality and mortality rates have declined by 95 per cent or more' (Goklany 2007).

It is not only in surviving natural disasters where we can expect economic and political progress to translate into a greater ability to withstand the harms associated with climate change. More prosperous and well-run countries can wring greater agricultural productivity from difficult climates (for example, Israel). They can manage the waters even in low-lying, vulnerable places (e.g. the Netherlands).

The last thing we would want to do in the face of an uncertain threat such as climate change, and a wide range of other potential risks, would be to erode our prosperity. 'In the face of massive uncertainty, hedging your bets and keeping your options open is almost always the right strategy. Money and technology are our raw materials for option' (Manzi 2010).

## Adaptation

To the extent that we do not mitigate climate change, we will have to adapt to it. Nordhaus (2008) studied a number of options to limit greenhouse gas emissions and found that even the most ambitious plan, limiting the rise in temperatures to 1.5 °C and costing over $27 trillion (2005 prices), would still allow nearly $10 trillion of harms (or nearly half of the harms expected in a scenario where no action is taken for 250 years). There is no practical scenario where we expect no significant warming.

The problem that we are most concerned about when it comes to global warming is an increase in the incidence of existing problems: drought in hot and dry regions, flooding in low-lying areas and more extreme weather of all kinds. Floods in Bangladesh are a problem worth addressing, regardless of what you expect from global average temperatures. There is no harm in getting some of our adaptation in early.

Adaptation can take place as and when the impacts of climate change start to be felt. It is therefore far easier for adaptation to adapt and improve over time. Lilico (2014) argues that by 'adapting as and when we need to, we cut down on the risks of doing something counterproductive by accident or of simply wasting our time and money.' We will be able to respond to the actual harms created by climate change, rather than those expected by scientists studying complex natural systems. Only in a small number of situations such as coastal defence and adapting transport systems are grand plans and long lead times likely to prove necessary.

Many of the changes that are needed will be made without any government intervention at all. If farmers are well informed and drought-resistant crops are available, they will use them. If it gets hot in the cities and people are not prevented from doing so by regulation, they will install air-conditioning.

The most dramatic measures that we might take in response to a warming climate are geo-engineering projects. They fit in a grey area between adaptation and mitigation. There is clearly the possibility that injecting large volumes of sulphur dioxide into the stratosphere or dumping large volumes of iron ore into the ocean could limit the harms created by global warming, but they might create a range of problems of their own. The unintended consequences could be severe. We should be doing our research, though, just in case we really are dealing with a potential catastrophe.

## Technology

The final area in which there is enormous potential for action is in producing new technologies that might help us adapt to or mitigate global warming.

Every ambitious strategy to mitigate climate change is at some level a technology strategy. There is no way that targets to decarbonise the world economy will be met without enormous reductions in emissions intensity. The sacrifices needed in living standards would be too severe. Politicians hope that, if they create the carbon market, then the technological developments will come.

The problem with that strategy is that, in the meantime, we are installing inadequate alternatives to fossil fuels, such as offshore wind turbines, on an enormous scale at huge cost. If it does not turn out that revolutionary reductions in the cost of offshore wind energy are possible (and so far progress has been much slower than hoped), then we will have wasted tens of billions of pounds in the UK alone.

We should support research into alternatives to fossil fuels (and other useful technology, such as geo-engineering techniques to limit catastrophic climate change) directly instead of by creating an expensive artificial market.

Of course, we already support new technology with the patent system. If someone invented a cheap alternative to oil as a motor fuel, they would make a fortune. However, I think that there is a pro-active role for governments, or at least for philanthropy.

This could be done by funding universities and other researchers with simple grants. Not all of those grants will pay off, but the amounts of money at stake are relatively small. A better alternative would be to establish a series of well-calibrated prizes for technological developments that could substantially improve our ability to mitigate or adapt to climate change.

Prizes have a long history of success in encouraging productive research to address specific needs, whereas patents support research in any area where there might be a market. They were effective in encouraging the development of new agricultural tools in the industrial revolution (Brunt et al. 2008) and in encouraging innovation in Meiji Japan (Nicholas 2013). The Longitude Prize in 1714 was a famous early example offered by the British government as a reward for the first person to develop a means to ascertain a ship's longitude. More recently, the X Prize led to the first manned private space flight. The X Prize was inspired by the earlier Orteig Prize, which saw $25,000 awarded for the first non-stop flight between New York and Paris. It is estimated that $400,000 was spent chasing that prize (White House 2011: 12).

Either way, the great thing about investments in R&D is that the costs are relatively small, in the tens of millions rather than the tens of billions, and you can therefore run lots of them. You can roll the dice many times and improve your chances. There are already a number of prizes relating to climate change. The Virgin Earth Challenge, for example, is a '$25 million prize for an environmentally sustainable and economically viable way to remove greenhouse gases from the atmosphere'. Other objectives for prizes should probably be more modest, but the idea has already been taken up.

There is no need for any international agreement. If we develop new technology that lowers the cost of cutting emissions or adapting to climate change, and other countries are then able to use it too, so much the better. Putting Britain's scientists and engineers to work developing new alternatives to fossil fuels for the future would be a much more effective contribution to reducing global emissions than deploying existing, inadequate alternatives now.

## Conclusions

There is no sense in continuing to insist on a monolithic global attempt to ration greenhouse gas emissions. That approach has failed so far. Developing countries have not signed up. Developed countries outside Europe have put economic growth before attempts to reduce emissions.

Yet European economies have so far made disappointing progress in decarbonising their economies. Its proponents always claim that the EU ETS is one reform away from functioning properly, but it is not. Renewable energy has proved so expensive that many member states have had to back away from extravagant subsidies, but they still face enormous bills. Green taxes are just an excuse to milk motorists.

Instead of trying to erect some kind of European memorial to the global deal never struck at Copenhagen, we should instead be thinking about a more realistic alternative. We need an approach in which policy can be adapted and changed as our understanding of the potential harms emerging from climate change evolves, and, just as importantly, we learn more about which technologies are the most promising, and which policy measures are the most effective.

Decarbonising modern industrial economies was always going to be difficult, and it is no indictment of politicians that they have made mistakes. The problem is that the mistakes are too large, the price is too high. In the face of enormous uncertainty, we should prefer solutions that can be adapted over time and allow us to roll lots of dice, improving the odds that some of them come up six.

There is an enormous opportunity to reduce the cost of climate policy. Energy markets could be rescued from their growing dysfunction. Rising pressure on family and business budgets could be eased. Industry could have a fairer chance to compete in international markets.

Whether or not you think this is possible within the EU, the key lesson is that good climate policy does not need the EU. The EU needs to show a new flexibility and accept a more modest, but more useful, role. Or this could be an area in which the UK could form better policy on its own.

# References

Atherton, P. (2010) The €1trn euro decade – revisited. Report, Citigroup Global Markets, London.

Atherton, P. and Redgwell, G. (2013) A crisis in UK energy policy looks inevitable. Report, Liberum Capital, London.

Brunt, L., Lerner, J. and Nicholas, T. (2008) Inducement prizes and innovation. Discussion Paper DP6917, Centre for Economic Policy Research, London.

DECC (2013) Investing in renewable technologies – CfD contract terms and strike prices. Report, Department of Energy and Climate Change, London.

Dunn, J. (2009) Relative transport spending. Report, TaxPayers' Alliance, London.

Europe Economics (2014) EU financial regulation. Report, Business for Britain, London.

Europol (2009) Carbon credit fraud causes more than 5 billion euros damage for European taxpayer. Press Release. https://www.europol.europa.eu/content/press/carbon-credit-fraud-causes-more-5-billion-euros-damage-european-taxpayer-1265 (accessed 15 September 2015).

Goklany, I. M. (2007) Death and death rates due to extreme weather events: global and U.S. trends, 1900–2006. Report, Civil Society Coalition on Climate Change, London.

Gummer, C. (2014) BASF looks to ride U.S. shale-gas boom. *Wall Street Journal*, 2 May.

Helm, D. (2009) EU climate-change policy – a critique. In *The Economics and Politics of Climate Change* (ed. D. Helm and C. Hepburn). Oxford University Press.

IEA (2013) *World Energy Outlook 2013*. Paris: International Energy Agency.

Kennedy, M. (2014) Stephen Harper and Australia's Tony Abbott won't let climate policies kill jobs. *Ottawa Citizen*, 9 June.

Knappenberger, C. (2009) What you can('t) do about global warming. Blog Post, *World Climate Report*. http://www.worldclimatereport .com/index.php/2009/04/30/what-you-cant-do-about-global-warm ing/ (accessed 21 June 2014).

Krugman, P. (2005) That hissing sound. *New York Times*, 8 August.

Lilico, A. (2014) We have failed to prevent global warming, so we must adapt to it. *Daily Telegraph*, 18 February.

Longitude Prize (2014) Longitude Prize 2014. http://www.longitude prize.org/ (accessed 22 June 2015).

Mankiw, G. (2006) The Pigou Club manifesto. Blog Post, *Greg Mankiw's Blog*. http://gregmankiw.blogspot.co.uk/2006/10/pigou-club-manife sto.html (accessed 21 June 2014).

Mann, C. C. (2013) Energy special: get ready for the 'fire ice' revolution. *The Spectator*, 15 June.

Manzi, J. (2008) Weitzman: formalism run amok. Web Article, *The American Scene*. http://theamericanscene.com/2008/01/04/weitzman-for malism-run-amok (accessed 8 June 2014).

Manzi, J. (2009) The socialism implicit in the social cost of carbon. *The Daily Dish*, 1 September.

Manzi, J. (2010) Why the decision to tackle climate change isn't as simple as Al Gore says. *New Republic*, 22 June.

Nicholas, T. (2013) Hybrid innovation in Meiji Japan. *International Economic Review* 54(2): 575–600.

Nordhaus, W. (2008) *A Question of Balance: Weighing the Options on Global Warming Policies*. New Haven; London: Yale University Press.

Nordhaus, W. (2011) *Estimates of the Social Cost of Carbon: Background and Results from the RICE-2011 Model*. New Haven, CT: Yale University Press.

Odell, M. and Pickard, J. (2012) Toll road plan runs into cost snag. *Financial Times*, 26 November.

Open Europe (2006) The high price of hot air: why the EU Emissions Trading Scheme is an environmental and economic failure. Pamphlet, Open Europe, London.

Osborne, G. (2006) Pay as you burn, not pay as you earn. Speech to the CBI Conference, London. https://toryspeeches.files.wordpress.com/2013/11/george-osborne-pay-as-you-burn-not-pay-as-you-earn.pdf (accessed 15 September 2015).

Pielke, R. A. (2010) A positive path for meeting the global climate challenge. *Yale Environment 360*, 18 October.

Pielke, R. A. (2009) The British Climate Change Act: a critical evaluation and proposed alternative approach. *Environmental Research Letters* 4(2): 024010.

Prins, G. et al. (2010) The Hartwell Paper: a new direction for climate policy after the crash of 2009. Report, LSE Research Online. http://eprints.lse.ac.uk/27939/1/HartwellPaper_English_version.pdf (accessed 15 September 2015).

Prins, G. and Rayner, S. (2007) The wrong trousers: radically rethinking climate policy. Essay, James Martin Institute for Science and Civilization, Oxford.

Rapp, T., Schwägerl, C. and Traufetter, G. (2010) The Copenhagen Protocol: how China and India sabotaged the UN climate summit. *Der Spiegel*, 5 May.

Renewable Energy Forum (2010) The renewable heat incentive: risks and remedies. Report, Renewable Energy Forum, London.

Renewable Energy Foundation (2013) Emissions savings' potential of wind and solar power. Blog Post, *REF Blog*. http://www.ref.org.uk/ref-blog/302-emissions-savings-potential-of-wind-and-solar-power (accessed 21 June 2014).

Rotherham, L. (2009) The price of fish: costing the Common Fisheries Policy. Report, TaxPayers' Alliance, London.

Royal Society (2014) Climate change: evidence & causes. Policy Project, The Royal Society and the US National Academy of Sciences, London.

Scott, K. and Barrett, J. (2013) Investigation into the greenhouse gas emissions of the UK service industries. Report, Department for Environment, Food and Rural Affairs, London.

Sinclair, M. (2009) The expensive failure of the European Union Emissions Trading Scheme. Report, TaxPayers' Alliance, London.

Sinclair, M. (2011) Industrial masochism. Report, TaxPayers' Alliance, London.

Sinclair, M. (2011) *Let Them Eat Carbon: The Price of Failing Climate Change Policies, and How Governments and Big Business Profit from Them*. London: Biteback Publishing.

Sinclair, M. (2013) Renewable subsidies after the Energy Bill. Report, TaxPayers' Alliance, London.

Tol, R. S. J. (2011) The social cost of carbon. ESRI Working Paper 37, The Economic and Social Research Institute, London.

US Energy Information Administration (2014a) Crude oil production. Statistical Data Set. http://www.eia.gov/dnav/pet/pet_crd_crpdn_a dc_mbblpd_a.htm (accessed 8 June 2014).

US Energy Information Administration (2014b) Natural gas gross withdrawals and production. Statistical Data Set. http://www.eia.gov/dnav/ng/ng_prod_sum_dcu_NUS_a.htm (accessed 8 June 2014).

Weitzman, M. (2009) On modeling and interpreting the economics of catastrophic climate change. *Review of Economics and Statistics* 91(1): 1–19.

White House (2011) A strategy for American innovation: securing our economic growth and prosperity. Report, National Economic Council, Council of Economic Advisers and Office of Science and Technology Policy.

Will, G. F. (2010) The energy future will look familiar. *Newsweek*, 11 October.

Worstall, T. (2010) *Chasing Rainbows: How the Green Agenda Defeats Its Aims*. London: Stacey International.

Wrigley, E. A. (1988). *Continuity, Chance and Change: The Character of the Industrial Revolution in England*. Cambridge University Press.

## 15 EU LIFESTYLE REGULATION

Christopher Snowdon

## Introduction

Public health, as traditionally understood, requires some degree of government action to protect the population from communicable diseases and pollution. Given the EU's commitment to the free movement of people, it is appropriate that member states work together to identify and tackle communicable diseases with initiatives such as the Early Warning and Response System.

The EU's health budget for 2007–13 was €321.5 million and has risen to €449.4 million for 2014–20. Much of this is spent on pan-European partnerships to deal with such issues as counterfeit medicines, radiation, organ donations and rare diseases (European Union 2011). Along with the European Health Insurance Card – which has become more controversial, thanks to concerns about 'health tourism' – these projects help member states achieve health goals that, by their nature, require collective action and international cooperation.

The case for EU action in relation to healthcare provision and the prevention of non-communicable diseases is less compelling. Member states have shown no great interest in integrating their health services, and the EU has no direct competence in this area. The UK government is satisfied with the current balance of competences that gives the EU a very limited role (HM Government 2013: 8). The bigger question is whether the EU has a role to play in 'lifestyle regulation' (Alemanno and Garde 2013: 7) to prevent non-communicable diseases such as cancer and diabetes. These diseases have been the focus of the new public health movement that emerged in the 1970s, with particular attention being paid to four risk factors: smoking, drinking, diet and physical inactivity.

Many of the favoured policies of the new public health movement are anti-market, including tax rises, advertising bans, minimum pricing and prohibition. This brings the lifestyle regulation agenda into conflict not only with personal freedom but with free trade and the internal market. Nevertheless, the EU could be useful to supporters of lifestyle regulation in three ways. First, by rolling out public health legislation across all member states under the guise of internal market reform. Second, by funding pressure groups to encourage member states to act unilaterally. Third, by reinterpreting the EU's 'fundamental rights' so they are used as a sword of the state rather than a shield for businesses and consumers.

## Competence and EU law

Article 168 of the TFEU states that: 'A high level of human health protection shall be ensured in the definition and implementation of all Union policies and activities.' Elsewhere, the EU says that it 'may also adopt incentive measures ... which have as their direct objective the protection of public health regarding tobacco and the abuse of alcohol, excluding any harmonisation of the laws and regulations of the Member States'.

The EU endorses the World Health Organisation's broad definition of health as being 'a state of complete physical, mental and social well-being and not merely the absence of disease or infirmity' (Official Journal of the European Union 2014: 86/1). Given this definition and the aspirational, but rather vague, assurances in Article 168, the EU might appear to have a great deal of scope for action, but this is not so. The important points to note are that the EU seeks a high level, but not necessarily the highest level, of health protection; in other words, health concerns are important, but they need not take precedent over all other considerations. Moreover, EU policies must complement, not override, national policies. The EU can encourage member states to take action, and it can encourage member states to cooperate, but it cannot harmonise policies between member states in the name of public health. As Howells (2011: 217) notes, this means that the EU has 'the power to enact a range of soft measures: however, it must look elsewhere for justification of harmonising measures'. The internal market offers the best justification for such measures, despite the 'inherent contradiction' between the internal market's objective of making trade easier and the public health objective of reducing the sale and consumption of 'unhealthy' products (ibid.: 218). Unless a public health policy can be justified on the basis of an appeal to the internal market, it is vulnerable to a legal challenge.

For example, setting limits on the amount of tar and nicotine in cigarettes has been justified on internal market grounds, since tobacco is widely traded across borders. Similarly, a ban on tobacco advertising in the print media has been justified on the grounds that a member state might prohibit the sale of a foreign magazine if it contains tobacco advertising.

In practice, these are anti-smoking policies, but it is imperative that internal market justifications can be found; several pieces of public health legislation have come undone without them. In 2000, the ECJ annulled the Tobacco Advertising Directive 98/43/EC, which implemented an almost total ban on tobacco advertising, because it could not be justified on internal market grounds. The ECJ ruled that bans on advertising in print and on television were legitimate (because they can cross borders), but bans on advertising and sponsorship in local markets (e.g. cinemas, billboards) could not (ibid.: 221). The subsequent Tobacco Advertising Directive (2003) was therefore less ambitious, excluding local advertising while banning tobacco advertising in print media, on radio and on the internet (television advertising had already been banned in the TV Without Frontiers Directive of 1989).

More recently, anti-smoking campaigners have faced the same roadblock when trying to ban tobacco vending machines and tobacco retail displays in shops. Regardless of the arguments for and against these prohibitions, they have no bearing on cross-border trade, and the EU therefore has no power to harmonise the market.

The precedents of anti-tobacco legislation are germane to the issues of food and drink, because temperance and obesity campaigners explicitly seek to emulate many of the same policies (e.g. advertising bans, warning labels, product modification). The EU has been most active in tackling tobacco, but pressure to legislate on alcohol has been mounting, and food that is high in fat, sugar and salt is increasingly coming under fire from public health lobbyists around the world.

To date, EU action on food and alcohol has been relatively tame. The EU's main piece of lawmaking with regards to food has been to bring about mandatory labelling (e.g. the 1979 Food Labelling Directive, the 1990 Nutrition Labelling Directive). Since these laws require ingredients and nutritional information to be clearly marked on food products in the same way across all member states, they can be seen as both pro-consumer and pro-internal market. These labels are not warnings, and they are not intended to deter purchase. It is conceivable that real warnings, including the kinds of graphic images seen on cigarette packets, could be mandated by the EU if it saw fit, but it has so far resisted calls for a 'traffic light' labelling system that marks food out as healthy or unhealthy.

In the field of alcohol, the EU has also held back from a legislative approach, with the exception of a few restrictions on marketing towards children, which are modest by British standards (European Parliament 2010). Instead, the Commission issued an Alcohol Strategy in 2006, which aims to spread 'good practice'.

This document contains only a few specific recommendations, such as random breath tests to combat drink-driving, and it is largely concerned with gathering data and spreading information. Even if the Commission were inclined to do more, it is hidebound by the principle of subsidiarity. It could not limit licensing hours or regulate the age at which citizens can buy alcohol, for example, because these are matters for member states and have no impact on cross-border trade. It can, and does, set minimum tax rates for alcoholic beverages, but these are set very low, partly because of the huge variation in incomes between member states.[1]

Public health campaigners, meanwhile, have developed a far tougher set of demands including minimum unit pricing (MUP), a policy that poses a direct threat to the internal market. Previous attempts by member states to introduce floor prices for tobacco and fuel have been overturned by European courts on the grounds that they represent quantitative restrictions on trade, but campaigners have been given a glimmer of hope by Article 36, which states that exceptions can be made for restrictions that are:

> justified on grounds of public morality, public policy or public security; the protection of health and life of humans, animals or plants; the protection of national treasures possessing artistic, historic or archaeological value; or the protection of industrial and commercial property.

On the face of it, this provides extensive scope for heavy regulation (arguments can be made for almost anything on the grounds

---

1   In theory, the EU could introduce a 'sin tax' or a minimum price on alcohol (or sugar, fat and soft drinks), but this would have to be set at the same level in each member state. If such a tax were to have any effect on consumption in rich countries such as Britain, it would have to be set at a rate that was punitively high in poorer countries such as Romania.

of health, morality or 'public policy'), but whilst campaigners for minimum pricing hope to get an exemption on public health grounds, it is questionable whether European courts, which have ruled against floor prices for tobacco, will view alcohol as a more deserving case. The European Commission has explicitly told the Scottish government that its minimum pricing proposal is likely to be illegal and has urged it to pursue policies that are 'less restrictive to intra-EU trade' (European Commission 2012).

At the time of writing, no final decision has been made by the ECJ on minimum pricing, and it remains possible that the court will allow minimum pricing under Article 36. If this happens – or if the matter is batted back to the domestic judges who make a similar ruling – it would be a significant win for supporters of anti-market lifestyle regulation. It would also set a legal precedent for other interventions. Judicial activism of this kind arguably represents the most promising avenue for public health campaigners if they are to overcome the obstacle of free trade.

In their book *Regulating Lifestyles in Europe*, Alberto Alemanno and Amandine Garde argue that the EU's 'fundamental rights' could be used as a 'sword' (of the state) rather than a 'shield' (from the state). They acknowledge that 'virtually all NCD [non-communicable disease] policies aim to reduce the consumption of goods that are freely traded across the world' (and therefore encroach upon international trade rules), but they suggest that various EU rights, including the right to health, the right to adequate food and the rights of children, could be invoked to trump trading rights (Alemanno and Garde 2013: 50). Couched in loose terms, these high-minded rights certainly lend themselves to judicial reinterpretation, and yet it remains doubtful whether a court of law will rule that 'junk food' advertising, for example, violates a citizen's right to health.[2] Legal precedents suggest that

2 The authors suggest that the 'right to adequate food' could be interpreted as a right to nutritious food, and that 'junk food' advertising somehow encroaches on that right (Alemanno and Garde 2013: 50). This requires two large leaps of logic and does

the ECJ is more likely to side with the advertiser in such a case, unless there were persuasive arguments that such a ban would improve the internal market.

## Ad hoc prohibitions

The central importance of market harmonisation to the EU's legal framework means that it is often easier to ban a product entirely than to enact more subtle regulation. This can be illustrated with two examples of tobacco legislation: the 1992 ban on snus and the looming ban on menthol cigarettes.

Snus is moist, fine-cut tobacco held in a small, tea bag-like pouch, which the user keeps under his or her top lip. It has been used in Scandinavia for hundreds of years, but it was virtually unknown in Britain until US Tobacco Inc. launched Skoal Bandits, a form of snus, in the mid-1980s. A legal loophole allowed the product to be sold to children in Britain and, despite there being little evidence that children were interested in the product, a media panic ensued. Action on Smoking and Health led a campaign to ban sales to minors. This soon morphed into a campaign for the product's complete prohibition. In late 1989, Parliament banned the sale of 'tobacco in fine cut, ground or particulate form or in any combination of those forms and which are for oral use other than smoking'. The Republic of Ireland did likewise.

These prohibitions attracted the attention of the EEC (as it then was), which expressed concern about the threat to market harmonisation of member states banning snus unilaterally. On 15 May 1992, Council Directive 92/41/EEC announced that 'the only appropriate measure is a total ban' on 'new tobacco products for oral use' across all member states (EEC 1992). The internal market provided the economic rationale for an outright

---

not appear to be legally robust. One could equally argue that 'fat taxes' and other policies that artificially inflate the price of food, including the CAP, are more meaningful violations of the right to adequate food.

ban, and concerns about snus causing oral cancer provided the scientific rationale. Both of these justifications soon fell apart.

First, in 1994, Sweden prepared for its accession to what had become the EU. With a long tradition of snus consumption, and with a quarter of the male population using the product, the prospect of a ban became a major talking point in the run-up to the accession referendum. Faced with the possibility that an arbitrary ban on an otherwise obscure tobacco product could jeopardise Swedish accession, EU officials swiftly abandoned their commitment to the single market and created an exemption. Sweden has been allowed to manufacture and sell snus within its own borders ever since.

Second, it had only ever been *assumed* that snus increased the risk of oral cancer (as many forms of smokeless tobacco do). It had never been proven. In the 1990s and 2000s, numerous epidemiological studies showed that there was, in fact, no link between oral cancer and snus use (Lewin et al. 1998; Schildt et al. 1998; Rosenquist et al. 2005; Boffetta et al. 2005; Luo et al. 2007). This evidence became so strong that the EU removed the cancer warning on Swedish snus products in 2001 because 'scientific opinion no longer supports a strong warning' (European Commission 1999).

Sweden's exemption from the EU-wide ban on snus made a mockery of the internal market arguments, just as the scientific evidence undermined the public health arguments. The case for a ban was further weakened when it became clear that snus use was the primary reason why Sweden had the lowest rates of smoking and lung cancer in Europe (Rodu et al. 2002; Foulds et al. 2003; Rodu and Cole 2009). Far from being a gateway to smoking, as campaigners had feared during the Skoal Bandits scare, snus has proven to be a gateway from smoking.

Having banned the least harmful tobacco product, the EU has had several opportunities to repeal the prohibition, but it has chosen not to do so. On the most recent occasion, in 2012, representatives of the European People's Party explained that 'it would be very harmful for the credibility of the European Institutions if the current rules would be liberalised' (Liese and Seeber 2012). This gets to the heart of the matter. Although the ban cannot be justified on the grounds of health, the internal market or proportionality, it would be embarrassing for Brussels to admit its error.

Tales of the EU's bureaucratic fervour are legion. From regulating the shape of cucumbers to making plans to ban unmarked olive oil bottles in restaurants,[3] European institutions have a notorious penchant for petty micro-management, which was much in evidence during the protracted negotiations over the Tobacco Products Directive (TPD) of 2014.[4] The European Commission wanted cigarette packets to be exactly 55 mm wide; it wanted all cigarettes to have a diameter of exactly 7.5 mm; it wanted flip-top lids to be mandatory on all cigarette packs; it wanted cylindrical rolling tobacco tins to be banned, but rectangular pouches to be allowed; packs of nineteen would be illegal, but packs of twenty would be approved; bottles of e-cigarette fluid would be limited to 10 ml, and so on.

Some of these trivial recommendations were enshrined in the final directive, and others were not, but in some respects it is the policies that were never put on the table that are most interesting. Bans on tobacco vending machines, on tobacco retail displays and on smoking in public places were high on the anti-smoking

---

3   It is sometimes claimed that EU regulation of bananas and cucumbers is a fiction dreamt up by eurosceptics. This is not so. Commission Regulation (EEC) No. 1677/88 regulates the shape of cucumbers and Commission Regulation (EC) No. 2257/94 regulates the shape of bananas. The proposal to ban unmarked olive oil bottles was abandoned after it drew unfavourable media attention in 2013.

4   The political process behind the TPD was not pretty. Among other minor scandals, a public consultation was ignored after it found significant resistance to further regulation, and the EU's Health Commissioner, John Dalli, was forced to resign after his friend allegedly tried to solicit a bribe from a snus manufacturer to overturn the ban on oral tobacco.

lobby's list of priorities and had already been implemented in some member states, including Britain; yet none of these policies appeared in the TPD.[5] Instead, the directive introduced an EU-wide ban on menthol cigarettes (to be implemented in 2022), despite no member state having seriously considered such a ban, much less having implemented one.

The explanation for this lies, once again, in the EU's legal constraints. There are many disparities in the way that member states regulate shop displays and vending machines, but they do not compromise the internal market, because they have no impact on cross-border trade. The 'mere finding of disparities between national rules is not sufficient' to require harmonisation (Alemanno and Garde 2013: 64–5). Conversely, the sale of menthol cigarettes across all member states does not threaten the internal market, but neither does a total ban. Given the choice between banning them everywhere and permitting them everywhere, the European Commission, supported by the European Parliament, chose to ban. It also came close to passing a de facto ban on e-cigarettes, and it is reasonable to assume it would do the same with tobacco vending machines and tobacco retail displays if it had the power. As yet, however, it does not.

Officially, the 2014 TPD was created as a response to the 'substantial differences between the member states' laws, regulations and administrative provisions on the manufacture, presentation and sale of tobacco' (European Parliament 2014: 2). In reality (and as its supporters openly stated) it was designed to reduce smoking prevalence by 2 per cent (Borg 2014). If market harmonisation was the true aim of the directive, it would legalise snus across the EU (or remove the Swedish exemption) and would not allow member states to have different packaging regulations. It does

---

5   With no competence to bring about an EU-wide smoking ban, in 2009 the European Commission issued 'Council recommendations on smoke-free environments', which encouraged member states to 'provide effective protection from exposure to tobacco smoke in indoor workplaces' (European Commission, 2009).

neither. In the case of packaging, the new TPD explicitly removes a limitation enshrined in the previous TPD on what member states can do, thereby allowing further 'substantial differences' to emerge.

The TPD provides an indication of how European institutions could regulate food and drink if it were so inclined. For example, it could plausibly ban a particular form of alcohol, such as absinthe, across all member states, and it could ban advertising for certain food products on television. However, it could not ban food advertising in domestic venues, such as cinemas, and, as we have seen, it would be unlikely to accept floor prices on products that are sold across intra-EU borders.

## State-funded activists: pushing the envelope

When lifestyle regulation policies cannot be justified on internal market grounds, the EU exerts its influence more subtly by encouraging member states to take action through their domestic parliaments. In addition to publishing guidance, such as the Alcohol Strategy (2006) and the Obesity Prevention White Paper (2007), European institutions fund activist groups in Brussels and elsewhere to formulate policy, organise conferences and influence the media. With very few exceptions, these groups are committed to the anti-market policies of restricting advertising, raising prices and limiting availability.

In the field of alcohol, the EU funds some surprisingly orthodox temperance organisations. For example, the European Commission paid Britain's Institute of Alcohol Studies (IAS) to produce research for its Alcohol Strategy (European Commission 2006: 7). The IAS is descended from the overtly prohibitionist nineteenth-century group, the United Kingdom Alliance for the Suppression of the Traffic in All Intoxicating Liquors, which became the UK Temperance Alliance in the 1940s. Methodist teetotalism is in the organisation's DNA (Rutherford 2012).

Similarly, the EU gives grants to ACTIVE (2012), which describes itself as 'a non-governmental organisation gathering European youth temperance organisations working for a democratic diverse and peaceful world free from alcohol'. ACTIVE is the youth wing of the International Organisation of Good Templars, another nineteenth-century temperance outfit that espoused (and continues to espouse) total abstinence from alcohol. Like the IAS, ACTIVE does not openly call for prohibition, but its policy recommendations include a total ban on alcohol marketing, minimum pricing, a ban on home-brewing and the exclusive sale of alcohol through state monopolies (ACTIVE 2010).

The Commission funds many similar organisations, including Alcohol Action Ireland, the European Alcohol Policy Alliance (also known as Eurocare), the European Network for Smoking and Tobacco Prevention and the European Public Health Alliance. The latter, a left-leaning pressure group that receives most of its income from the EU, has been particularly vocal in its support for 'fat taxes', minimum pricing and plain packaging, despite these policies being inconsistent with the principles of the internal market.

The money of European taxpayers is used not only to promote anti-market policies in member states, but also to attack critics of these policies, including academics and privately funded think-tanks (Gornall 2014; Snowdon 2014). The EU's generosity towards a select group of special interest groups ensures that supporters of lifestyle regulation can loudly promote anti-market policies, which the EU could neither implement nor endorse directly.

## Implications of a 'Brexit'

At first glance, the EU's public health legislation appears to be incoherent. Policies that are keenly supported by health campaigners, such as smoking bans, are absent, while marginal issues such as menthol flavourings in cigarettes are addressed with outright prohibition. The European Commission warns member states about the probable illegality of minimum pricing while funding groups that campaign for the policy. This confusing picture only comes into focus once it is understood that the EU does not officially produce public health legislation. It does what it can within 'the art of the possible'. There are plenty of indications that European institutions are inclined towards bans and bureaucratic regulation, but they are often unable to do more than encourage 'the exchange of best practice and self-regulation' (Alemanno and Garde 2013: 100). In some instances, such as the challenge to minimum pricing and the free movement of alcohol and tobacco across borders, EU legislation actively hinders attempts at lifestyle regulation. The legal framework of the EU as it exists today means the public health lobby fights with one hand tied behind its back in Brussels.

This mixed curse for anti-market campaigners is a mixed blessing for consumers. British drinkers and smokers have probably gained more than they have lost from EU membership. Tobacco and alcohol duty is exceptionally high in the UK, but it would probably be even higher if shoppers did not have the option of buying in other member states (Rabinovich 2009: 78). Moreover, at the time of writing, the existence of Article 14 of the TFEU has so far prevented the implementation of minimum pricing, which would make off-trade alcohol still more expensive.

In the field of lifestyle regulation, the British government is usually more draconian than the EU. In recent years, British (and Irish) politicians have prided themselves on 'leading the way' by introducing public health policies that have little appeal to mainland Europeans. Far from tempering the EU's bureaucratic zeal, Britain has encouraged European institutions to embrace the kind of top-down lifestyle management that has become de rigueur in English-speaking countries since the 1990s. If the UK left the Union, British consumers might not have to abide by the EU's petty regulation of e-cigarettes and might be able to buy snus, but this would only happen if Westminster were more enlightened than Brussels. This seems a forlorn hope when one considers that the EU banned snus only after the UK banned it, and that the Department of Health initially favoured a system of medical regulation for e-cigarettes that was rejected by the European Parliament. Plain packaging for tobacco was rejected by MEPs in Brussels, but was supported by MPs in Westminster. The European Commission has warned member states against introducing minimum pricing, but Wales and Scotland are pursuing it nonetheless.

In short, British consumers of alcohol, tobacco and 'unhealthy' food would benefit from leaving the EU only if their own politicians were more liberal. There is little evidence that they are. This could change – the EU could acquire more powers, or British politicians could become less interventionist – but there is little reason to believe that Britain outside the EU would be a more liberal country in which to eat, drink and smoke.

## Conclusion

Those who hope that Brussels will produce more restrictive laws on food, drink and tobacco are faced with as many challenges as opportunities. On the one hand, the EU offers public health lobbyists a chance to bring about legislation across most of Europe with greater ease than if they had to persuade 28 governments individually. The European Commission is unelected and there is a large bureaucracy to turn policy into law. Legislation must be passed by the European Parliament, but MEPs can only vote on what is put in front of them by bureaucrats, and legislation can be altered by committee after it has been approved. As with the World Health Organisation and the UN, political processes in the EU take place at a sufficiently safe distance from the electorate to be appealing to campaigners who are aware that their policies are often unpopular with the public (WHO Europe 2004).

On the other hand, European institutions have a very limited competence in the field of public health. The anti-market approach favoured by many campaigners clashes with the EU's commitment to free trade between member states. Some health policies can be advanced under the guise of market harmonisation, but there are limits as to how far this approach can be taken.

The claim that 'fundamental rights' could be reinterpreted in such a way as to compel the EU to extend its competence into the domestic affairs of member states is speculative and unconvincing. If the lifestyle regulation agenda is to progress at EU level, perhaps the best hope for campaigners lies in the exemptions set out in Article 36 of the TFEU for 'the protection of health'. If risky lifestyle products are considered to be special cases, they might be subject to a different set of rules. Minimum pricing will provide an important test case. If the ECJ (or a national court) rules in favour of the Scottish government on the basis of Article 36, British public health groups expect it to 'set an important precedent that could encourage Member States to introduce further public health legislation' (HM Government 2013: 40). It would be a groundbreaking victory for lifestyle regulation over the single market, with implications that extend far beyond the field of health (Article 36 also mentions 'public morality' and 'public security' as possible grounds for exemption). Theoretically, the internal market could become riddled with so many exemptions granted to special interest groups that it becomes like a Swiss cheese.

So far, however, the ECJ has been unwilling to sacrifice the internal market in the name of health-based lifestyle regulation. Judicial activism cannot be ruled out in the future, but in the meantime, those who seek to control what Europeans eat, drink and smoke must work around existing laws, with policies designed to reduce the sale and appeal of products being introduced – paradoxically – through legislation that is ostensibly aimed at facilitating trade.

# References

ACTIVE – Sobriety Friendship Peace (2012) Turning popular opinion into public policy. Press Release, 25 April.

ACTIVE – Sobriety Friendship Peace (2010) Alcohol policy program.

Alemanno, A. and Garde, A. (2013) Regulating lifestyles in Europe: how to prevent and control non-communicable diseases associated with tobacco, alcohol and unhealthy diets? Report, Swedish Institute for European Policy Studies, Stockholm.

Boffetta, P., Aagnes, B., Weiderpass, E. and Andersen, A. (2005) Smokeless tobacco use and risk of cancer of the pancreas and other organs. *International Journal of Cancer* 114(6): 992–5.

Borg, T. (2014) Commissioner Tonio Borg delivers a keynote speech at the 6th European Conference on Tobacco or Health Istanbul. Keynote Speech, 27 March, EEAS.

European Commission (1999) Proposal for a Directive of the European Parliament and of the Council on the approximation of the laws, regulations and administrative provisions of the member states concerning the manufacture, presentation and sale of tobacco products (recast version). 1999/0244 (COD), 16 November: 43–51.

European Commission (2006) An EU strategy to support member states in reducing alcohol related harm. Communication from the Commission to the Council, the European Parliament, the European Economic and Social Committee and the Committee of the Regions.

European Commission (2009) Council recommendation of 30 November 2009 on smoke-free environments. *Official Journal of the European Union* 2009/C296/02: 4–14.

European Commission (2012) Communication from the Commission. SG(2012) D/52513, 26 November.

European Economic Community (1992) Council Directive 92/41/EEC of 15 May 1992 amending Directive 89/622/EEC on the approximation of the laws, regulations and administrative provisions of the Member States concerning the labelling of tobacco products.

European Parliament (2010) Directive 2010/13/EU of the European Parliament and of the Council of 10 March 2010 on the coordination of certain provisions laid down by law, regulation or administrative action in member states concerning the provision of audiovisual media services (Audiovisual Media Services Directive).

European Parliament (2014) Directive 2014/40/EU of the European Parliament and of the Council of 3 April 2014 on the approximation of the laws, regulations and administrative provisions of the member states concerning the manufacture, presentation and sale of tobacco and related products and repealing Directive 2001/37/EC.

European Union (2011) EU Health Programme: working together to improve public health in Europe. Brochure, European Commission.

Foulds, J., Ramstrom, L., Burke, M. and Fagerström, K. (2003) Effect of smokeless tobacco (snus) on smoking and public health in Sweden. *Tobacco Control* 12: 349–59

Gornall, J. (2014) Under the influence: 1. False dawn for minimum pricing. *British Medical Journal* 348: f7435

HM Government (2013) Review of the balance of competencies between the United Kingdom and the European Union: health. Report, July.

Howells, G. (2011) *The Tobacco Challenge: Legal Policy and Consumer Protection.* Farnham: Ashgate.

Lewin, F., Norell, S. E., Johansson, H., Gustavsson, P., Wennerberg, J., Biorklund, A. and Rutqvist, L. E. (1998) Smoking tobacco, oral snuff, and alcohol in the etiology of squamous cell carcinoma of the head and neck: a population-based case: referent study in Sweden. *Cancer* 82: 1367–75.

Liese, P. and Seeber, R. (2012) Tobacco Products Directive. Briefing Paper, European People's Party.

Luo, J., Ye, W., Zendehdel, K., Adami, J., Adami, H. O., Boffetta, P. and Nyren, O. (2007) Oral use of Swedish moist snuff (snus) and risk for cancer of the mouth, lung, and pancreas in male construction workers: a retrospective cohort study. *Lancet* 369: 2015–20.

Official Journal of the European Union (2014) Regulation (EU) No. 282/2014 of the European Parliament and of the Council of 11 March 2014 on the establishment of a third programme for the Union's action in the field of health (2014–2020) and repealing Decision No. 1350/2007/EC.

Rabinovich, L., Brutscher, P.-B., Vries, H., Tiessen, J., Clift, J. and Reding, A. (2009) The affordability of alcoholic beverages in the EU. Technical Report, Rand Europe.

Rodu, B., Stegmayr, B., Nasic, S. and Asplund, K. (2002) Effect of smokeless tobacco use on smoking in northern Sweden. *Journal of Internal Medicine* 252(5): 398–404.

Rodu, B. and Cole, P. (2009) Lung cancer mortality: comparing Sweden with other countries in the European Union. *Scandinavian Journal of Public Health* 37(5): 481–6.

Rosenquist, K., Wennerberg, J., Schildt, E. B., Bladstrom, A., Hansson, B. G. and Andersson, G. (2005) Use of Swedish moist snuff, smoking and alcohol consumption in the aetiology of oral and oropharyngeal squamous cell carcinoma. A population-based case-control study in southern Sweden. *Acta Otolaryngol* 125: 991–8.

Rutherford, D. (2012) A conversation with Derek Rutherford. *Addiction* 107: 892–9.

Schildt, E. B., Eriksson, M., Hardell, L. and Magnuson, A. (1998) Oral snuff, smoking habits and alcohol consumption in relation to oral cancer in a Swedish case-control study. *International Journal of Cancer* 77(3): 341–6.

Snowdon, C. (2014) Costs of minimum alcohol pricing would outweigh benefits. *British Medical Journal* 348: g1572.

WHO Europe (2004) Seventh Futures Forum on unpopular decisions in public health. Background Document, Copenhagen.

# ABOUT THE IEA

The Institute is a research and educational charity (No. CC 235 351), limited by guarantee. Its mission is to improve understanding of the fundamental institutions of a free society by analysing and expounding the role of markets in solving economic and social problems.

The IEA achieves its mission by:

- a high-quality publishing programme
- conferences, seminars, lectures and other events
- outreach to school and college students
- brokering media introductions and appearances

The IEA, which was established in 1955 by the late Sir Antony Fisher, is an educational charity, not a political organisation. It is independent of any political party or group and does not carry on activities intended to affect support for any political party or candidate in any election or referendum, or at any other time. It is financed by sales of publications, conference fees and voluntary donations.

In addition to its main series of publications the IEA also publishes a quarterly journal, *Economic Affairs*.

The IEA is aided in its work by a distinguished international Academic Advisory Council and an eminent panel of Honorary Fellows. Together with other academics, they review prospective IEA publications, their comments being passed on anonymously to authors. All IEA papers are therefore subject to the same rigorous independent refereeing process as used by leading academic journals.

IEA publications enjoy widespread classroom use and course adoptions in schools and universities. They are also sold throughout the world and often translated/reprinted.

Since 1974 the IEA has helped to create a worldwide network of 100 similar institutions in over 70 countries. They are all independent but share the IEA's mission.

Views expressed in the IEA's publications are those of the authors, not those of the Institute (which has no corporate view), its Managing Trustees, Academic Advisory Council members or senior staff.

Members of the Institute's Academic Advisory Council, Honorary Fellows, Trustees and Staff are listed on the following page.

The Institute gratefully acknowledges financial support for its publications programme and other work from a generous benefaction by the late Professor Ronald Coase.

*New Private Monies – A Bit-Part Player?*
Kevin Dowd
Hobart Paper 174; ISBN 978-0-255-36694-6; £10.00

*From Crisis to Confidence – Macroeconomics after the Crash*
Roger Koppl
Hobart Paper 175; ISBN 978-0-255-36693-9; £12.50

*Advertising in a Free Society*
Ralph Harris and Arthur Seldon
With an introduction by Christopher Snowdon
Hobart Paper 176; ISBN 978-0-255-36696-0; £12.50

*Selfishness, Greed and Capitalism: Debunking Myths about the Free Market*
Christopher Snowdon
Hobart Paper 177; ISBN 978-0-255-36677-9; £12.50

*Waging the War of Ideas*
John Blundell
Occasional Paper 131; ISBN 978-0-255-36684-7; £12.50

*Brexit: Directions for Britain Outside the EU*
Ralph Buckle, Tim Hewish, John C. Hulsman, Iain Mansfield and Robert Oulds
Hobart Paperback 178; ISBN 978-0-255-36681-6; £12.50

*Flaws and Ceilings – Price Controls and the Damage They Cause*
Edited by Christopher Coyne and Rachel Coyne
Hobart Paperback 179; ISBN 978-0-255-36701-1; £12.50

*Scandinavian Unexceptionalism: Culture, Markets and the Failure of Third-Way Socialism*
Nima Sanandaji
Readings in Political Economy 1; ISBN 978-0-255-36704-2; £10.00

*Classical Liberalism – A Primer*
Eamonn Butler
Readings in Political Economy 2; ISBN 978-0-255-36707-3; £10.00

*Federal Britain: The Case for Decentralisation*
Philip Booth
Readings in Political Economy 3; ISBN 978-0-255-36713-4; £10.00

*Forever Contemporary: The Economics of Ronald Coase*
Edited by Cento Veljanovski
Readings in Political Economy 4; ISBN 978-0-255-36710-3; £15.00

*Policy Stability and Economic Growth – Lessons from the Great Recession*
John B. Taylor
Readings in Political Economy 5; ISBN 978-0-255-36719-6; £7.50

## Other IEA publications

Comprehensive information on other publications and the wider work of the IEA can be found at www.iea.org.uk. To order any publication please see below.

### Personal customers

Orders from personal customers should be directed to the IEA:

Clare Rusbridge
IEA
2 Lord North Street
FREEPOST LON10168
London SW1P 3YZ
Tel: 020 7799 8907. Fax: 020 7799 2137
Email: sales@iea.org.uk

### Trade customers

All orders from the book trade should be directed to the IEA's distributor:

NBN International (IEA Orders)
Orders Dept.
NBN International
10 Thornbury Road
Plymouth PL6 7PP
Tel: 01752 202301, Fax: 01752 202333
Email: orders@nbninternational.com

### IEA subscriptions

The IEA also offers a subscription service to its publications. For a single annual payment (currently £42.00 in the UK), subscribers receive every monograph the IEA publishes. For more information please contact:

Clare Rusbridge
Subscriptions
IEA
2 Lord North Street
FREEPOST LON10168
London SW1P 3YZ
Tel: 020 7799 8907, Fax: 020 7799 2137
Email: crusbridge@iea.org.uk